How To Upset
A Goliath
Book Biz

PublishAmerica:

*The Inside Story
of an Underdog with a Bite*

PublishAmerica
Baltimore

First printing

Photos by Andrea Higgins

ISBN: 1-4137-9096-8
PUBLISHED BY PUBLISHAMERICA, LLLP
www.publishamerica.com
Baltimore

Printed in the United States of America

I gratefully dedicate this book to PublishAmerica's staff, whose tireless professionalism, love for books, and loyal commitment to our shared purpose fill all of us with pride,

and to the victorious legion of PublishAmerica's authors whose names are listed at the end of this book, one by one, as the most potent exclamation point that I could think of.

Introduction

PublishAmerica, Cavemen, Gutenberg, and the New Stone Tablets

I consider it a privilege to introduce to you the fascinating success story of how PublishAmerica has forever changed the publishing industry. To found this company, we poured our entire livelihoods into pushing the publishing industry toward changing into something more forgiving, something more fair to new authors, and something that could actually reward the often life-changing endeavors undertaken by new authors.

And the publishing world will never be the same.

The results of our efforts have been more than spectacular. Many thousands of authors now proudly hold their books in their hands, most of whom stood little chance of being traditionally published elsewhere.

PublishAmerica has forever changed the publishing industry. PublishAmerica is the first company to use on-demand printing to bring the reality of traditional publishing to tens of thousands of previously unpublishable authors. Never again will new authors have to remain unpublished. And never again will authors need to endure the stigma of paying to be published.

As is happening in the music industry, the walls of the publishing industry are now being scaled by thousands of first time authors, the vanity/subsidy publishing industry is already showing signs of decline, and even mainstream publishers are increasingly printing books on demand.

But this was all easily predictable, really.

Ever since we founded PublishAmerica, it has not been difficult to predict the future of the publishing industry. And, it's especially easy when your company is leading a revolution that is making that prediction come true.

Normally, when you revolutionize an industry, you have opposition. You have people, groups, companies, industry titans, and various pundits who disagree with you. They have an opposing opinion, a different outlook, they come from differing environments, and they have different predictions. And, most importantly, they have all sorts of well thought out reasons for why they are right and why you are wrong.

But PublishAmerica has had none of that.

Subsidy publishers, vanity publishers, and other publishers who charge authors money for services have already started to falter, and they, certainly, are not happy about PublishAmerica publishing first-time authors at no charge, as they continue to try to charge for the same services. But other than them, PublishAmerica has had no opposition worthy of mention.

Everyone agrees that the direction PublishAmerica is leading the industry is inevitable. Everyone else is moving in the same direction too. There is no other direction for the publishing industry to go, other than toward on-demand printing. Interestingly, we have all watched parallel patterns happen in other industries as technologies advance, consumer demands evolve, and raw materials become more costly.

PublishAmerica's largest customers are, in descending order, Barnes & Noble, Borders, Books-A-Million, and Amazon. It should not be difficult to determine whether or not their corporate executives and those running other major corporations would agree with my prediction for the future of the publishing industry.

Barnes & Noble sees that the future is in printing on demand. Just a couple of years ago, the company bought their own print-on-demand equipment, and experimented with doing their own on-demand printing.

Additionally, Barnes & Noble also owns a vanity, pay-to-publish company that prints books on demand.

Xerox Corporation sees that too. An expensive ad run by Xerox during Super Bowl halftime espouses print-on-demand as a means for new authors to be published. Xerox also manufactures print-on-demand equipment, as do IBM and Sharp. Many others are joining this trend too, and hoping to compete.

Borders agrees also. Borders was the first to experiment with putting print on-demand equipment in bookstores. Also, Borders has sold vanity publishing kits in their bookstores, the works of which are printed on demand.

Random House would also agree. It also owns a vanity, pay-to-publish company that prints books on demand.

The always forward-thinking Amazon apparently thinks so too. Amazon bought its own vanity, pay-to-publish company that uses print-on-demand. And, Amazon is providing products to consumers in much the same way that PublishAmerica is providing books to Amazon and other customers. From Amazon's point of view, it acquires products only as the demand arises. Amazon has no warehouses storing clothing, jewelry, musical instruments, or books. Like PublishAmerica, Amazon provides its products on demand.

Perhaps most significantly, Ingram Books, the world's largest book wholesaler, the company that makes PublishAmerica books available through any bookstore in the United States and most of Europe, also owns its own print-on-demand facility, where many of PublishAmerica's books are printed, along with the books of many mainstream publishers.

All of these companies, and many more throughout the world, see the future of publishing moving toward being on demand.

A very similar on-demand revolution is occurring in

many other industries. The same phenomenon happened with the music industry decades ago, and then more recently to the movie industry. A brief look at the history of these industries makes the trend seem very obvious. The physical products of both industries are now produced on demand, and the companies who pioneered the changes are now household names.

More revenue is now produced by people renting movies to watch "on demand" than by people going out to movie theaters. The music industry saw the same phenomenon occur a few decades ago when more people began listening to music in their homes than going to live performances. The invention of record albums enabled this revolution, where millions of people could listen to music "on demand." CDs and the advent of digital music simply made on-demand music more convenient. The on-demand revolution had already happened in the music industry long ago. Many other unrelated industries are moving in this direction too, toward providing their products as the demand arises.

As the first company to make traditional publishing profitable using on-demand printing, PublishAmerica is pioneering parallel changes in the book industry, and publishing the works of tens of thousands of authors in the process. It is little wonder, really, that we have achieved such success.

The reason for producing books, or any product, on demand is very simple. Instead of printing thousands of books, putting them in a warehouse and hoping they will sell, PublishAmerica prints them digitally, as the demand arises. More and more publishers, including the largest mainstream publishers, are moving in this direction. Publishers who used to do initial print runs of 10,000 or 20,000 books now print just 1,000 books. Then they wait to see how the book is selling. If is not selling well, it moves to being produced on demand, and the publisher has not spent money on books sitting in warehouses. Increasingly, mainstream publishers are doing smaller and smaller print runs, and are thereby taking less and less financial risk.

PublishAmerica took this notion, long before it became a trend, to a radical new length. By producing books only as the demand arises, PublishAmerica does not have to warehouse books, and is therefore able to afford to publish, at a profit, the works of tens of thousands of first time authors.

PublishAmerica started out with no influx of capital, with Willem and I working 16-hour days doing everything from making coffee to licking stamps in the mailroom. Now we run America's fastest growing publishing company. In less than six years PublishAmerica has grown to 13,000 authors and 80 employees, and now publishes over two percent of all books published in the United States. As of this writing, over 130 authors ask to be published by PublishAmerica, each day.

PublishAmerica has had no bank loan or any capital

investment, yet it has grown steadily throughout its history. In terms of the rate of publishing new titles, PublishAmerica is now the largest publishing company in the United States. And, even though a very small minority of the 150-175,000 books published each year can be found on bookstore shelves, many hundreds of PublishAmerica titles sit proudly on bookshelves across the nation.

This is no measure of success, however, as the vast majority of books sold in the United States are not sold in physical bookstores. Amazon and others are pushing this trend, and succeeding. At a recent cocktail party at Amazon headquarters, I mentioned to a young Amazon staffer that our top three customers, above Amazon, are brick and mortar bookstores. This, of course, is not what Amazon wants to hear from a publisher. I found her reply priceless: "Bookstores are sooooo twentieth century...."

- - - - - - -

From an early age, I knew that I wanted to be a writer, and I had a proclivity toward taking adventures a few steps further than most others. So I got degree in English literature, set out to see the world, and ended up terrified, arrested, sick, detained, and harassed in some of the most unstable, primitive, and violent areas of Africa.

This adventure turned into something so unique, so unlike anything I had ever heard of anyone else doing, that I wrote a book about it, as it was happening. It came as a surprise to me, then, that I could not find a publisher who was interested in it.

I tried very hard, read books about how to do it, took a course on how to do it, and even met with an editor at Random House. I was told, over and over, the same phrase that was told to many authors who later became famous, that my book "lacked commercial potential."

I found out that only a very small pecentage of authors are ever published in the United States, and that there was little that I could do. I knew I was in good company, though, since the list of well-known published writers who were given the same basic message is very, very long. Mark Twain, Shakespeare, Steven King, Agatha Christie, George Orwell, and many others were given similar messages about their writing. This list goes on and on.

Ultimately I failed, gave up on that project, and wrote another book about an area of New York City called Little India. This book, I thought, had more "commercial potential." But again, I could not find a publisher. This time I was determined not to fail, however. I wrote this book with commercial viability in mind. So I tried again, and this time I failed again.

A different approach was clearly appropriate. So I read books on how to self publish, I printed the book myself at home, bound the copies myself with glue, and used pants hangers to hold them together. My pants lay wrinkled on the floor, and my books hung proudly in the closet.

But again, I ultimately could not succeed, so I decided to call this a notable failure, and plunged forward into another career.

But I was plenty annoyed at the publishing industry.

Years later, I met Willem Meiners. During discussions of many different business models, we tried to figure out a way to publish authors without charging a fee, and to use technology to our advantage. Charging authors anything at all was anathema to us, since it would leave the stigma of paying to be published, no matter how low the fee. So we decided to try using a new printing technology called print-on-demand to experiment with publishing large numbers of authors in traditional fashion, without charging them any money at all.

- - - - - - -

A quest toward this type of printing technology has been a major influence in the publishing industry's history. More importantly, the use of this printing technology will dominate the publishing industry's future.

But most importantly, this new printing technology represents the next of several major milestones in world history. The first such milestone was cave painting, the next, stone tablets, then papyrus reed painting, then Chinese printing presses, then Gutenberg, and then print-on-demand.

Neanderthal people 35,000 years ago, sitting around a

fire in their cave, had the same reasons that we do for wanting better print technology: more cave people could "publish" their ideas to make them available to others.

At that time, the only way to "publish" ideas was verbally. And that method was very labor intensive. Better printing methods - that is, the advent of cave painting as communication - meant wider distribution of ideas at a lower cost. Today the objective is still the same: to publish written works in order to make them available to as wide an audience as possible.

Before the Neanderthals, the only way to communicate, to preserve ideas, or to propagate ideas was verbally, which is tremendously inefficient.. They needed a method that was cheaper, in terms of labor, and more efficient, so they invented cave painting. Suddenly, their ideas were available to a far wider audience, without the expense of verbal communication.

This was extraordinary, from the standpoint of enabling people who had something to say, to say it and have it remain said, and available for others to see. This could be done, obviously, without extra effort by any person, such as the effort needed to propagate ideas by word of mouth.

Cave painting was far cheaper than verbal communication, but unfortunately it was still expensive.

Then, 6,000 years ago, someone invented chiseling language into stone tablets. The written word was then portable. But it was still expensive.

So, 4,000 years ago, the Egyptians brushed written

language onto papyrus reed paper. And, suddenly, communication was even more portable. But it was still expensive.

Then, 1,000 years ago, the Chinese invented movable clay type. And again, suddenly, the written word was even more portable. But it was still expensive.

Then, just 600 years ago, Gutenberg invented the printing press that quickly spread throughout Europe. And again, suddenly, the written word was even more portable. But it was still expensive. Gutenberg's invention was wildly popular and partially alleviated the problem, but did not solve it.

The publishing industry still lives with the same basic problem. There has not been an invention as radical as Gutenberg's in the last 600 years.

That is, until recently.

Up until recently, it remained, just as 600 years ago, very expensive to propagate books. Advances were made, of course, but most printing presses today remain labor intensive and therefore expensive to set up. Because of the financial risks involved, publishers are reluctant to publish the works of first-time authors whose books have no track record of sales.

Gutenberg would not have had much difficulty in predicting the result: a publishing industry, 600 years later, that publishes a small percentage of all books written, the industry dominated by a very few large companies who can afford to take the risks involved, thousands of other publishers competing furiously, but remaining in obscurity, and many frustrated writers who can not manage to find a book publisher. And only a very small percentage of authors who write ever being published. Gutenberg could have predicted all of this.

It is obvious that publishers need to select only books that they think will sell in the tens of thousands. It doesn't take very many warehouses full of unsold books to put a publisher out of business. Of the 50,000 book publishers in the United States, a few are so dominant that they are household names. Most of the rest are not growing, and remain obscure. The reason for this is that they are still, basically, printing the written word on stone tablets. The printing technology used for the past 600 years, including its advancements, represents that latest in stone tablets.

Gutenberg is not famous today because he invented the printing press. Others invented it too. The Chinese invented it hundreds of years earlier. Willem Meiners, who is Dutch, will tell you that the printing press was actually invented by a Dutchman. Gutenberg is famous today because he was the first to make that new printing technology economically viable in a Western economy. Partly because of his location, his printing contraption quickly spread throughout Europe.

Like Gutenberg, PublishAmerica is the first to popularize the next step in printing. Like Gutenberg, PublishAmerica is using the next step in printing technology to enable people to be published whose voices otherwise would not be heard. Thanks to Gutenberg, thousands of people across the Western world could suddenly read what authors had to say. And the same goes for PublishAmerica.

PublishAmerica is doing the same thing that Gutenberg did, with printing on demand.

It is not difficult to predict the future of the publishing industry. Machines exist today that take in a computer file at one end and, minutes later, spit out a finished book at the other end. Such machines will soon be found in bookstores, and will alleviate bookstores' perennial dilemma of deciding what small percentage of published books to stock.

Most published books can not be found on the shelves of any bookstore. For bookstores to stock all published books would mean adding 15 feet of shelf space each day. Stocking all published books soon will not be a problem, however. If the book that you want is not on the shelves of your local bookstore, the clerk will simply press a button, the machine will make a soft whirring sound, and out will pop your book.

The book industry is simply following in the footsteps of the music and movie industries, and undergoing its own on-demand revolution. On-demand technologies will cause many industries to evolve their competitive advantages. Current book printing methods are already going the way of stone tablets and cave painting.

Picture a family of Neanderthal people standing in their cave, considering how best to share their ideas or their cave paintings with the family in the next valley. Would they have wanted to print thousands of copies on a printing press? Or would the Neanderthals have preferred their cave paintings on demand?

No one who knows the publishing industry is predicting anything other than on-demand printing dominating the future. The evolution of on-demand products that is taking place all over the world, and becoming a part of our culture, is unstoppable.

Up to now, very few books written were ever published. Publishers only published books that were forecasted to sell tens of thousands of copies. Authors worked for years, and often for decades, to write a book about something very dear to them, and until PublishAmerica changed the industry, they had little hope to ever be published.

Now, thanks to PublishAmerica and on-demand printing, that is no longer the case. Tens of thousands of happy authors now proudly hold their books in their hands, and hundreds of thousands more will follow. Like the Neanderthals painting on their cave walls, the Egyptians writing on papyrus, and Gutenberg with his printing press, PublishAmerica is leading the latest revolution in publishing, and it is very apparent that the publishing industry, and the world, will never be the same.

LARRY CLOPPER

Foreword

This is the story of an adventure that turned into a purpose. It is the tale of an underdog publishing company that, on the eve of the new millennium, set out to introduce the entire book publishing world to the twenty-first century. Nothing more, nothing less.

For those who wonder if that's a big deal: America buys 4.5 million books *every day*, 1.6 billion books per year—more than five per average individual, or twenty books per family. Americans amount to only five percent of the total world population, yet they purchase thirty-five percent of all books that are sold *worldwide*. That's one-third of all the books in the whole wide world. America and books: you bet it's a big deal!

This is the story of two entrepreneurs, two bibliophiles, two true author advocates who realized before anyone else did that the time for democracy in authorland had arrived.

Gone are the days when those who have written a good book are either routinely rejected or required to pay hundreds, sometimes thousands of dollars to see their work in print. Gone are the years when readers did not have the kinds of options and choices that an increased supply of books, written by thousands of new authors, makes available.

It is the story of the first free ride for authors ever, the story of what some call *The People's Publisher*, of literary Independence Day, of a revolution in a domain that used to be ruled by a book elite of self-crowned kings and queens. There are millions of finished book manuscripts in circulation; some say six million, others say the real number is closer to sixty million. That is millions of real people, individuals, law-abiding citizens—and much more than ninety percent of them never stood an honest chance of getting their book published. The gates to becoming a published author, to being invited to an equal opportunity of success, greatness, recognition were kept hermetically closed.

This is the story of how that was changed, almost overnight. The reality of book publishing will never be the same again. Because someone opened the gates.

But much more than this being the chronicle of two men, and of the magnificent, loyal, and highly professional staff that supports and sustains them, it is the saga of the true heroes of this campaign: the thousands upon thousands of writers who heard opportunity knocking on their doors, who walked through the gates, and who made their dreams come true. Writing this book was one small step, but what, together, they have achieved is the giant leap that defines all great movements.

How to Upset a Goliath Book Biz is primarily about and for these heroes. It is as much the story of them as it is the tale of the band of happy warriors who are currently the most hotly and energetically debated innovators in the traditional publishing industry:

The story of PublishAmerica.

Chapter 1

"A week ago I received the notification that all aspiring authors dream of. PA accepted my manuscript for publication. I cried, I shook and I got goose bumps! This has been my dream since I was 15 years old. I struggled over this book and rewrote it many times only to keep getting it rejected. The feeling over PA willing to give my book a chance is indescribable! All of you out there waiting for this feeling, please don't give up."

—Cynthia M. Hickey, author of *Pursued by Evil*

D-Day

First there was an idea, a thought, a belief. We knew what we wanted. There were a thousand others like us, we figured, maybe even a hundred thousand or more. Regular folks such as ourselves who had written a book, or who wanted to write one. People with a story, a talent, a dream. Writers without a publisher. Ignored, refused, denied. Authors who were "not good enough," but who knew better than that. What we wanted was to give them a free ride and a home.

The birth of PublishAmerica was not very laborious. The only blood that was shed came out of the succulent medium-rare steak that the two founders were merrily digging into during their very first lunch together. We were having fun. This was the groundbreaking ceremony, the start from scratch, two guys sensing that they were on to something. The place was called Red River Steakhouse. Not unlike many once-sizzling landmarks of the old publishing world, it does not exist anymore. It did not survive the onset of PublishAmerica.

We also knew something else. There is no way in the world that you can accomplish something great all by yourself. You need helpers, a support group, people with a similar mindset. Adventurers, risk-takers, kindred souls. Young people preferably, open-minded, or at least young at heart. With a love for the written word, a nose for the smell of books, and a knack for working with computers, IT savvy. If we wanted this to go anywhere at all, we were going to need a solid team, a tight organization, dedicated troopers.

The concept of publishing books is not difficult. You need to find talented authors, so you've got to have an acquisitions team. You must edit a manuscript and format a text, so you are going to establish an editing department. You also need designers who will come up with top-notch book cover art that attracts the eye and invites the mind. And then, not unimportantly, you need a printing press. Get these four ingredients together, and you've got yourself a publishing house.

The concept of publishing books *differently*, that is something else. Everyone can reinvent the wheel, and all already invented book publishing wheels run on money. Almost every new start-up in publishing follows the path of least resistance: they ask someone else to foot the bill. That's why the modern publishing landscape is strewn with vanity houses, where the author is required to fork over the dough, varying from a few hundred dollars to more than a month's worth of paychecks. It's the beaten path of make-believe, where the real publisher of the author's book is actually the author himself. Vanity publishing, subsidy publishing, hybrid publishing, on-demand publishing—at the end of the day these are ordinary, routine, humdrum synonyms for what it really is: self-publishing. Which itself is a euphemism for maxing out your credit card.

THE BUCK STOPS HERE

We did not want that. We were not going to ask our authors to pay for anything at all. What we wanted to abide by was a new take on an old saying: "The buck stops here." We were going to pay for the whole process ourselves, down to the last penny. No author contributions, no fees, no charges. In fact, we spent no more than five minutes on deciding that we were going to ask for no one's money, period. No banks, no loans, no investors. It was going to be sink or swim. If we were going to fail, we wanted to owe no one a dime. If we were going to succeed, it would be because of our own investment of money, countless hours, and tireless work. It was going to be old-school risk-taking, a key ingredient of old-fashioned traditional publishing. That's what we were going to be all about. Traditional book publishing, taking all the risks, footing all the bills, and earning our keep by selling books only.

What we were certainly not going to be was mainstream publishing. Main Street publishing, that's what we were after. Publishing those authors who were denied access to the mainstream houses. A somewhat puzzling and deceptive term, mainstream publishing, for what exactly is so mainstream about an industry where only five publishing conglomerates control eighty (!) percent of all book sales, and where the top twenty publishers control ninety percent? It is an elite industry dominated by the few, with little or no access afforded to the many.

There are numerous book writers who are keeping a

scrapbook of refusal letters. For years, sometimes decades, they had doggedly and stubbornly submitted their manuscripts to those mainstream houses. And while their labors of love were gathering dust in desk drawers all over the fruited plain, they were gathering "not good enough" letters as far as the eye could see. No place in the inn for them. No seat at the dinner table. In *Seinfeld* speak, *"No soup for you!"*

Those were going to be our people, the ones we were going to need the most, the talented story writers without whom there would be no book publishing, period. They were the underdogs of Publiland, literary fugitives, banished souls, authors whose only alernative to being refused and unpublished was to spend a few months' rent on being refused and vanity published, only to quickly find out that now they were stigmatized even worse. We were going to champion them; we were going to publish America. Main Street writers with a manuscript in their hand, or in their head. And we were going to pay for it all.

Together with them, we were going to take on a Goliath. It was the Fall of 1999. PublishAmerica was born.

A PERFECT MATCH

And so was what I believe to be a remarkable partnership. At first glance Larry Clopper and I would be considered two unlikely partners. We are both distinctly independent souls, both strong-headed, and some would insist that our egos are well-developed, too. Our backgrounds are totally different, and so are the cultures and histories that formed us. But unlikely or not, we turned out to be the perfect match. And while perfect matches may create perfect days, or an occasional perfect storm, they also breed perfect results, because their personalities, tempers, and talents complement each other ideally. With perfect matches, one plus one equals a lot more than two.

Larry is very much a doer, someone who rolls up his sleeves and gets things going. He invents stuff. As a thirteen-year-old paper boy, he designed and implemented a "fly-band" technique for newspaper delivery, using a specially designed hands-free bicycle, which resulted in a fifty percent reduction of delivery times. He's the efficiency man, a leader, an innovator. When he was seventeen and a restaurant dishwasher, he designed and implemented a dishwasher loading method which enabled the restaurant to use one employee rather than two. He became probably the first dishwasher in modern history to be offered a raise, and I'm sure that he accepted it with his trademark grin.

Like me, he is a traveler, fond of seeing something new. But whereas I bought myself a luxury RV when I was in my twenties and drove it all around Europe for a year, Larry took the jungle route at that age. He traveled Africa from north to south, got himself arrested in Sudan, accused of being a spy, interrogated, and then deported. He was detained by separatist tribal guerrilla warriors for wearing their style of sandals, then released after he agreed to learn the proper African spear-throwing technique. He was offered babies for ten bucks by starving people, was beaten by another tribal chief for refusing to give him a gift, and was ostracized by white South Africans for insisting that black people use his first name, instead of calling him "Boss" or "Master" as they had been instructed.

I did not invent things, and when traveling I preferred comfort. I am the son of a preacher man, and in my teens I played the organ in my dad's church in the Netherlands, by ear only because I can't read scores. I became a newspaper reporter and made an early career in journalism. And when I traveled, I was always looking to eliminate waiting times, and if that was not possible, to travel as comfortably as I could, to make it feel effortless. As soon as I discovered the difference between coach and business class, I resolved to beat the business class travelers at their game, and that's what I did. I found ways to always fly first class without betting the house, and let others fly it, too: whatever is available to some of us should be accessible by all.

Like Larry, I am the presiding type. I ran my newspaper's foreign desk when I was 24, became the managing editor at 32 and the editor when I was 37. I taught business college, chaired boards and committees, and ended up running a psychotherapy practice on the side. That's where you tell other people to follow their dreams, and one day when one my of patients asked me if I, too, was doing that, I said, "Actually, no, but thanks for bringing it up," and I closed the practice and moved overseas to do what I wanted to do most.

Maybe more than anything else, Larry and I are both storytellers. I know that he is very good at it, better than I am, which is arguably also why he is better at teaching than I am. We are both writers—more specifically, book writers. I wrote a dozen books, and my dream was the same as Larry's after he returned from his two-year trek through Africa and had written books of his own: we wanted to get involved in book publishing, be in charge of what we wanted to get in print, be independent of anyone else's decision about what we could and could not turn into a published book.

When I met Larry, something clicked, fell in place, matched. Two lone wolfs, two independent soloists who would think long and hard before committing themselves to sharing business fate, future, and ultimately also power with anyone else, decided to do exactly that, within a matter of minutes. Over a medium-rare steak.

I came to America in order to be published. Instead, Larry and I talked each other into publishing America.

Chapter 2

"Thank you for making such a dream so simple!!"

—Gretchen Anne Gundel, author of *Welcome to My Yesterday*

A Claim to the Throne

On one of our desks is a framed picture of a lighthouse in the stormy dark. It is captioned, "Giving: One of life's greatest rules... 'You can not hold a torch to lighting another's path without brightening your own.' " This is true. We are no philanthropists; PublishAmerica is in it for the money. But we decided on a business concept that puts giving above receiving—like every parent would do, which is why this business concept is also a life concept.

Parents are unselfish in providing a life for their children, in creating opportunity, wholesomeness, a healthy start. And what they receive back in return is a fuller life of their own. Before brightening our own road, we were going to light someone else's path, by holding the torch of publication to their book. And only if that book was going to find readers would our own benefit materialize.

Those who demand nothing may hope to expect everything.

The beauty of this concept is that it is so simple, transparent, and basic. When simplicity is your base, it will immediately permeate everything you do. It allows you to structure your entire organization in an open way, and, more importantly, it affords transparency to everyone you deal with—authors, readers, customers. It is what America has always embraced in its true entrepreneurs: show me who the real risk-takers are, who are putting their livelihoods on the line, who are willing to give all and risk to lose all. Those are the entrepreneurs who will receive.

THE RIGHT TIME, THE RIGHT PLACE

Nothing about the PublishAmerica concept is secret or hidden. But also nothing about it guaranteed success beforehand. Having a lofty ideal and a back-to-basics business concept is a great place to start, but success requires more than that. For every one enterprise that succeeds, there are a thousand that fail. We did not want to be among the thousand. We wanted to be the one.

This is easier said than done. Everybody wants to be the one that succeeds, but not everyone comes in at the right time, in the right place. That's what we had going for PublishAmerica. It was the right time, and we entered the industry in the right place. A new era of printing was just emerging, with digital technologies rolling into printing facilities like a tsunami. Offset printing had been king for decades; digital printing now became the crown prince with a firm claim to the throne.

In the history of printing, most developments and inventions have been the result of printing press builders trying to do it quicker and cheaper. All changes in printing technology, ever since it was invented in the fifteenth century, were aimed at making the process more efficient and less costly for the printer, so that he could print more copies faster, with fewer employees, and get more profitable as a result. But this one, the invention of digital printing, was different. It made printing actually more expensive, and it aimed at printing *fewer* books. Digital printing, one could say, came about as a service for publishers, and not so much for the benefit of the printer, at least not on the short term.

What is digital printing? Think of it as your own desktop printer at home, because it works pretty much the same way. A digital press is a very big desktop printer, connected to a personal computer that informs it what to print. It is not really sitting on a desk, of course, because it may run the length of a large room or more, and it is fed either by high stacks of paper sheets or by paper on a roll, a web. There are professionals behind consoles checking, commanding, correcting, and what is coming out of the printer at the very end would be an unusual sight for those of us who regularly use our desktop printer at home. The digital press spits out book block after book block, paper printed on both sides, each sheet in the right place, a few books per minute, depending on how many simultaneous books the particular machine can handle. They cost a million dollars or more, and the more you're willing to invest, the more your digital press can do for you.

ON-DEMAND: NEED ONE, MAKE ONE

In most digital printing facilities, the book blocks, or text blocks, are manually transferred to a binding machine, where the book's laminated cover, produced on what is by and large a desktop full-color laser printer, is already waiting. The text is glued and bound, the book is trimmed to size, and there we have it: a digitally printed book. Same quality as an offset printed book, same feel, same look, only a little more expensive.

So why would a publisher prefer to have a more expensive book coming off the press? Answer: if he needs only one, he can now order only one. In the past, regardless of how many books he thought he was going to sell, existing printing technologies forced him to print at least one or two thousand copies of that particular title. If he sold only a few hundred, he was stuck with many hundreds that would never sell. For the longest of times, publishing meant needing large storage spaces to stock inventory that never sold.

The arrival of digital printing changed the math. If printing two thousand books on an offset press at $3 per copy meant that you'd be stuck with a thousand unsold copies, what you were really paying for your merchandise was then $6 a piece. So if you first print only 100 books at $5 each, and after that only as many as you really needed, you'd be money ahead no matter how you sliced it. A new phrase was born: print-on-demand. From now on forward publishers needed no inventory if they didn't want to have one, plus their upfront cash outlay was dramatically lower. A new era in publishing had arrived.

And PublishAmerica arrived with it.

The founders knew that they could not possibly fulfill the publishing dreams of thousands of writers if they had to pre-print and stock books for all of them. There would be no storage space large enough, or at least affordable enough, to hold a million books or more. But more importantly, printing that many books upfront without a certainty that they would all sell reasonably soon was utterly unsustainable. And that's exactly why all those mainstream publishers never touched those authors we were going to serve.

But now there was digital printing. Books would be printed on demand as the demand came in, and the whole inventory issue that had dogged, bothered, and overwhelmed publishers for centuries had dissolved overnight.

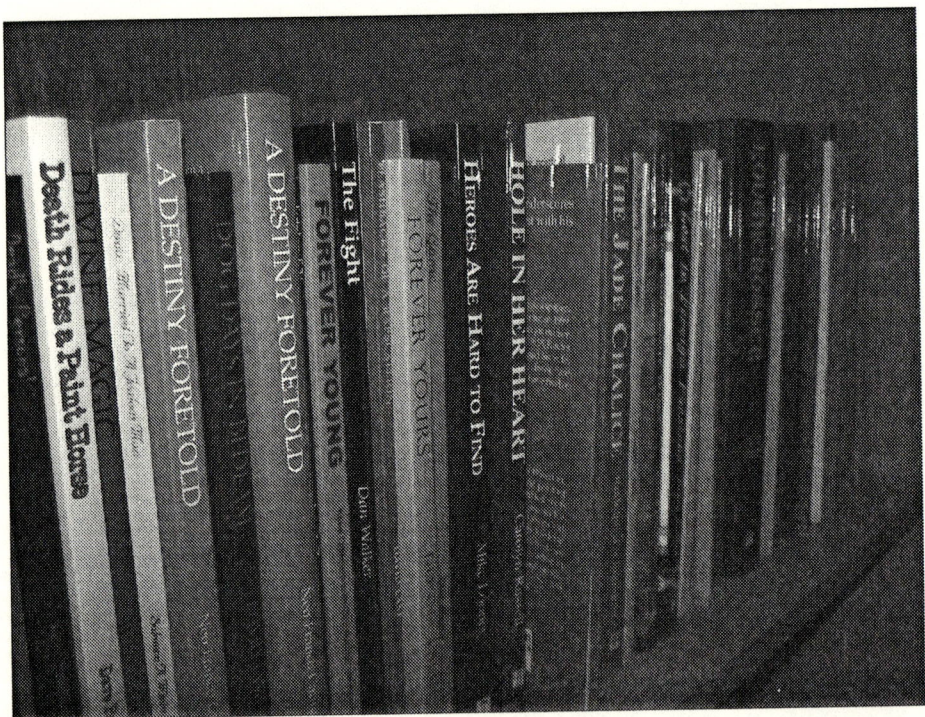

Chapter 3

"Yesterday I received my dollar in the mail. I framed it immediately. I am so excited. It is hanging on the wall directly across from my bed. I can see it as soon as I open my eyes every morning. What a gratifying feeling. Thanks PA, for assisting me in my quest to be published. I am an author. It sounds so good."

—Pamela deLeon, author of *Smiling Thru the Tears*

The Dollar Dance

We came in at the right time, reacting immediately to the outbreak of the digital printing era, and in the right place, nestling in the one niche that all publishers, every single one of them, had overlooked—not inadvertently, but knowlingly. We were going to do what no one had ever done before.

So all we needed to ensure was that we did it the right way. If we wanted to be the one that succeeded, and not among the thousand that failed, we would have to keep our eye on the ball, work harder than everyone else, stay focused within our niche, deliver on what we promised, provide quality service and quality products, grow as fast as we possibly could in a controlled manner, be confident, be smart, and do all of this with a big smile, and mean it.

It sounds easy and not quite self-depreciating looking back, but the truth is that we knew all along that we were going to succeed. It was not a matter of if, but when, and to what degree. Ours was a killer concept, impossible to ignore. If we were going to fail, it would be because we screwed up. And that we were determined to avoid. We knew that authors would love the PublishAmerica idea, the fact that finally there was a publisher who was going to take their manuscript and turn it into a real book, for free, with nothing expected back from them in return!

HOW CAN YOU DO IT?

When we first announced PublishAmerica, people asked us, "How can you do it? How can you succeed where others failed?" And our answer was always the same: we don't succeed where others failed; we succeed where others never tried. Really, it wasn't rocket science. Every other publisher, mainstream or otherwise, could have done what we did. They just never got around doing it. Why? Because they were hungry. Some big houses, such as Random House and Time Warner, actually did dabble in the new author pool for a while, but they wanted to do it risk-free and see upfront money, so they became involved with vanity publishing. Their efforts failed. Authors did not like it. They never have, and they never will. Authors want to be treated the old-fashioned way. They want to be paid.

This was our first major business decision. Not only were we not going to charge our authors anything, we were going to pay them up front. An advance. No fortunes, no gold mine, but one dollar. No more than a score of dimes, but to our authors it would make a world of difference. Yes, it would be a symbolic payment, but a payment nonetheless. Receiving a check would be the 180-degree opposite of writing one. In fact, we quickly decided to send not a check to our newly contracted writers, but the real dollar bill, legal tender, the greenback. If our authors were in any way going to be like us, they would want to keep it, treasure it, maybe even frame it, their very first payment for a book they had written. Such a monumental moment ought not be cheapened by us sending them a check, a piece of paper that costs us 10 cents to print. We decided that the least we could, and should, do was send, and spend, the full dollar on this symbolical gesture. Real, tangible money.

Our authors would appreciate it. And boy, were we right about that. Case in point: author Jacki Ortiz, who penned *Heart Aches & Rainy Days*. She told us, "When I first found out that I was accepted and the dollar would be arriving, my husband went out and bought me a beautiful frame and a mat to go with it. I polished that thing for weeks! I have my dollar framed and hanging right up where I can see it."

Said Mario S. Fedele, a gifted writer whose book *Stories for a Stormy Night* seamlessly echoes our "hold a torch" motto mentioned in the previous chapter, "I had thought I'd been the only one to frame their dollar. Obviously I'm simply following a long standing practice."

ALL-RISK AUTHORS

Looking in from the outside, this does not seem like much of a big deal, a publisher mailing one dollar to each new author. Once you have contracted, say, a thousand authors, your upfront payment to all authors is only that, one thousand dollars. Any publisher could afford that, right? Of course they can. Then how is it that no publisher, except PublishAmerica, is spending it on all-risk authors?

First of all, because that's what the legions of unproven, unpublished authors are. They are all-risk. The few times that a major commercial house in New York decides to publish a no-name, a non-celebrity, a debut writer, they first have made an in-depth assessment of what return they can expect to see on their investment. If it's iffy, they pass on the no-name. Too risky, too much of a chance that money spent will be money lost. However promising and talented the new author may seem, if he comes with an unquantifiable risk, he's stuck on Main Street, with no access to mainstream.

And then there's the vanity industry. All-risk does not exist in their book. It's not a word in their vocabulary. They are masters of elimination by having the author check all risks at the door. They assure themselves of a profit, no matter what happens, by charging their hefty entry fee. And if they are clever, which most vanity publishers are, they lure the author into paying even more once they're inside. There are extra charges for extra services—a couple hundred bucks for some guidance here, a few hundred dollars for some assistance there, an upgrade fee for this, a star charge for that. By the time a vanity publisher actually prints the first copy of a new book, the entire process has been padded with green.

In other words, that simple, ordinary, plain one-dollar bill that the new PublishAmerica author receives sends a clear message, and it is a major one. It tells them that they will receive, not give. That they are invited, not denied, refused, disallowed. That their publisher will pick up all tabs, underwrite all expenses. And that however all-risk they may be, PublishAmerica believes in their books' ability to sell at least enough copies to make it worth our trust, and our effort.

The founders expected that new authors would respond to this feature of our concept with great enthusiasm, and we were right. Until this day, the dollar experience remains one that authors write us emotion-filled letters about. When their author advance arrives, it is a high moment, a thrill, a unique day of poignancy that they will always remember. PublishAmerica authors frame their first Published Author Dollar, they keep it, treasure it, hang it on their wall, tape it to the monitor of their PC, show it to their children, their neighbors, their friends. To them, it is much more than a hundred pennies. It captures a rite of passage.

GOOSEBUMPS

No one confirms this sentiment more than Sophia Loran Brown, author of *My Husband's Mother.* "I can't believe it. I'm getting goosebumps as I am writing this. I received my first dollar advance in the mail. My books is on its way to be published. I keep pinching myself to make sure that I'm not dreaming. I finally did it. I can finally say, I have accomplished the one thing that I wanted to do most in my life."

Good for her. And good for PublishAmerica, for believing what no eyes had seen yet: that one simple dollar would mean the world to thousands. Like a diploma hanging on the wall, a certificate of graduation. "My dollar was framed the same day I received it," said Kenneth Chambers, author of *Dying to Believe.* "I have it hanging above my computer desk with a ceramic white wolf standing by it." Neil Milofsky concurs, "I have my book cover and dollar matted and framed together and hanging very near my computer for inspiration and motivation."

The same inspiration and motivation that he put into his wonderful book *A Symphony to Finish*. The kind of inspiration that all writers need and feed off of. After all, writing a book is a tough journey, an endeavor that comes from within, and it is always lonely. Therefore, in the same vein, Mary Rose, who put countless hours into her first book *Link Detonator*, knew immediately what to do when she received The Dollar in the mail: "I've already decided to hang my dollar in frame on the wall above my computer. It's the first dollar I've made for writing and, hopefully, it will serve as encouragement for later endeavors."

It is because of sentiments such as these—dreams that have actualized, fulfillment that has come to pass, a writer's vision that has become reality—that PublishAmerica has never withheld the advance amount from later royalty payments. We could, but we didn't, not because, "Oh well, it's only a dollar," but because we have always been mindful that sometimes even a dollar is sacred. One does not ask someone else to surrender and return a token of such beauty.

Chapter 4

"Got the books today and wow! They look great! Thank you for making a dream come true."

—A. K. Barnes, author of *Mosby's Gold*

"Maybe it's just my imagination but I'm sure this is the finest looking book I've ever seen!! I think I'll take your advice and go out and celebrate."

—Sharon Rose, author of *Missed, by a Hair*

Things We Couldn't Do

So we had the right time, the right place, and we also believed that we had the right attitude. Or did we?

Our attitude was that we were going to be self-sufficient, self-reliant, self-sustained. No loans, no banks, no investors, no vanity, no subsidy. We were going to pay all the bills ourselves, plus we were going to do as much as we could in-house. No outsourcing, no farming out, no depending on others. We were going to hire all these editors, designers, book shippers, and other assistants, and we were going to put them to work. Lots of work. Hard work. We were going to be incredibly busy. Oh, and by the way, we were going to print our own books as well. Or so we thought.

Right. What were we thinking? Looking back now we can not imagine what possessed us then, but at the time it seemed to make all the sense in the world. This major undertaking, the printing of books, it was something we certainly could quickly learn to do ourselves, we estimated. Printing was expensive; professional printers were going to charge us between five and six dollars for an average 225-page book. If we did the whole manufacturing process ourselves—the printing, binding, and trimming—we could maybe shave at least one dollar or more off our cost per unit. For two guys who figured that one day they'd sell a million books, that seemed worth attempting, or at the very least experimenting with.

It was not like we were novices, we boldly told ourselves. After all, we were men with experience in printing. In his younger years, Larry Clopper had self-printed and self-bound two books he had written. He had investigated what it took to put a book together, using trousers hangers to hold it while the glue dried, and he thought he'd done a pretty darn good job. Mainstream publishers that he had submitted his books to didn't agree, but, heck, what did they know? And I, well, I had actually learned how to run a small offset press decades ago, way back when a bunch of friends and I had fooled around with our own little printing shop that we ran out of my barn as a hobby. We could do this, we insisted. After all, how hard could it be, really?

GLUE, INK, AND BOOKMAKERS

We started to do what we thought was homework, and looked into the magic world of paper stocks, laminators, printers, copiers, trimmers, binders, glues, and inks. We went to Florida to see the InstaBook Maker, then much talked about, but not very impressive when challenged to do a professional job. We went to see and examine glues, and learned how to read the color of a hot adhesive. We tested awe-inspiring trimmers with their frightening, razor-sharp blades, and heard the awful stories of body parts that have gone missing as a result of amateur use. We compared laminators, learned the difference between run-of-the-mill applications on the one hand and layflat lamination on the other, and actually ordered one. We bought and studied paper of various weights, colors, and grains, and, more exhaustively, we ran tests with printers, both laser and jet.

Though we quickly learned to admit that, in fact, we were novices, undergraduates, laymen, we figured that we could actually do the job after all if we could overcome the one hurdle that has plagued digital printers for many years: curly paper. It was relatively easy to install a battery of home PC printers and make them print book pages, even on both sides. It was also doable to let one or two color laser printers spit out full-color covers that we would then run through our laminator for protection and gloss. And for less than sixteen thousand dollars we could obtain and operate a binding machine that would bind the text blocks inside the covers. A fancy trimmer would trim each book to size. As a matter of fact, in our innocence we thought that this entire process could be run by one person.

That was us, the free musketeers of PublishAmerica, the guys who were going to rock the boat not only in the publishing world but in the printing universe as well. If only we could get the paper to do what we wanted.

Everyone who has a laser printer knows what we are talking about here. You run a regular sheet of paper through your printer and it comes out hot and wavy like a rippled pond. It undulates, waves, crimples. Run a hundred sheets and you have a stack of ripples. It just refuses to stay flat. We tried everything from placing the stack under a big brick overnight, to burying it under a load of heavy books, to putting it in a more damp basement. We tested all kinds of paper qualities—light paper and heavy paper, medium paper, and paper in between—even examined if maybe the color made a difference. We tried it with laser printers and ink jet printers, cheap printers and expensive printers, even with copiers. And each new day when we came to the office hoping to see that the night had performed a miracle, we were disappointed. Waves and ripples all over the place. The paper wouldn't listen.

BLESSING IN DISGUISE

When you publish books, you want them to look like real books. This was one of the proud claims of digital printing—that the book it produced could not be distinguished from a book that came off an offset press. Only master printers could tell the difference, and only because their sharp, trained eyes could spot if a text was printed with ink or toner. Everything else was the same— the cover quality, the paper weight, fonts and font sizes, the clarity of printing, the overall feel of the book. Unless your paper rippled.

Book pages must lay flat; the text block must look smooth and solid. When you lay it level on a table, all pages must sit straight inside the cover. We tried everything we could to get this accomplished, but it just wouldn't work. Experts told us that we'd have to get ourselves a digital press of at least a hundred thousand dollars, possibly even a million. Heavy machines with heavy brand names such as Xerox, Kodak, Oce, IBM. We did not have a hundred thousand dollars, let alone more than that. So we swallowed our pride and abondoned the idea. Like all other publishers, we now had to rely on an out-of-house company printer to do the printing for us.

As it turned out, this was a blessing in disguise. Not only because we had underestimated the investment of time and resources in printing our own books, but also because we miscalculated the sheer volume of books that we were going to need, and the pace at which we were going to need them. Plus we underestimated Murphy's law. When you start building up an ambitious organization such as PublishAmerica from scratch, crafting something where nothing was before, you'll have your hands full with just about everything, anything, even if you focus on only being a publisher, and not a publisher who also wants to be a printer. All that could go wrong did indeed go wrong, not just once but repeatedly. From managing postage to folding direct mail letters, from losing book illustrations to shipping books with the wrong covers, from hiring staff to finding enough parking spaces in a crowded downtown area, even in a small town like Frederick, Maryland. Each a minor headache issue, but a big and nasty migraine when combined.

A lot of things went right, though. One of them was the printing company that we eventually picked. Another was that, as it turned out, at the eleventh hour the seller made an administrative error with that laminator order: we escaped having to purchase a fancy machine that we'd never use.

Chapter 5

"PublishAmerica has a great team and it is such a blessing to work with such wonderful people."

—Timothee Ntouba Mboule, author of *The African American Association of Mass Return*

"How About That, Isn't That Something!"

In business, inefficient organizations don't survive. Inadequate processes tend to die in their infancy. Ineffective systems are train wrecks waiting to happen.

What works in government certainly does not work in the real world. Government departments and institutions are as a rule of thumb Inefficiency City. They are oversized pyramids, with everyone reporting to a superior who is reporting to a supervisor who is reporting to a deputy manager who is reporting to a manager, and then you're still only at the base of the pyramid. While working in government, having stamina is more important than having merit. Stay around, show up each day, keep your desk reasonably clean, produce a pile of paperwork, and accept a future of no more than two promotions, three at best. On the plus side, your job is virtually safe.

Government organizations are not in the business of risk-taking; in fact, they are not in business at all. And we don't want them to be. Government is supposed to be of the people, to represent and serve us. We don't want government to take any risks; we want it to be the one predictable entity that society has, stale as a funeral parlor. Unfortunately, with predictability comes a glaring absence of incentives to be innovating, cutting-edge, efficient. Government wastes endless amounts of time and money, but since it has no competition in a marketplace, there is no built-in pressure to do a better job. Where such pressure is absent, people become averse to change; therefore, each time something new needs to be tackled or implemented, government tends to add more people. Organizationally, it feeds on itself. It always grows bigger, never smaller. If government were a business, it would go broke before a court could issue Chapter-11 protection.

Both PublishAmerica founders had previous experience with government environments. Larry had been hired as a consultant who was to teach defense specialists how to network their computer systems, and what he had seen there had baffled him. And I had a past in Europe, and had therefore been spoon-fed the cradle-to-grave attitude. We both knew firsthand the difference between efficiency and inefficiency. We also knew that PublishAmerica could only come off the ground, and stay there, if we made efficiency our top priority.

RE-INVENTING THE CATAPULT

I have often said this to people, and I say it again: Larry Clopper is the supreme master of efficiency. And not only that, as I mentioned before, he is also a master teacher. I remember all those instances of us sitting at our conference table together, which was also our shared desk, listening to him predicting, spotting, identifying inefficiencies in what we were trying to set up, where I believed that we were looking at concepts that were already highly effective and systematic. No, he would say, this will lead to time loss; why don't we remove this step, or that? And he was always right, without exception. Larry could look at a certain production procedure and detect ways to simplify it or make it less labor-intensive and more time-effective. He actually studied those kinds of things; he tested them, trial-and-errored them, then documented the best steps.

I should not have been surprised. After all, this was a man who had a patent certificate hanging on his wall, as the inventor of the hexadecimal abacus. And if you asked about it, he would show you the abacus and teach you how to make calculations, not with a base-10 number system, but a base-16. And you'd actually understand it, too. The man has a master's degree in computer science, where they work with binary numbers and bytes, and since bytes usually contain eight digits, it is easier to refer to them in hexadecimal terms than in decimal lingo. That's what inspired him to develop a device that combines modern technology with ancient Chinese culture, even though he would be the first to admit, with that grin, that it has repeatedly proven itself to be almost entirely useless. "How about that," he would say. "Isn't that something!"

Also, this was the man who was fascinated by inventions made centuries ago, such as those pyramids, or the trebuchet. So fascinated that he had assembled his own mini catapult, and he used it to explain to staff and visitors how something so seemingly simple and obvious had affected and changed world history by making medieval castles and walled cities effectively defenseless.

It was a relevant metaphor for what we, in all modesty of course, hoped PublishAmerica would accomplish, and just so we would be well prepared, we actually practiced slinging pennies, marbles, and coffee creamer through the office. That was fun.

THE BEELINE MAN

No wonder that he was on top of these efficiency issues; he loved finding the shortest way from A to B. As a young backpacker, by the time he had arrived in North Africa and had made up his mind that he wanted to see South Africa, he did what very few others would do. Larry crossed the entire continent from north to south, in a virtual beeline, even if it required passing through the most formidable and grim disease-ridden war zones. He braved fevers, infections, and nights in warlord prisons; he dodged bullets, escaped captivity, ate inedible food, and when he arrived at his destination, he dusted himself off and taught English literature to both the privileged and the poor.

A guy like that can be trusted with efficiency, and it showed at PublishAmerica. A patient teacher by nature, a man who actually loves to teach and instruct, he made it a point to sit down with each individual employee who asked for help, or who was caught being less than effective, and he walked them through all the steps of their particular task until they understood it, and each time they tried to insert an extra step that they believed made life easier, he explained why they were wrong and made them do it the right way. Initially, with little funds to spare, we were hiring mostly young people, kids just out of school, and we entrusted them with big responsibilities. Not every one of them succeeded, but those who did thanked it in no small degree to Larry Clopper, who had leveled their playing field for them. Those who didn't, it is safe to say, were beyond help.

Today, PublishAmerica is a template of efficiency, an all-smooth organization, a beehive of beelines. This has Larry's fingerprints all over it.

Chapter 6

"This is a dream come true. Thank you all so much!"

—DJ Marshall, author of *The Alpha Treaty*

Hitting the Ground Running

People often wonder how we got started so fast. How were we able to hit the ground running? On top of my two decades in newspaper publishing, I had already a few years' experience as a book publisher, and I had learned some things the hard way. Contrary to Larry, who had steadfastly refused to have his own books published the vanity way, I had once been published by a vanity publisher, at a whopping price of more than six thousand dollars. I hated it, and I hated to have to depend on other publishers to begin with, which was at the time the only reason why I started my own little publishing company out of my basement. I wanted to continue to write books, and I wanted to always be assured that I'd have a publisher. So I became one.

Having no clue as to how to do it any differently, I charged my early authors a fee. That didn't work; it made nobody feel right, so I first charged them, but then paid them back. That made nobody rich either. I started to publish for free, but couldn't get the scale right. All of this was pre-PublishAmerica. It was a learning curve, an education, discovery. By the time Larry and I first met, I knew what a dead-end street was. Fortunately, that's also an essential ingredient of acquired wisdom.

I had hired a smart young lady who came from Germany, where she had been working for Bertelsmann, the publishing giant that today also owns Random House. She took care of building the bare foundations of an infrastructure that a publishing company of any size needs: she set up arrangements with wholesalers such as Ingram and Baker&Taylor, and with vendors such as Amazon and Barnes and Noble; she composed necessary instruments such as author questionnaires, and she talked to bookstores, arranged book signings, and organized a slick book shipping system. Though I was stuck in the end, at least I knew what didn't work and what did, plus I had an idea or two about what might work in the future, and also there was a seed of infrastructure that could be handed over to our new company.

That, and shelves filled with hundreds of manuscript submissions that I had not been able to afford to publish, from authors who were in my own old category, who could not find themselves a decent publisher. They had run across the name and address of my first company and thrown a Hail Mary. My basement office had been their wide receiver.

STUMBLING BLOCKS, STEPPING STONES

There were about six hundred of those manuscripts sitting on stack after stack, pile after pile, and they had not been touched by me or my old team. Today we receive more than that many submissions every week, but at the time we thought it was a whole lot—and it was. I showed them to Larry, and together we wondered how many of these authors would welcome an offer to have their book published at no cost to them. All, half, only a few? Here we had the perfect opportunity to test our concept. Instead of first trying to find authors who might be interested, we could skip that step. We already had our test group, our focus group, right here on the shelves in my basement. Almost all of them had included an email address, so we were going to review their work, and if we liked what we saw we were going to send them an acceptance message.

By that time the founders had already decided that our niche was not primarily going to be decided by a book genre, but by who our authors were. If they were one of the refused and rejected, then they were our group. We could loosely define their profile: they were persistent people with an artistic streak, who had tried again and again to get their work published, who had not succeeded to date, but they were unyielding so they kept trying. These were folks who in the face of adversity worked hard to turn stumbling blocks into stepping stones. Almost by a rule of nature, this had to be what their books were about, too: characters who overcame a major obstacle, a challenge, a barrier. So there was our genre niche as well: we were going to publish works that dealt with characters overcoming a hardship, both fiction and nonfiction.

We worked our way through those six hundred manuscripts, and we were lenient. In the next round, for our own sanity, we would quickly adopt stricter guidelines about what and what not to accept, but in those early weeks we were excited and hungry to get the ball rolling, so we said "OK" to roughly five out of six books: five hundred or so authors received an email, the other one hundred or so manuscripts failed to make the cut and ended in the recycling bin.

Living in the twenty-first century we have almost forgotten how life was before we had email, but really it was a different life. Publishers communicated with their authors by regular mail, and the term snail mail had not yet been introduced because there had been nothing better and faster to compare it to. It took days, often weeks, to correspond about decisions, which not only made everything slow, but it prevented most things from happening on a mass scale as well. It is hard to imagine, but email and internet did not tip over to being universally embraced until as recently as 1996. After that, nothing was the same, especially in the media world. Book publishing is part of that media world.

CONGRATULATIONS

We sent out our acceptances in groups of twenty-five, sometimes fifty or sixty. We had put a skeleton website together that explained who we were and what we had in mind, and also what an author realistically could expect, and our acceptance letters referred to that site. We attached the general text of our contract, boilerplate agreement language that had been time-tested long before we adapted it to our circumstances and peculiarities, and that had gone through the fingers of a trizillion lawyers, so we knew that it was standard, fair, and transparent. Of course, we also stressed that we would pay the entire bill.

Our acceptance message read as follows:

"Dear [author]:

I am happy to inform you that our Publisher has decided to give your book, [title], the chance it deserves. Attached you will find a sample copy of our contract for your careful review. Upon receiving your e-mail in acceptance with the terms, we will forward the final contract documents to you via regular mail for your signature.

The main terms of the contract are that we will pay you climbing royalties starting at 8%, you retain the copyright, and we will produce the book within 365 days. A symbolic $1 advance underlines that all financial risk is carried by the Publisher, as we firmly believe it should be.

After both parties have signed the contract, you will be contacted by our production department with a list of questions and suggestions. Please feel free to e-mail any concerns or questions dealing with the terms of the contract to [our email address]. Also, please visit our web site at www.PublishAmerica.com for a full understanding of who we are and what we do.

Welcome to PublishAmerica, and congratulations on what promises to be an exciting time ahead. Sincerely, etc."

It was a powerful text that covered all the bases, an acceptance letter that every author must have dreamed of back when they had put the first word of their book on paper. In fact, the message was so succinct, compact, and all-encompassing that over the years we have modified it only slightly, and today it is still in use.

The first responses came in within minutes. Authors accepted our offer one after the other—five, ten, fifteen, and it soon became clear that there are three categories of authors. The first group accepts the offer immediately. They briefly glance through the contract, and they are so happy that they would probably accept virtually any contract terms, which is heartwarming but also unwise. They are the largest group, and today we repeat telling them, more than once, to ask us any contract questions they might have before they sign, if for no other reason than that it saves us time down the road, when those questions come up anyway.

The second category is more careful. They are our time savers; they know what to look for in a contract. They thank us for the offer and announce that they will read it thoroughly, and then they come back with questions. They also end up accepting offer and terms eventually; they just need a little more time so they can be thorough and complete.

And then there is a minority group of funny people. They are suspicious of everything unexpected that comes their way, good or bad, and immediately start making demands, frequently of an outrageous nature. They require advances of tens of thousands of dollars or more: in the very first week there was a woman from Texas who wanted five million down, and another five million when the book came off the press, plus first-class plane tickets for a first-class book tour, with a chauffeured limo and bodyguards. This group never signs our contract, mostly because we withdraw our offer as soon as we detect their troublemaking natures. We want to publish regular people, not jerks.

We discovered a pattern that stayed with us consistently for the first two, three years. Two-thirds of the authors we accepted accepted us in return. Over time, the percentage moved closer to eighty—an incredibly high yield. Within a few months PublishAmerica had signed up more than three hundred authors.

We were in business.

Chapter 7

"I am still a bit in shock that my book is actually getting published. I have just signed the contract and finished with my final editing / author questionnaire. When they asked for photographs for the back cover, that's when it hit me; that this is FOR REAL! It's been a long road, but the ten-year process has paid off. It's very exciting and I am thankful to God for opening this door with PA and I am looking forward to my future as an 'author,' no longer an 'aspiring writer.'"

—Joanne M. Kerzmann, author of *Shadowed Remembrances*

"Before I heard about PublishAmerica, I self-published four of my previous books. I had to, because

many of the major publishers don't want to take a risk on people who aren't already widely known. I love PublishAmerica because it doesn't require talented writers to get agents or jump through ridiculous hoops in order to get their work published! To all the aspiring writers out there who read books in bookstores and say to themselves, 'Geez, I'm a better writer than a lot of these guys': PublishAmerica is the answer to your prayers."

—Eugene Williams, Jr., author of *I Am the Darker Brother*

A Norman Rockwell Troupe

Who were those authors, and who are they in general? Years after we signed up our first three hundred, we have a pretty sharp picture of them; we know what they want, think, hope, believe, fear. Though we had more than roughly thirteen thousand authors under contract at the moment of this writing, we had over the years been communicating with more than forty thousand others who wanted to come onboard, and we had reasons to believe that this number would exceed a hundred thousand by the end of 2006. At PublishAmerica we are writers experts. Not the celebrity, 50-city book tour, all-glamor writers, but the regular folks—your next-door neighbor, someone's brother, sister, niece, cousin, daughter, son, grandparent, mom, dad. In other words, America.

They all have that artistic streak, obviously. But they also harbor a drive to teach, educate, explain, instruct. They have something to say, and writing is their best means of communicating it. Most of them choose fiction because it allows them what poetry allows the poets: the tool of words, images, perceptions that, when used in fiction, may go beyond their everyday meaning and lift the hearts and minds of their readers to a different plane and sphere. Only a minority write nonfiction.

They tend to write about themselves, basically. About what they have experienced, felt, done, learned. They have seen things, gone through challenges that transformed them, met people and situations that changed them. They have been at a certain place in life, and a spark inside, a glow, instructs them to mention and share it, because that is what human instinct is all about. Our collective experiences become roadmarks that others after us may use while continuing down man's path. Writing them down, being a storyteller, passing the baton—it is the stuff that educates the generations.

Ask them the question and most will confirm that it also helps to know that part of their minds and souls will live on beyond their lifetimes. But this is not their primary drive. What motivates them more than anything else is that writing makes them aware of being alive among the living. They have something to say, and they want, need, crave feedback. Very few writers compose something that they don't want to be seen until after their death, unless it is their will. They want their work published, which means becoming public, open, available, known, part of society. They want it to be discussed, debated, used, and liked, and they want to live to see this happen.

BOOKS ARE FOREVER

There is something about the book as a physical phenomenon that is appealing to virtually everyone. It is one of the most basic and indispensable elements of our culture, which to most is a Judeo-Christian or Muslim culture where the ultimate Story has been handed over from generation to generation in the form of a book, a scripture, a text on sheets of paper. The word Bible means "book," Qur'an means "recite, read," Torah refers to a "book of laws." In our collective awareness, a book is the primary tool of revelation and discovery, and those of us who feel the urge to add to collective knowledge are intuitively inclined to choose the book as our platform.

As an aside, I hasten to add here that, for this very basic and millennia-old reason alone, reports of the upcoming death of the physical paper-based book, bound in a paper-based cover, as a storytelling product, are greatly exaggerated. The e-book, touted by some as the Second Coming in book publishing, faces a challenge of epic, if not biblical, proportions if it wants to overcome approximately three thousand years of book-dominated culture any time soon. It's just not happening.

Our authors have dreamed of penning a book with their name on it for more than a few years. Their average age exceeds forty. They are predominantly baby boomers. They are almost equally divided between the sexes, with a slight tilt toward women, and the time spent on writing their books varies widely. Some wrote them within only a few months; others tell us that they needed more than thirty-five years, though those are exceptions. Rarely have our authors sat down for one particular stretch of time to write their books from cover to cover, in part because everyone's batteries of imagination need maintenance and a frequent recharge, which causes interruptions in productivity, but also, and mainly, because writing is not their day job. Outside journalism, writing is a full-time profession for only a very precious few.

Our authors are teachers, musicians, homemakers, professors, truck drivers, librarians. They are waitresses, doctors, travel agents, sheriffs, lawyers, inn keepers, bank tellers, newspaper deliverers, receptionists, preachers, military personel, or inmates. We know them to be students, schoolbus drivers, janitors, nurses, psychologists, accountants, clerks, cooks, pilots, cab drivers, grocers, store owners, politicians, booksellers, dieticians, and croupiers. Or inventors, bankers, bakers, farmers, veterinarians, used car salespeople, pharmacists, cashiers, pizza deliverers, flight attendants, news anchormen, retirees. And that's just off the top of my head, based on the thousands of query letters that I have seen.

They write during the quiet hour before sunrise, or at night when the day is done. They find time in weekends only, or during lunchtime at work. Some write on a laptop during their daily commute, others when the baby is asleep or while the kids are in school. There are those who write in a very disciplined manner, each day one or two pages, and there are others who write in fits and starts. Some take time off from work to write day after day; others can bring themselves only to write during vacations. And many write while they are actually supposed to be doing something else, when no one looks over their shoulder, simply because it is a stronger duty and they just can't help themselves.

A MAIN STREET LINE-UP

In other words, they are regular folks, people like you and me. Let us watch a small parade to make the point. Occasionally our authors share their professional backgrounds with the rest of the world, usually on our website's message board. One asks all the others, "What else have you done beside writing?" and there they come, a true line-up of Main Street America, a Norman Rockwell sketch of what this country is all about. A sample:

Carol Benning, author of *Unspoken Dream*: "At one time, before gambling was legal in Missouri, I worked with a company that was hired out to do gaming nights for different organizations. I used to deal blackjack. I also was a restaurant manager, bank teller, typist for two different insurance companies, worked the counter at a discount smoke shop. I guess we all knew we had a niche out there somewhere but weren't sure exactly what that was. We found it, folks! We are authors! No wonder we have had so many jobs. Just took us all a while to figure out what we could do."

Either that, or it's because one needs to have seen more of the world than just one job before serious stories can take root in an author's head. Kelli Deister, who wrote *Embracing The Storm:* "I've managed a couple of fast food restaurants in Waikiki. I started babysitting when I was twelve, worked for the Alaska state payroll when I was fourteen, worked in a local grocery store, was a preschool teacher's assistant, worked in a life insurance company, as a dental assistant, and am currently an assistant instructor for deaf students entering college."

Donna Laird, author of *Forever Yours*, said, "I worked for Wal-Mart several times. What can I say, I'm in Wal-Mart country...." C.J. Wilkes, author of *Daddy, I Forgive You*, was a cosmetologist, then "a credit union teller, photographer for Kiddie Kandids, nurses aid for Alzheimer's patients, worked fast food joints, computer tech, was a phone survey person, and was director of human resources." And Melanie Rutan, who penned *In*

Walks Love, used to work "in a shoe store, and a underwear sewing factory when I was going to college. Now I work in boring old insurance. No, I don't know why your claim wasn't paid!"

Very few have an actual background in writing, but Jim Woods is an exception. "I worked as staff editor and editorial director for one magazine house in Los Angeles," he says, "and from home as field editor for another magazine conglomeration based in San Diego, each position good for about six years. I worked in the aerospace/defense industry for many years as an engineering writer and technical editor. One of my early jobs while in high school was with a magazine distributor. How could I possibly ever become a book author?" Anyone's guess indeed. Jim wrote *Honk If You Love Geese.*

"I was a bouncer at a topless bar when I got out of the Navy, got tired of being beat up, so I quit," says Kevin Clark of *Children Growing Funny*, and Tarra Young, of *Druxel Manor*, adds that she "used to be a Tupperware consultant, even though I'm shy and don't like speaking to groups of people." Robyn Whyte, who wrote *I Call Her*

Mom, says, "I was a body repair estimator here in Michigan—there were only approximately five other women in the state doing the same line of work." And Sam Joy vividly remembers that "I once carried Nick Cage's bags to his private plane." He wrote *Legend of the Spear* and *And From the Ashes*. Sam, that is.

Then there are the ones who can't help shaking their heads looking back, such as author Steve Harrison. "The first paying job I had was pulling tobacco for $1.85 an hour when I was thirteen. Do this for one day and you will run back to your current job in relief," he says. Steve wrote *Undeserved Trust*. When he was sixteen he worked "as a clerk in the layaway department at Zayres, a now-defunct discount department store. At 10 PM I had to announce on the intercom that the department was now closed, while twenty people in line realized they had waited in vain. One lady hurled a big wheel at me, but I faked left and went right. I also worked as a copier repairman, surgically removing accordion-folded paper jams and patiently explaining the need to insert the power cord into the socket. By far the worst job I've ever had was Army recruiter. I had to make thousands of phone calls, mostly to people who really didn't want to discuss their future options. There are a multitude of people who want to join, but there are even more rules barring them from doing so. The next time you encounter a military recruiter, be nice to them, please."

GETAWAY CARS AND CAR HOPS

Of course, there's also the folks with the gazillion jobs, the people with the dazzling resume such as Rudy Girandola, author of *The Jade Chalice:* "OK, I'll confess, I played hooky in the fourth grade, got a job scraping carbon off engine pistons at 10, sold magazines and had a paper route (mornings up at 4 AM, finish by 6 AM, Sundays end at 8AM), was an usher, soda jerk, cook, pool hall racker, state highway maintenance worker, landscaper, auto mechanic, garage attendant, store clerk, mail clerk, aircraft factory kitchen helper, phys ed instructor, sports coach, tennis pro, teacher college, high school, elementary, school administrator, guidance counselor, actor, writer, political writer, editor, reporter, sports writer, education executive, driver (getaway cars), tutor, song writer, poet, radio announcer, summer camp counselor, lifeguard (and couldn't swim), insurance clerk, magazine writer. Oh, when I had my sixth child, I had four full-time jobs: teacher, editor, tutor, and political canvasser."

Betty Fasig, of *Wooffer*, has been "a bookkeeper, bartender, babysitter, bank teller and book seller, an obit writer, proof reader, a dispatcher, and a convenience store operator, a forklift operator, waitress, a basket painter, and door-to-door salesperson (hated that), a house cleaner, a mother, a grandmother and a great-grandmother, a plant grower and a pond planter and now an author. I am still a grower of plants and own a nursery business and plant ponds. I am new at being an author, a book signer and a book marketer." And the author of *Richard, The Legacy*, Roger Sitaric, has been a "hamburger joint waiter, janitor, baker, handyman, factory worker (one job assembling bikes and another job working in a warehouse sorting, receiving, and shipping veneer), nurses aid, salesman, security guard, immigrant aid worker, day care, elementary school sub, painter (walls, not paintings), kennel worker, petting zoo assistant, personal assistant, sales associate."

And the parade goes on, and as you can see, it is very easy to connect with these authors. They are your cousin, your neighbor, and some of them are simply exactly like you. Tessie Chapman was "a babysitter at age 11, a waitress at 18, homemaker at 21, Certified Electronic Solderer for Litton ATD at 35, nutritional service clerk in Three Rivers Hospital in 2003, and now I am back as a solderer in a local electronic company here in town." She wrote *The Enchanted Island*. And Linda Oness, of *The Tinkerers* and *Ghost Stories from Beyond the Grave*, who hails from Canada but is no less Rockwellian, "worked as a car hop at A&W. Remember when you used to park in the lot, and those girls would bring you your food on a tray that fastened to your car window? Juicy teen burgers, and a large root beer foaming over the top of the perfectly chilled mug? Would you like an apple pie with that? A big smile, and the ching-ching of the change machine? Yup, that was me. Then I worked as a manager for a winery, then became a certified welder, and then a computer tech."

Glenn Ross Johnson wrote *Sila and the Dog from Hell*. As a youngster, she "mowed yards, packed potatoes for a grocery store, and waited tables at a dairy and local restaurant. When old enough, I worked weekends and summers as a 'ware boy' for a local pottery. While in college, I worked at the cafeteria and student center, delivered mail during Christmas holidays, and spent summers working as a pipe benders assistant in a factory. After college, I served two years on active duty with 3rd Armored Division and eight years as a public school teacher, assistant principal, and principal. Then I worked 30 years as a professor at a major research university, during which I was a department head, implemented and directed a faculty development center, and served as an associate editor for an academic journal."

"...AND FATHER"

Andrew Huddleston, who wrote *Heart & Iron,* was a "drive-in theater worker, credit bureau clerk, furniture delivery, infantryman, karate instructor, shoe clerk, industrial relations, safety director, human resources manager, and father." And Melodie Rogers, of *Follow Me,* "took tickets at a racetrack, worked in my parents' restauraunt at the age of 14, bartender, housekeeper, cake decorator, deli manager, waitress, among others. I once worked in a bar that was half in Canada and half in the US. It was called the Halfway House and had a line down the center of the floor. It's still there, just closed now."

Walt Lange, author of *Trawlaine,* remembers that his first job was a paper route, and "back then we walked and carried papers in a contraption that went over our shoulders. I mowed everyone in the neighborhood's lawns with a people power mower. In high school I was what could be called a soda jerk, made sodas and burgers, etcetera at a counter-type lunch stand for a whole $5 a week, big money then. After high school I went to work as a mail clerk in a bank, then into the U.S. Navy. I was released from active duty ten days before the Cuba Blockade. Went to work as an insurance underwriter, then factory worker for aerospace, owner/operator of a Red Wing Shoe franchise, machinist in both aerospace and oil field equipment. House painter, worked in a rock quarry, bagging roofing rock and chicken grit, owned a small earthmover and dump truck and cleared acreage for weed abatement. Industrial catering (Roach Coach, Lunch Wagon), licensed contractor, machine parts inspector, FAA repairman, back to painting, retired, and now I am an author."

The Bull's author Patrick Shanahan "started out small selling used hub caps and wheels to garages and salvage yards. I graduated to working as a collection representitive for a neighborhood businessman who specialized in short-term loans. After spending a brief time behind the wire I retired from that occupation and went into union organizing. That was fun but after a while you become a target of law enforcement and wherever you go, unprovable stories seem to follow." And Joe Wellman's "first job was baling hay for 50 cents a day. In high school I worked in a factory. I've been in the army, a radio announcer, a reporter and finally a teacher for thirty-five years. Oh, and I also taught flying. And now I'm writing." About teaching, obviously. Joe is the author of *The Private Lives of Teachers*.

"I walked beans for 25 cents an hour," says Donna Beeler. "Then I worked in a lumber yard doing books for 25 cents an hour, but most of the time I just worked for free on the farm. In other words, I was working for the bank, the implement company, and the fertilizer seed company. That was fun, though, and it was always in the fresh air and sunshine—that should count for something. Then I worked for an attorney in an insurance company for thirteen years. Now I work for myself—and I don't do much of that." Donna wrote *Passed Through the Window on My Way to Life*.

And then there's Edd Voss. "I sold papers as a kid, no paper route, just, 'Hey, mister, want to buy a paper?' I was maybe 8 at the time. I worked for Brooks Brothers as a store porter, I worked in sales for Sears, both during high school, then I became infantryman, U.S. Army photographer, ditch digger, photo lab tech for Colorado State University. I sold cars, oil investments, water conditioners, photo plans, signs to businesses, I took photos for PCA doing the old K-Mart routine (traveling from store to store), Olan Mills, I worked doing church directories, and school photos (up to 500 kids a day). I was an exterminator, then I started driving trucks, and happened to write a book along the way." The book's title is *A Tree for America.*

Author Robbie Riley, of *The Creaking Stair Step* fame, "chopped cotton, picked cotton, picked strawberries and tomatoes. Worked in grocery store, helped build houses, cleaned motel rooms, was a waitress, drove tractor, combine, 2-ton grain truck. Raised hogs and turkeys. Used a chainsaw, owned a small pizza place, worked as accounts payable clerk and coordinator. County commissioner, town alderwoman, helped part-time in graphic design business. Gee, did I forget something?"

And Carol Troestler, who wrote *Flow On Sweet Missouri,* "organized stuff and wrapped presents in a dry goods store, waitress, office mailroom and parts ordering department for a large company, English teacher, school social worker, counselor, trainer, group facilitator, ran my own business, writer."

STARRING IN THEIR OWN BOOKS

Like many, Carol also highlights what she calls, "my most important job: mom and grandma." Because that is what our authors are first and foremost, real-life individuals, professionals, parents. That's the source that they draw from, the well they tap into. It is the basis, the foundation, the origin of their storytelling. They often use fictional characters to describe their real-life selves. Their stories reflect their own dreams, hopes, fears, or past experiences. Their main characters almost always possess, in an abstract way, their own genes. They have the author's qualities and flaws, but in the end they mostly possess the author's strengths.

Their fictional characters allow them to be more honest and open. They make it possible for the author to reveal elements about him or herself that, when exposed in a nonfictional manner, could be embarrassing. A common example is that few people are willing to openly discuss sex scenes in which they participate, but many feel unrestrained to describe those very same scenes, in detail, using the alias of their fictional characters.

There is a risk involved with describing one's world this way because there is a line of separation that can not be crossed if a sufficient degree of "observership" is to permeate the story. The skilled writer is able to look at his life from an elevated vantage point, as an observer with a helicopter view, and hover over it like a hand that barely touches gently waving grassland. The less skilled writer is someone who has not yet achieved that observing distance, and who is more likely to portray his world with the very same intentions as his more seasoned peer, but now the hand does not caress or brush, but it is stuck in a tightly fitting glove, inside of which every little detail and nuance is still acutely felt.

But who is to judge this? Who better than the author knows what message, image, sensation she wanted to convey? Who determines where this or that book's line of separation is, or should be? And at the end of the day, do observing and distance make or unmake a book? These are tough questions, and our authors are always searching to find the correct answers, *their* correct answers. When is someone skilled? Who will take their measure?

Some will say that this is up to the larger audience out there. That they are the ultimate judge of quality in a book, that they ultimately resolve such questions, and while this is debatable, at least it is the larger audience that will decide the size and impact of the splash that a book will make. And that's where PublishAmerica comes in.

PROSECUTION, JUDGE, AND JURY

For the public to even be able to know that there is a new book out there, it must be published first. Who determines skill and quality? The answer used to be that mainstream publishing does, the old powers that be. They played prosecution, judge, *and* jury, and that was the end of many authors' dreams, right there. Millions upon millions of writers throughout modern history never stood a chance of having their books published because their residence happened to be on Main Street, and the dukes and duchesses of mainstream never go there. Case in point: after my own dad died a decade ago, we found under his desk five meticulously typewritten manuscripts: a thriller, two novels, and two history books—never published, and under a stack of old newspapers in a corner of his office we saw why. A small stack of rejection mail: "Not good enough," "Needs a total overhaul," "Try a different hobby." Prosecution, judge, and jury. And like my father, there were, and still are, maybe a million or more others.

So PublishAmerica chose to give these writers a break, a chance, an opportunity to present their cases to the public. And our authors appreciate this. It's the break they had been hoping for for a long time. Living is all about sharing, so what good does it do if someone spends months or years writing down their thoughts, their experiences, their acquired growth, and there is no one to share it with, no one to benefit from it all? A book written ought to be a book shared, period.

Not all books will be shared through PublishAmerica, clearly, and in the next chapter I will explain why. Also, not all books will be shared with large audiences. In America alone, each year some 175,000 new books are released. That the public at large will not see all of them is the understatement of the year. Very, very few books make it to the bestseller lists, and that is not even taking into account how poorly designed those lists are: if your book is not published by the nation's top ten publishing houses, you will not even be considered for any list. Example: according to the renowned book marketing expert John Kremer, who followed such lists in 1996, the much-ballyhooed bestsellers list in *Publishers Weekly* contained only one book from a non-top ten publisher. One. *In the entire year!* The rest were simply not considered—ignored, disregarded, haughtily overlooked.

For almost all writers this means that fame will be

limited. They won't become a celebrity, and certainly not overnight. Their success, triumph, victory will be celebrated within a relatively local circle of a few thousand, or even just a few hundred who will know them by name, who will cherish them, who will pay admiration and respect. There will be exceptions to the rule; an occasional author will break through and hit a bull's eye somewhere, and everyone will cheer them. In fact, everyone wants to *be* them, but it is the exception. The rule on Main Street is that success echoes a few blocks, and not up and down the entire street because it is crowded there. Unless it is your local Main Street. Then it rings with deafening clarity, and everyone in the valley can hear it.

Our authors know this, and most of them proudly settle for it. It is more than they had even dared to hope back when all doors were slammed in their faces.

Chapter 8

"After my wife and I submitted our book it took only two weeks to receive a reply. After we received the notice that our book was accepted by PublishAmerica we were so excited that we threw a party. We both are from New Orleans and people here will throw a party for just about anything. We are so excited about being accepted by PublishAmerica that we are still partying to this day."

—Prince and Gaynelle Kaywood, authors of *An Unbelievable Story*

"I had been aimlessly writing [my book] for four long years, uncertain of its future and doubtful of any success. PA changed all that. It gave me hope and a

reason to keep working on my dream. Thank you for inspiring me to get it done and work on the rest of the series."

—Joel Segler, author of *The Afterburner*

Jerks And Heroes

There is no traditional publisher in the whole wide world who will publish just about everything. They can't. There are genres that require a specialization, a specific production and distribution background if you want to be able to market them properly. There are certain books that, by their sheer topics or dimensions, are special-needs books. Coffee table books, for instance, are not automatically touched by all publishers. Too many special needs, such as size, paper weight and quality, illustration demands. Also, frankly, there are certain authors that you don't want to touch. And there are books that a publisher simply can not agree with because of what they advocate. And, finally, there are books that are badly written—so badly that they are beyond editorial help.

PublishAmerica receives on average roughly a hundred and thirty new submissions per day, each day, at the time of this writing, spring of 2005. That is approximately thirty thousand submissions on an annual basis, considerably more than the almost twenty thousand submissions that we received in 2004. Of those submitted books, we must unfortunately refuse all the works that are children's picture books, and that's a great many. I am a grandfather who enjoys telling wild stories to his grandkids, yet I am stunned to see how many mothers, fathers, grandmothers, and fellow grandfathers there are out there who have a story to tell about a bird, a bear, an apple, a purple truck, a pony, a choo-choo train, a llama, a kangaroo, a cicada, a pair of tennis shoes, or a Egyptian mummy that wants to be an astronaut.

We can not publish them. We tried it for a while, but we were not happy with the final product. Those children's books look alright enough, but alright is not good enough for PublishAmerica. They are also disproportionally expensive to print, since digital color printing is not really cost-effective just yet. The color quality itself is fine, very fine actually, but for best results you want to see it on heavy, glossy paper, and this is prohibitively uneconomical. Each day we receive submissions for children's picture books. After experimenting with the genre for a few months, we decided to close the door on that one.

Then there are books that we simply, plainly, unceremoniously don't want, period. Books that advocate bigotry, hate, violence. Books that champion immorality, which is by definition an arbitrary field, but sexuality involving underage kids is a good example of stories that we refuse out of hand. Books that frivolously insult are on our taboo list as well, and so are books that go overboard in disparaging others. We have refused books that scandalized George W. Bush just as handily as we have rejected books that smeared Bill Clinton.

Book publishers ought to always be cautious and scrupulous when they go about denying an author. We exist by the grace of the First Amendment, and free speech ought to be sacred. Those of us who have visited countries where writers are persecuted for speaking their minds know how precious this right is. Those of us who have actually lived under such repressive regimes know and value this a hundred times better. And those of us who personally know writers who have been banished, exiled, chased away by their governments, and who have sat down with them to listen to their hair-raising and mind-boggling stories of being oppressed and tyranized for merely putting their thoughts on paper will go to great lengths to help ensure that everyone who has something to say is at least allowed to say it.

ANNE FRANK, A NEIGHBOR

For that reason alone, PublishAmerica continues to donate a percentage of its proceeds from *The Published Author's Guide To Promotion*, written by scores of our own authors, to a special fund that PEN, the non-political, non-governmental worldwide organization of writers, dedicates to supporting and defending "writers and journalists from all over the world who are imprisoned, threatened, persecuted, or attacked in the course of carrying out their profession," as PEN describes these haunted souls.

Also, I was born just blocks from where Anne Frank hid, where she was betrayed and arrested, and from where she was deported to die in a Nazi death camp. She was not allowed to breathe, to speak, to write. When you read her diary and you see her describe the houses and the streets that were your own childhood's setting, when you learn from your parents that this was in fact the real girl next door, believe me, it gets your attention. It makes you want to fight for equal rights for everyone.

That said, however, a right is not an obligation; in fact, it is the opposite of an obligation. While we defend everyone's right to express themselves, PublishAmerica is under no obligation to publish everyone and print everything. We reserve our right to be selective, and we execute this right every day.

For instance by not letting writers in who during the process of discussing their contract forget their manners. If someone behaves like a jackass during the acceptance stage, he will usually end up being a major pain in the rear down the road, and nobody needs that. These are of course exceptions; the vast majority of the author population is nice, kind, and civilized—folks who are happy that they will soon see their book in print—and they treat you the same way you treat them. Only a very small minority behave like jerks, and true jerks waste no time showing it, which is a good thing because we can kick them out the door before they are even inside.

People are basically the same everywhere you go in the world. I spent four decades living and working in Europe, I have traveled in more than fifty countries, I have been in America for fifteen years now, and I can safely say that wherever one goes, people will behave similarly under similar circumstances everywhere. Each sings his own song, of course, but Russian mothers dote on their children just as lovingly as American moms do, Japanese boys play with the same toy cars that German boys play with (each made in China), French girls giggle just like Mexican or Moroccan or Moldavian girls do, and Irish guys drink their beer just as cheerfully and loudly as men in Iceland, Spain, or Canada. Most people are good and decent people.

But some are not. They treat you bad; they are angry, idiots, stupid. Somewhere in life they lost it, for whatever reason. You reach out to them by accepting their book for publication at their own request, and they bite your hand off. These people always assume the worst—that everyone else is out to get them. You tell them, 'Congratulations, we will publish your book at no cost to you at all,' and they respond, 'I don't think so, no way, do you have any idea who you are dealing with here, I want to talk to your superior, I know what you guys are after, you want to steal my book and sell it to Hollywood.' Aarrgghh. Grrrr. Bark, bark. And that's after they had sent us their book for consideration at their own initiative, unsolicited. We have no patience for such people, and we don't let them in.

THE WAY UP, OUT, AND BEYOND

As for genres, we will consider most. PublishAmerica is not a genre niche publisher. Our typical author is our niche, and, as portrayed earlier, our authors have a life attitude that can be found back in the content of their books. Almost every single one of those books deals with individuals facing and overcoming hardships, characters who succeed by being persistent and by turning stumbling blocks into stepping stones. There are exceptions to this rule, but they are rare. Whether the book was written in the adventure genre, or in cooking, dieting, education, fantasy, general fiction, health, history, horror, or humor, whether it is inspirational, mystery, general non-fiction, philosophy, poetry, romance, or science, or if it is sci-fi, self-help, a collection of short stories, spiritual, sports, suspense, thriller, western, or young adult, in virtually all cases, the book is about a challenge, and the author who has been on a life-long search points the way up, out, and beyond. It's fascinating.

Those are the books that we are looking for, these are the authors we stand up for, this is what PublishAmerica is all about. Wanna sneer at this or that author's particular language, at her story angle, at his style, at their perceived lack of sophistication, finesse, or worldliness? Go ahead, be my guest. You will be in a very small minority. Our authors represent America. They may come from afar, they may be raising their families in remote places, they may live in small towns or big cities, they may have unusual or regular jobs, and their backgrounds may be as varied as all the colors and shades on the nation's cultural spectrum. But they all have their studios, their ateliers, their writer's lodges on Main Street, and that's where most Americans live.

Chapter 9

"I just want to tell you what you have opened up for me by publishing my book, My Time to Care. *Not only have you fulfilled a dream for me but you have opened so many doors at this time of my life. Thank you for the beautiful job all of you, from my first contact to the finished product. It has been such a delightful experience. At 72 I have helped start a Care Giver Support Group in our church and our community. I have had calls from all around the country. My book is now in the Aging Information Resource Library in the Administration on Aging in Washington, DC. I have been asked to go to the International Conference on Family Care in Washington at which time I will report on my experiences in care giving and the support group at our church. I have been written up in the* Senior News, *a newspaper that covers the state of*

Georgia and have been asked to speak to several groups. You have made my life so fulfilled and I am doing what I wanted to do, help others in the care giving process."

—Barbara Winters, author of *My Time to Care*

"I was thrilled PublishAmerica decided to publish my book after being rejected over 10 years by 60 other publishers, most of whom never bothered to read my novel. Since then, I'm in my local Barnes & Noble. Now I've discovered I'm listed in Great Britain and New Zealand. That's all thanks to the efforts of PublishAmerica. They took a chance on me and that's all I asked. I have four other books ready and I'm starting to have faith (once again) in the American Dream!"

—Jeffrey Hauser, author of *Pursuit of the Phoenix*

Something to Talk About

Sometimes people ask us where all these PublishAmerica authors come from. It is not a question about their backgrounds, their walks of life, but about the sheer fact that so many found us, and about their apparent hunger to join us. Truth be told, both founders did not foresee or expect the actual size of PublishAmerica's massive success back when they first sat down putting the company together. Larry and I hoped for a thousand authors, maybe two or three thousand, numbers that would be astonishing enough if that's what PublishAmerica were to grow into. The entrepreneur's mind says, "Well, if three thousand, why not aim at five thousand then?; and if five thousand, why not ten?" and this is true in the sense that ambition is always a sound adviser, but the actual size of our spectacular growth was not really what we expected at first.

However, we could have known better, and soon we did. First of all, after we got to know the industry a little better we discovered how many thousands of writers were being taken in by vanity publishers. Initially, we could not understand why so many people were willing to pull their wallets and fork over hundreds, and often even thousands, of dollars just so they could see their book in print. But then two things dawned on us. One was that what we were looking at had to be the tip of an iceberg, the second that the seas would surely part if those same writers would be aware of PublishAmerica's existence.

If six thousand writers were willing, or able, to pay substantial fees to what was at the time the nation's most successful vanity publisher, XLibris in Philadelphia, there had to be at least sixty thousand others who couldn't, or wouldn't, spend that kind of money. That's where the rest of the iceberg was. And if all those folks would know about the alternative of PublishAmerica, where the only ones who were spending money were Larry Clopper and me, and where becoming and being a published author was free of any fees or charges, it was not hard to guess how they would vote. The iceberg would change course and make waves.

There was also a second development that told us that we were on to something big, and it reinforced our belief that our iceberg theory was right. Writers started to find us within weeks of us setting up a website and explaining and detailing our fundamentals. Not because Google searches were leading them towards us—it is a widespread myth that, on the internet, "if you build it, people will come." Any search keyword with "publish" in it would typically lead the searcher straight into a jungle of tens of thousands of websites that were related to publishing. For a long time, PublishAmerica was nowhere to be found on search engines.

WORD OF MOUTH

No, writers started to find our website because someone else told them to go there. As soon as our first small band of new authors had signed their contracts, they started to talk about it. Word of mouth got underway, and it was spreading like a transmittable condition, something so contagious that when you heard about it, you couldn't resist it. Writers contacted us out of the blue, leaving emails, dropping their manuscripts in the mail, and we had no clue where they were coming from. Later, we started to ask them how and where they had found out about us, so that by now we have a detailed understanding of all the different paths that lead to PublishAmerica, but in the beginning we could only guess. And all guesses led to a single answer: word of mouth.

It had to be. We were not advertising PublishAmerica anywhere. We had been tossing around a thought of maybe harvesting email addresses of authors who convened on the internet in chat rooms or in newsgroups, and alert those people to the fact that we existed, but we had decided against it. We deemed it low-class, kind of ambulance chasing, and we figured that most authors would agree with that assessment, and that they would not want to be part of a publishing family that angles for more members like a pay-to-pray televison ministry. Larry and I made a decision early on that we would not solicit any authors. We would do everything we could to make PublishAmerica known, but in a passive manner, and not by actively pursuing individual authors. There was one exception—an author that I personally set out to bring onboard—but I will save that story for later.

We were right, it was word of mouth. Newly contracted

authors were so happy with the course that their lives had taken that they immediately shared the news with anyone who would listen. And listen is what people do when someone tells them that they have written a book that soon will be published. Many writers are reluctant to share the fact of their writing with too many others while they are still in the process of composing their books. When it is still incomplete, it's still vulnerable. It is also not yet real—not good, solid, mature enough to be shared with others. But when the book is ready, and a publisher has decided to publish it at *the publisher's* cost and not the author's, that's when authors typically can not keep it quiet any longer. They want the whole wide world to know, and they find, to their delight, that people actually listen.

Most people are impressed when they discover that their friend, relative, co-worker, boss, friend's friend, fellow church member has written a book, because it says something about that person, about their substance, their intellectual baggage. They look at the newly announced author with new respect, with admiration and awe, and, yes, occasionally also with envy. They will listen, and many of them will spread the word. And somewhere, some day, the word reaches another author, another writing soul who is still unpublished, and for that writer the name PublishAmerica also becomes the key that opens a door where all doors had remained locked year after year.

"WE WANT YOUR BOOK, NOT YOUR MONEY"

Today, almost six years later, this same word of mouth is amplified by hundreds, even thousands of articles in newspapers, magazines, newsletters, journals, and author interviews on radio and TV stations. Not a day goes by without a local newspaper somewhere, in some town, region, or big city, writing a story about a PublishAmerica author, and this of course helps our name recognition greatly. Our staff sends out dozens of news releases every day, each time we have contracted a new author or released a new title. Some of those press releases are picked up by the media, others are ignored until the authors themselves contact their local reporters— which, by the way, most journalists find very hard to ignore—and the net result is this continuous stream of media attention.

But it has not always been that way. PublishAmerica and its current fame have been built from the grassroots up, by regular folks who told other regular folks, because they had a real story to tell, a success story, a story of happiness and achievement. It was a story of doors opening up, of opportunity knocking, of new horizons beckoning, and it planted seeds wherever a mind was fertile. When we now look at our database with its many thousands of names and book titles, and we see the column "How Did You Hear About Us?" it is simply fantastic to read all those names of individuals who have been listed by our authors as their source of information and referral.

Later, we started to do our share of advertising, just to make certain that new writers would know about PublishAmerica, to make sure that they were aware of their options. We learned how to communicate with one-liners. Larry came up with, *"We treat our authors the old-fashioned way—we pay them,"* a motto that still crowns all of our web pages. And I coined, *"We want your book, not your money,"* which we used as a slogan in many of our ads. We advertised in magazines, newsletters, seminar brochures, and on the internet. We discovered, as most entrepreneurs do, that most advertising does not work, but that some does, and we spent a small fortune on locating the difference. But whatever we spent, and wherever we spent it, this was the key message: author, whoever you are, if your book is any good, then do not ever spend a single dime on getting it published; you shouldn't have to, and today you have a choice.

This, more than anything else, drew authors to PublishAmerica. It did when our name was only a rumor, and after we acquired the means to spread and control our message, it did so even more. Today, more than a thousand authors ask to be admitted every two weeks. Our website registers three hundred thousand hits *every day*.

Chapter 10

"Way to go, PublishAmerica! I'd like to thank everyone! PublishAmerica is the way!"
—David Anthony, author of *In Search Of Dorothy*

"After 9-11 many book publishers stopped accepting manuscripts from unpublished authors. This made the task of searching for a publisher extremely difficult. I kept the search up and prayed that God would let me find a publisher. Without fail, He did. He led me to PublishAmerica. I couldn't have asked for a more experienced and professional team."
—Cherrie Ann Moses, author of *Erin Landers and the Phantom Peril of the Night*

From Venus

"After we acquired the means to spread and control our message": since nothing lasting in life happens

129

overnight, it took PublishAmerica at least two years before we could even set aside a meager, less-than-modest advertising budget for furthering our name recognition. In the beginning, money was always scarce, by design.

One difference between PublishAmerica and vanity publishers is that we had to finance the entire operation until we could start selling books, which was a full eight months. Vanity houses have their operations financed by their authors. Pre-funded, that is. The very first action an upstart vanity house takes is to deposit its very first check, written by an author, long before any production activity takes place. At PublishAmerica, in contrast, we were the ones who wrote the checks.

Another difference is that the big vanity publishers also benefitted from big investment money. Venture capital has flowed to places such as XLibris, AuthorHouse, and iUniverse like the Mississippi to the ocean. Seeing who the real owners are in vanityland is like reading the *Who's Who* of the rich and the mighty: publishing giant Random House, bookselling behemoth Barnes & Noble, Warburg Pincus, Johnson Ventures,

Gazelle TechVentures are all reported to be deeply involved with publishing the books of an approximate 50,000 poor souls who have been required to shell out their own money in return for seeing their book in print. Cumulatively these investors have put tens of millions of dollars—reportedly more than fifty million—into vanity outfits, which would indicate that, on average, the big ticket folks have been willing to risk one million dollars for every one thousand authors they would attract.

That is a lot of money, but not if you may assume that a thousand authors will pay you a thousand dollars each for the privilege of being associated with you, which is what the basic concept of vanity publishing is all about. And when you are the vanity guy who wants to start a vanity house, heck, life is a lot easier when it comes to building your company, compared to the challenges that the founders of PublishAmerica faced when they knew that every penny, dime, nickel, and quarter would have to come out of their own pockets.

Larry Clopper and I were by no means members of the rich and mighty society. We had each seen both successes and failures in our previous occupations, and we had both been fortunate enough in that we were not up to our eyeballs in debt. But it was not like we had money to burn, absolutely not. We knew that if we wanted our concept to work, we would have to build it up on the cheap because that was all we could afford. And as I have stated before, we took the old-fashioned, old-school approach: we refused to take any loans or accept any outside investing.

COOKIE MONSTERS

Ironically, investors came knocking on our door repeatedly as soon as they got wind of what we were doing—both private investors and venture capitalists. We listened to them politely and gave them coffee. We heard them say nice things about us and about our company, and about all those authors out there whose books would be a safe investment, and we dutifully nodded when they insisted that our lives would become so much easier if only we let them come in. And after they had said what they came to say, we thanked them and told them no.

There was no way in the world that we were going to sell part or all of the company just so we could fund what we knew we could, and should, bear by ourselves. Angel investors are rare. The guys who came to talk to us wanted more than just a piece of PublishAmerica. They were cookie monsters; they wanted the whole nine yards, and who could blame them. They saw what we saw—a great opportunity—and they wanted to buy it, run it, own it. But that was the thing that we wanted to do ourselves, to own it and to run it, because we knew it was going to be great, and it was going to be fun, and we were the right guys to do it. We had what it took. That's why we built it ourselves.

The publishing world has been a major showroom of mergers and takeovers for many years now, and more of the same is to be expected. Huge slices of the pie are owned by foreign companies—German, Dutch, British, Australian. Some of it has been good for business, some has been questionable, and among the questionable investments are some that have been paid for by venture capital infusions, in particular those that occurred in vanityland. When guys with a publishing background are shoved out the door to make place for money men whose primary task it is to protect their investment, something vital gets lost. You lose a connection with your authors, and with the readers of your authors' books. A publishing company needs to understand the author's mindset, needs to know what motivates and moves her, what makes him tick, needs to speak the language of the author's heart. If it doesn't, sooner or later a disconnect will show, and one day it is going to hurt business.

PublishAmerica's founders wanted to owe nothing to anyone—no money, no percentage of the decision making, zero, zip. The only thing we were happy to owe would be gratitude—to our authors who would entrust us with their books, whose works we were going to make available to a larger public. That was going to be our sole source of income: books. We believed that we spoke our authors' language, that we understood them, that we were one of them, and that America's authors would recognize this.

PILLARS OF STRENGTH

We built our organization step by step, hiring staffers as we needed them, editors first, then cover designers, then our sales team, our shipping operators, and tellingly enough, our accountants last. Since we would not be bringing in any money until we'd sold our first book, there was no need for a bean counter until the very last, no need until there would be beans to count to begin with. Up until then we would only spend, out of our own pockets, and that is exactly what we did.

We hired a few strong people first, all women who knew what they were doing, and who knew what was required of them. Some of them became pillars of strength that to this day are still integral to PublishAmerica, people who have become household names here and among many of our authors—Miranda, Nikki, Pat, Marleen, Loretta, and soon also Sarah, Jaime, Andrea—all cornerstones of our company, all still going strong, stronger than ever before, all in positions of primary significance and responsibility. The fact that they are still here says something about PublishAmerica, but certainly also about them. They are the ones who helped build this company since early on; they saw the promise in something that had yet to be developed, yet to grow, yet to establish itself. They immediately understood it when we explained and outlined it to them. They loved books, writing, and writers, and they wanted to be a part of this adventure.

They joined us for the fun of it, the excitement, the challenge, and certainly not because of the pay. PublishAmerica could not afford to pay top dollar. If our new hires were after big paychecks, they were at the wrong address. Washington, Baltimore, Philadelphia, New York—that's where the high salaries could be found in the mid-Atlantic area, not in small-town Frederick, Maryland, not at PublishAmerica, at least not in those early times. And the funny thing is, pay rarely became an issue during the many job interviews that Larry and I have conducted over the years, and after we had delegated the hiring process to our managers, this did not change in any meaningful way. PublishAmerica appeared to attract job applicants for whom their paycheck was important, but not the most important thing. The character of their work, their work environment, and the audience they worked for, all that came first.

Publishing companies often create their own special ambiance; it is a different habitat, the climate is unconventional, it's something else. The people working there are a little unusual. They have an uncommon streak to them, and they have always known this. In school, in college, among friends they have always been just a tad different, and people often told them that they were dreamers, unfit to join the dog-eat-dog world. Their priorities in life had always been somewhat incongruous with what they noticed around them, but when they come to join a publishing company they suddenly see that they are not the only unconventional person in the world. They quickly feel at home.

PublishAmerica is no exception to this rule, and neither to that other rule which says that publishing attracts more women than men. Some sociologists have suggested that because the world of books represents mankind's softer, gentler side, women are more likely to spend their entire day in it, simply because they're from Venus, and we guys are not. I don't know if this is true. I have an extensive background in newspaper publishing, and I have seen the same thing develop there since the late sixties, early seventies. In fact, my newspaper won award after award for hiring more women than any other paper, and I have always considered that a little silly: we had job openings, women applied, and if they were the best candidate, we hired them. Newspaper journalism, once an alpha male bastion, does *not* represent mankind's softer side, and least of all its gentler side, but I am told that today the average newsroom is inhabited by more women than men. There is something about the combination of paper and the written word, about the expression of thoughts, the powerful innocence of the pen, the strength of the vulnerability of arguing with words only that attracts them, more so than men.

PUBLISHAMERICA'S HENHOUSE

PublishAmerica has never had less than eighty percent women on its staff. So many that at some point our managing editor, who is overseeing a department of more than 35 text editors, came to us asking if we could *please* hire more men. She was managing a henhouse, she said, and it would really, definitely, undoubtedly be better for morale, she insisted, if we would infuse a little more testosterone into the department. This appeal coincided with our decision to delegate her department's hiring to her, as we were adding five new jobs to her staff at the time, part of an overall growth rate that the founders could not continue to supervise in practical terms of doing all the interviews.

Two weeks later she reported back to us. She had received a stack of resumes, almost solely from women, and among the male applicants there were zero who fit the bill of what we were looking for. Our own experience exactly. A few years later, despite her best efforts to boost gender diversity, there have never been more than four male editors working at PublishAmerica simultaneously, which occasionally makes men almost look like an endangered species, at least under our roof. At PublishAmerica, Mars is vastly outnumbered.

Of the guys who have come and gone, most would say that the working environment is a little unusual, but pleasant, and the fact that they were surrounded by above-average intelligent women with a variety of college degrees has a lot to do with it. Occasionally, a male staffer may have overreacted, like the guy who always brought a Superman costume in the trunk of his car, or the man who resigned and went back to live with his mother when it dawned on him that his supervisor was a woman.

But then again, we had our share of funny girls as

well. There was the one who wanted to get pregnant so desperately that, after seeing her boyfriend during lunch, she was caught laying down on the floor in her office with her hips elevated on a pillow and her legs at a 90-degree angle because she had read somewhere that this would boost the upstream mobility of what she had just collected. That was not what got her fired: she got booted after she was caught giving herself a raise by stealing rolls of 37-cent stamps from the mailroom. And there was the bookkeeper who cut a $900.00 check and mailed it overseas, then found out too late that she had forgotten the decimal point. Or the young lady who was an accomplished soprano, who used that voice to yell at her superiors—a falsetto that got her fired.

But these are the exceptions. As a rule PublishAmerica has been very lucky with its staff, and with the unusually low turnover that we have seen to date. Some departments have a higher burnout degree than others, but there is nothing abnormal about that, given that some sections of work are more taxing and stressful than others, as is the case everywhere. By and large, PublishAmerica has always been, and today still is, populated by a dedicated and loyal staff, scores of women and men who are without exception highly qualified professionals. They like where they are, they love what they do, and whenever they see the physical results of their efforts—the newly printed book of the author that they helped succeed—the air around them is thick with satisfaction.

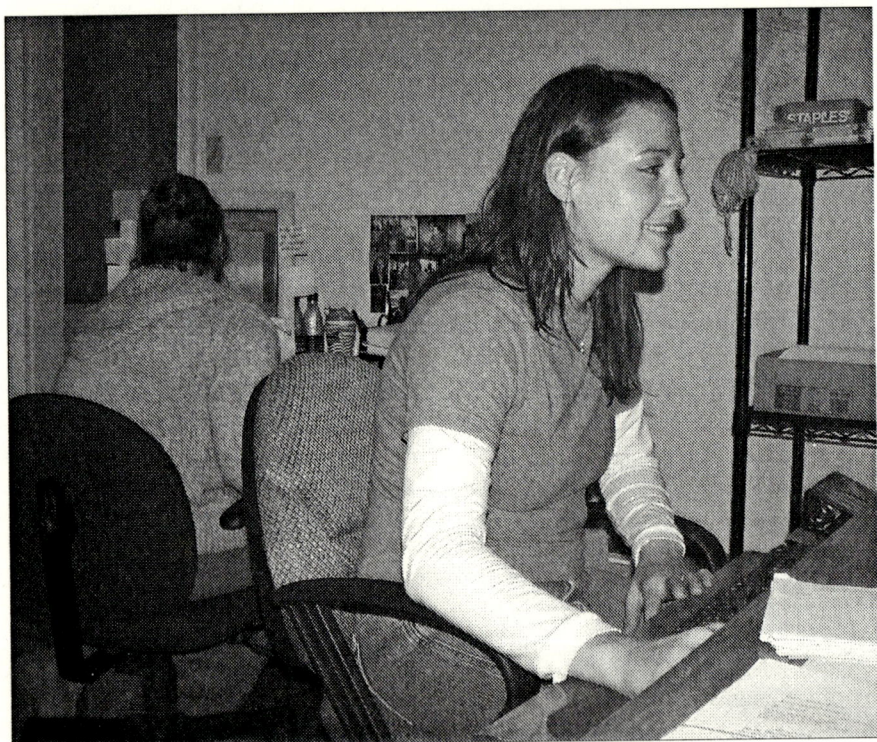

Chapter 11

"Throughout my experience with your acquisitions department, your pre-production department, your text production office, your editorial staffers, your cover design department, and your author support team, I was consistently met with focused and qualified individuals whose patience and kindnesses I will never forget. If I could walk into your office today, PublishAmerica, I would bring with me a big smile and a heart filled with gratitude. I would invite all of you to lunch and we would celebrate the praiseworthy fruits of spirited teamwork; I have never seen a greater example of it."

—Jettie C. Hess, *The Rose Within My Heart*

Traffic Control

PublishAmerica's structure is basically divided into six areas. There is an acquisitions/marketing department, there is an author support team, there is pre-production, text editing, cover design, and ordering/shipping. Naturally, there are also people dealing with tech issues, computer and website maintenance, accounting, and office management, but our basis is the six main areas that every author at some point gets to deal with. Though we do a spectacular lot of sales, there is no sales department per se, for reasons that will become clear in later chapters.

Every aspiring new author enters the door through the acquisitions/marketing department. Whether they contact us through our website, or send us an email or a letter through regular mail, they all end up on the desks of our acquisitions editors who study, sift, debate, and select them. Most submissions come in the form of a query letter, with no manuscript attached or enclosed, just like all writers' guides suggest—those appear to be well-read by most authors who apparently find them in their local bookstore or the library. Most query letters are carefully composed. They contain information about the book and the author, they are well-written and easy to understand,

and they make it simple for us to decide whether we want to see the entire manuscript or not. There are some, however, that are in a category of their own. Case in point, the following two samples.

"My story begins at my time of birth, because I am an extra-terrestrial. I was born into this world from a being of light which I witnessed coming from a space ship, beaming into a little baby, by the name of [author], born on May 30, 1954, in McKinney, TX, USA, on planet Earth. Before I get too far into the experiences, I wish to tell you my education and background, and to state that I am mentally stable. I do not partake of any drugs or mind altering substances. The only medication I regularly take is for my thyroid. I used to drink on occasion and stopped drinking in 1999. I have seen several psychotherapists since this has begun in order to make sure that there is nothing wrong with my mental condition, for sometimes it is difficult to tell the difference between third dimensional reality information coming in from other realities and dimensions. I feel that at times I have walked a thin line between sanity and insanity, trying to sort all of this out. All of the counselors I have seen have

stated I am mentally stable and a very healthy functioning individual." Phew. Could have fooled us.

And this one, unplugged: "*my name is [...] and im a first time writer . my book is called what if? its about what if john wayne and bruce lee and elvis presley and james dean were cloned and brought together to stop a man from cloning hitler and reuniting the nazi party. there are two words in the English language that when put together can make the human mind wander in many different directions. two words that at first glance seem so very insinifigant and so unimportant that most of us have a tendency to just ignore them with out thought. alone they don't hold much allure at all but when combined and given great thought they can make sense of the most improbable of things. i know it sounds like the rumblings of a madman but its true. the two words I'm referring to are what if? SEEMS HARMLESS RIGHT SEEMS LIKE NOT MUCH CAN BECOME OF IT DOESN'T IT. that's exactly what i thought at first too till i started thinking. what if there was life after death? what if aliens did exist? [...] your probably thinking who am i and how do i know all this stuff. lets just say i wasn't there but i have good sources who know the truth and i was a unwilli ng witness to things that would forever make me say what if. here's the story as it was told and even witnessed by me."* Fortunately the guy took his subsequent rejection well.

"HUH, ME?"

Better at least than the woman whom we asked to take a second look at her manuscript before we could accept it. Her language rambled, the story went nowhere—it simply needed serious revisions before it could be considered. Her less-than-enthusiastic response was, *"What type of revisions? What is it you want to change? It took you this long to ask me for a change? Then you want me to resubmit? Lady, you must be on something truly strong! How could you possibly sugarcoat an experience as grim as that. Everyone is not Martha! You have truly pissed me off. DOES THAT NEED EDITING? What are your requirements? Bambi finds a husband! I thought you had an editing department. You keep a copy of this email because my manuscript will* sell and when it does I will personally take a copy of this email and dedicate it to you! Merry Christmas!"

On the other hand, authors who do receive an acceptance mail from us sometimes react with equal passion, albeit in a more elated fashion, such as this guy who wrote, "*It's hard to describe the emotions one goes through when their dream becomes reality. The simplest description is all of 'em! That's precisely what happened to me last night. Slowly but surely each emotion had its turn as the evening rolled over to greet the dawn. No wonder you never heard from me yesterday, quite simply I was in no fit state. I was unable to sit down, rather I was pacing up and down with the energy of my five-year-old. The boldest of them all was excitement—uncontrollable excitement where the rush of feeling was so intense I swear it felt as though my whole body was being thrown into the air like molten lava spewing its way through a severed vein. I was bubbling inside, so much so, the steam protruding from my ears was the only reason I didn't explode. What can I say— nothing really but to let you know this man is grateful for the opportunity you and your colleagues have presented.*"

Once we have accepted a book and the contract has been signed, author and book become like an airplane that is guided through an assigned corridor and gets to be overseen by one traffic controller after another. The acquisitions editor who signed up the book launches the first post-contract event by asking the author for names and email addresses of their local media reporters, something that all of our writers invariably find exciting, because this will be the first time the world will hear about their status as a soon-to-be-published author. The acquisitions/marketing department issues news releases to all these local media, between twenty and fifty every day, telling them that a new local star is born in their town, county, or state. This frequently yields immediate local news attention, and for many authors this is the first time they are interviewed about anything in their whole life.

DIRECT MAIL

The next thing the author knows is that he is

contacted by our pre-production people with our extensive Author Questionnaire, which does what the name suggests, as it asks questions, but it also comes with a ton of guidance.

The AQ wants to know obvious things such as, for our records,

"1. a. Your legal name.

1. b. Your name as you wish it to appear on the title page (pen name, pseudonym or nickname).

2. Title of manuscript, plus subtitle if applicable.

3. Your date and place of birth.

4. Citizenship and social security number (for tax purposes only).

5. Home address (please include zip code and city).

6. Home telephone number and e-mail address."

Then it also asks for a list of names and addresses of no more than 100 people "who know you well enough to be interested in your success as a writer: personal friends, colleagues, relatives, etc.," so that we may send them an announcement by the time the book comes off the press. This is a great device, and though it is entirely optional, more than ninety percent of our authors embrace it with gusto because it adds a special touch to what they did themselves when they found that their book was going to be published: it confirms to their daily world that indeed there is a real publisher out there who decided to take a chance on their friend's book.

PublishAmerica has mailed more than one million announcements to people all over the continent and beyond, at an estimated expense to us of half a million dollars or so, with one purpose only: to help spread the word about our new releases. There is an element of science behind this direct-mail effort, because one of the most elementary questions that any direct mailer has to answer is: how do we make the recipient actually read the announcement?

We found the solution early on. We decided to print the announcement on a regular sheet of paper, black on white, nothing fancy, and address it to "Dear friend of [author's name]," like a regular letter, on our own letterhead. It says that the author has written a book, that it is about to be released, what the book is about, that more details can be found on our website, and it offers a discount to those who want to obtain a pre-release copy.

We put the letter in a regular envelope, stick a real 37-cent stamp on it, make no effort to make it look like it comes out of a mailing machine, put a sticker with the recipient's name and address on it, slightly skewed, and thereby almost force the recipient to open the envelope because it stands out between the load of unsolicited mail that everyone receives in the mail every day, and because it looks like a piece of mail that comes from an individual, which is pretty much the truth.

All of our release announcements are individually put together. The only mechanical part of the process is that we have a little miracle machine that folds the letter, stuffs it inside the envelope, and wets the glued line for sealing. Each letter is hand-composed and printed on a regular desktop laser printer, each address sticker and each stamp is attached manually, and all letters are hand-delivered to the post office. We have done this more than a million times, one by one.

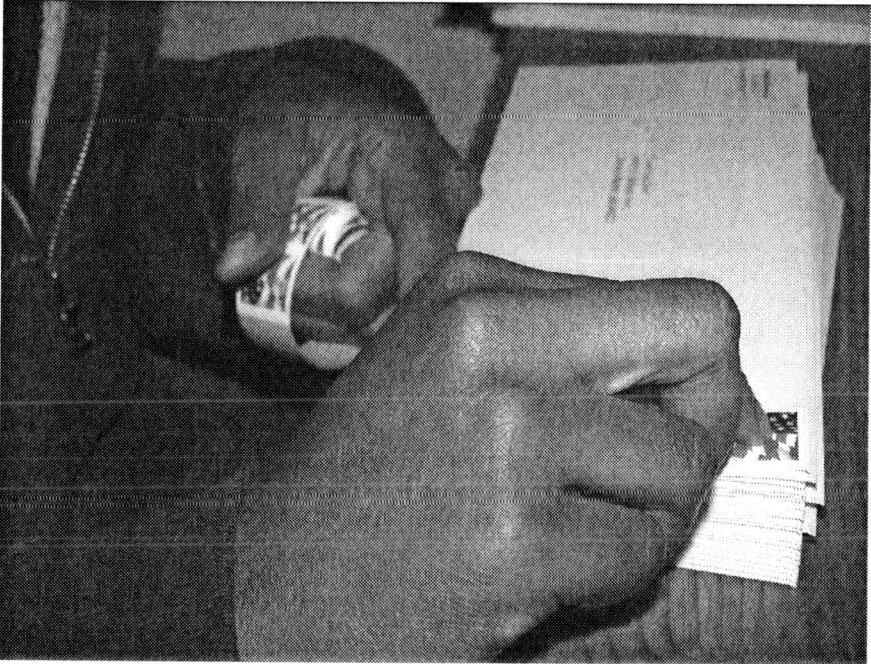

At first we figured that this was something that may be handled best by a direct mail company, but we were wrong. All mail that goes through those companies looks like junk mail. It has bulk rate stickers on it, it lacks personal care, and these folks are thinking quantity, not quality. The quality of our letters is that they look unprofessional, odd as it may sound. They look like they are manually handled. One day we had lunch with the pros, guys who do nothing but distribute direct mail. Their advice was: don't change a thing. Fancy-looking bulk mail typically has a response rate of less than one half of a percent. The fancier it looks, the lower the response rate. PublishAmerica's response rate is eighteen percent.

And that is only the directly measurable response, coming from individuals who actually buy a copy of the author's book—eighteen out of a hundred contacted, which in the larger scheme of things is a meaningless sales number, even though it is important to the author, for obvious reasons. But the other eighty-two recipients also read the letter, and though they may not be into impulse buying, they do participate in spreading the word. That's why our book announcements are such a great tool. They make everybody happy: the author, the recipient who feels that she was deemed important enough to be singled out to receive the great news about their friend, and us, not so much because it sells us a few books, but because it has been a fantastic instrument to communicate our name, our existence, and our Main Street affiliation.

GIVING GUIDANCE

Back to the Author Questionnaire. It also asks the author how he wants the book to be summarized on the back cover, and if there are any design suggestions he may have. Many authors do. They have had images of their cover design in their heads ever since they wrote their first chapters, and they will let us know. But they also realize that designing book covers is a special art; therefore, they gladly leave producing the final look up to their publisher who, by the way, requires by contract that all matters dealing with production and design remain the publisher's responsibility.

The author's suggestions in the questionnaire help our artists to come up with a cover image that not only does right to the book content, but to the author as well. This is an often forgotten element, but one that is of keen significance to the author, whose first book this often is. You want to make it a monument, a tribute, a testament to what the work stands for, and to what and who the author is and was when he developed, conceived, and created his labor of love.

However, the questionnaire does not only ask, it also guides. When it finally requests the author to submit a final version of the manuscript, with all its last-minute revisions and changes in a completely clean format, it also provides an elaborate set of rules, hints, and tips about language, spelling, and grammar. We always attach a style guide, the product of years of learning and fine-tuning on our end. Our editors have seen too many *theres* and *theirs, its* and *it's, should ofs* and *should haves, thens* and *thans, tos, toos,* and *twos, lays* and *lies* to not be prepared for a little oversight or two, or more, on the author's part.

"We are aware that many authors are more in the business of storytelling and not in the minutiae of grammar rules and sentence mechanics. However, these are important areas in manuscript preparation and presentation because, very often, the author's original meaning can be lost with a misplaced comma or improper quotation format," is what the style guide says. "In other words, standard word mechanics can ensure that your book says exactly what you, the author, wish it to say." After all, "when an author finishes writing, only he or she knows exactly what was intended. Standard grammar and usage ensures that it can be understood and enjoyed by everyone."

A publisher should always allow for unusual language, deviant constructions, and other idiosyncracies that define the author's chosen tongue, but since the book is written for the benefit of its readership, more so than for the welfare of the author, it does not hurt to keep in mind what the average reader will reasonably expect to see language-wise when he opens a book. Hence our reminders to our newly contracted authors, compliments of our pre-production staff.

One more example of why these reminders are no luxury in America? Okay, here's another gem: *"There son David was born at home in Ruth's mothers house a three bed roomed council house in the suburbs of Newcastle upon Tyne quite a nice place at the time soon as the baby was born he was rushed to the hospital and placed in a incubator the doctors came to talk to Ruth and Ronnie we don't hold out much hope for the survival of you child he has yellow jaundice and has a very weak chest (asthma) I am very sorry explained the doctor that first night passed without any problems next morning little David was still here."*

This one didn't make the cut either.

Chapter 12

"I liked my editor at PA. I bothered her so much that I got to know she's a grandmother. Now that's working commas pretty close, wouldn't you say!"

—Rudy Girandola, author of *The Jade Chalice*

"My editor did an excellent job on the final draft."

—Rob Sargeant, author of *Lost Ark Found*

"A few days ago I noticed a punctuation mistake I had made throughout the manuscript. I contacted author support to let them know I wanted to fix them all, and I was told to get in touch with my editor when she contacted me. Lo and behold, when I opened my proofs a little while ago, the corrections had already

been made. I'm not talking about a few scattered mistakes here, folks, I'm talking about hundreds. Anyway, just thought I would share that with you. Anyone who claims PA editors don't do much have no idea what they are talking about."

—Steve Harrison, author of *Undeserved Trust*

Dotting the I's, Crossing the T's

Let's talk a little bit about our text editing department, by far our largest team. Roughly forty editors strong, they occupy ten separate offices on one entire floor in our 12,000 sq. ft. office building. It is a quiet floor. When you come up the stairs and walk into the central hallway, what's striking is the tranquility of the place. Dozens of people, as I said mostly women, are sitting behind their computers, lost in the stories they are working on. Every single one of them is a text specialist.

They love words, grammar, spelling, correct idiom. It is always a joy to talk with them, because what you get back is above-average coherent language, sound prose, and a choice of words that comes from an oversized vocabulary. They speak how they write and edit: in full sentences that actually go somewhere, with a beginning and an end, and with words that they select by the nuances they represent. Our editors generally don't lose themselves in cool-speak; you don't often hear them say words such as "awesome," "kewl," or "da bomb," and no one is a Randy Jackson "dawg."

They are accomplished writers in their own right. Without exception, they write excellent letters, as thousands of our authors will confirm, but that's just the beginning. One of our editors was already a PublishAmerica author when she applied for the job, another is to be published shortly, and when we asked two other editors to write prologues to anthology books that had been written by our authors (one a tribute to our authors' mothers, the other a summary of their book promotion experiences), they came up with chapters so delicate and thoughtful, and so maturely written, that we can hardly wait for the day when they have finished their own first books.

It appears that they are all like this. Occasionally we hear them discuss their own poetry, or their plans for a work of romance, or, strikingly indicative for people with a knack for writing, their plans, hopes, or dreams of traveling far distances. Not all travelers are writers, but most true writers are travelers. It is a universal source of inspiration, and it can and always will be found back in the books they write. Our editors, many of whom have their own writing on their minds, are no exception to this rule.

At first Larry and I had not been entirely sure what we could expect from such a large crowd of text readers/correctors/editors, whose combined names read like a pink baby name book: Briana, Tasha, Adrianne, Nicole, Colleen, Bonnie, Janice, Jennifer, Lynn, Linda, Andrea, Theresa, Marta, Melissa, Jaime, Tarah, Brenda, Sarah, Katherine, Anne, Lucie, Claudia, Sherry, Carrie, Jeannette, Natalie, Sandra, Virginia, Pam, Julie, Christen, Paula, Iris, Laura, Connie, Cornelia, Jackie, Pam, Sandee, Julia, Carol, Joanne, Jackie, Deb, Angie, Heather—and that's just the names that my memory

quickly reproduces. Wouldn't they get bored quickly, sitting at those desks, working through books they had not written themselves, trudging from comma to quotation mark, plugging along from an em dash here to an ellipsis there? Should we not expect a high turnover rate? And could they be safely left to their own devices, without our personal supervision, or would it be a girls' dorm chaos?

TIP OF THE WEEK

But our concerns were unfounded. This was a quiet crowd with a high sense of responsibility. What once started out as a small group of merely four soon doubled, quadrupled, tenfolded, and the more were added the more serious they seemed. Turnover was, and remains, low, much lower than we had expected. Virtually each new addition to the team appeared to simply love this kind of work, which was arguably helped by the fact that we used to give each new editor no fewer than three months to grow into her job. Today, given our constant rate of growth, we must require her to do it a little faster.

As the department grew, we also learned to adjust its structure. It was not enough to have one manager oversee it; she needed a pair of supervisors who could train and coach all newcomers, who occasionally arrived three or even five at a time. All promotions were done from within, as has been our company policy from the start, and all were resounding successes.

We quickly found out that at the basis of their success was a self-designed, self-developed internal stay-on-the-ball system of education. What to some may seem needless and redundant (everybody knows his English, right?) turned out to be a key ingredient in keeping dozens of editors, all professionals with English backgrounds, sharp. The system was simply called *Tip of the Week*, the result of both new and veteran editors showing a constant curiosity as to what the official, and always changing, rules of their mother tongue are. Instead of refreshing one editor's mind, the manager and her supervisors decided to renew everyone's acquaintance with what they once had learned in school. Begun as a once-a-week thing, they developed it into a full-fledged spelling and grammar guide.

Here's an elementary sample, something everybody with a high school education is supposed to know:

"We'll be discussing hyphen usage in relation to two or

more words serving as a single adjective. This one is huge! I see it done wrong every day!

RULE: Use a hyphen to join two or more words which serve as single adjective before a noun.

EXAMPLES:

correct: blue-eyed woman

incorrect: blue eyed woman

correct: mud-caked shoes

incorrect: mud caked shoes

correct: coming-of-age story

incorrect: coming of age story

correct: five-year-old child

incorrect: five year old child

correct: 300-year-old curse

incorrect: 300 year old curse

RULE: When the first of the words is an adverb ending in "ly," do not use a hyphen. Also, do not use a hyphen when a number or letter is the final element.

EXAMPLES:

correct: freshly painted barn

incorrect: freshly-painted barn

correct: Grade A milk

incorrect: Grade-A milk

correct: number 360 sandpaper

incorrect: number-360 sandpaper

RULE: When words forming the adjective come after the noun, do not hyphenate them.

EXAMPLE: Jaime's shoes are mud caked."

Simple stuff, isn't it? Or did you catch yourself thinking at some point, *Ah, I didn't remember that one?* It is okay to admit it, because it is safe to assume that ninety-five percent of all Americans with an average or above-average education have forgotten some of these rules. We can see it every day in the manuscripts that we review, the amazing number of basic spelling or grammar errors in an otherwise great piece of prose. Though they have access to one of the most efficient languages in the world, and arguably in the history of the world, Americans are lousy spellers, poor followers of grammar, and masterful at breaking basic rules. In fact, they are so good at disobeying idiom laws and at creating their own vocabularies that one sometimes has to believe that they do it on purpose, though in the vast majority of all cases it appears to simply be a matter of carelessness or a genuine lack of knowledge.

Here's another example from our editors' in-house spelling and grammar guide:

"Capitalization of degrees and titles often go hand in hand, as both appear frequently throughout our back cover text files and books. A good rule of thumb with capitalization is less is more. Our authors tend to go hog-wild with capitalization, so be on the lookout. Don't be afraid to make words lowercase!

———————

When referring to degrees in a general way, do not capitalize them. Note that bachelor's and master's end in 's.
EXAMPLES:

a master's in chemistry

a bachelor's degree

a doctoral degree

doctorate

_____

When full titles of degrees (Bachelor of Arts, etc., in place of bachelor's) are used, they should be capitalized. However, "degree" should never be capitalized.

Also notice that it is not necessary to capitalize the specific discipline unless it is already a proper noun (i.e., English, French, etc.).

EXAMPLES:

Master of Science in environmental engineering

MS in environmental engineering

a Bachelor of Science degree in chemistry

BA in English

_____

When a title appears before a person's name, it is capitalized. When it appears after a person's name, it is lowercase.

EXAMPLES:

Professor Englebert

Professor of History Herb Englebert

Herb Englebert, professor of history

the professor

Mayor Smith

Sarah Smith, mayor of Tinseltown

the mayor

Senator Rochelle Long

Rochelle Long, senator of Maryland

the senator

Captain Hook

the captain

Lieutenant Ryan

the lieutenant

Doctor Carroll

the doctor

Reverend Higgins

the reverend

EXCEPTION: In dialogue, a title can be capitalized

without a name if it is being used as direct address.

Correct:

* "Top o' the morning to you, Reverend!"

* "Top o' the morning to you, Reverend Higgins!"

* He yelled a greeting to the reverend.

Incorrect:

* "Top o' the morning to you, reverend!"

* He yelled a greeting to the Reverend."

BEHIND THE SCENES

The reason for sharing these very basic examples is that it helps demonstrate what a core job it is that our editors are doing when they go through a PublishAmerica book. And it's all behind the scenes. No one, except the author, ever sees what they caught, removed, and replaced. The average book page counts ten changes made by our editor. Tiny changes, and occasionally less than tiny. Multiply this by the number of pages that the book counts and you'll know how often a human intervention occurred. And that is without using a computer spellcheck. We don't like them; they are unreliable, an editor's nightmare.

Our editors receive tons of praise for their work. Each day brings twenty or so thank you notes like this one: "YOU are my hero! I can't tell you how much I appreciate it... It was a joy having you as my editor!" Or this: "Thanks for doing a terrific edit task in the first place and adjusting where necessary. This is my first major editing experience on anything other than a short story and I can't imagine that it could have gone any better. If PublishAmerica ever foolishly accepts another novel of mine, I couldn't hope for a better, more professional editor."

But no one summed it up better than Dr. Gerald Roe, author of *Terror in the Steel Mountains* and *The Curse of Red Wolf Valley*:

What I have to say is long overdue.... I approached your firm as I assume did the majority of your other clients: discouraged by previous rejections, but confident in the value of my work. The manuscript I submitted was fifteen years old. For all those years it had produced nothing but enough rejection letters to paper my living room wall. While I never flagged in my belief in the manuscript, I had all but given up on the possibility of ever seeing it in book form. PublishAmerica changed all that by seeing in its pages what I had seen for over a decade. You accepted it! Then, just as promised, you worked with me to make what I had written better than it was, then put it into print.

As to the editing process, I found PublishAmerica to be careful, detail oriented, and, on occasion, rather tough. It was obvious to me in the several "back and forths" with my own manuscript that a fine-tooth comb was applied to my every word. As a college professor, I deal with editing, grading numerous student papers. The work is tough and exacting. There are times when even the closest scrutiny fails to spot every editorial need. Perhaps those who complain the loudest should spend more time developing their own editorial skills. We do, after all, claim to be writers....

I came to PublishAmerica as a completely unknown commodity. In reality, we are first-time authors, unknown to the market and industry, well informed of the difficulty of our chosen pursuit, fortunate enough to have been published by a traditional, royalty paying publisher, willing to gamble on our success. It seems reasonable that even Hemingway would have been grateful for such an opportunity in his early days. I am grateful to PublishAmerica for all you have done on my behalf. I look forward to a long and successful relationship with you as my publisher. It is a particular joy to grow alongside someone else.

IGNORING THE CONVENTIONS

Truth be told, not every author appreciates our level of thoroughness equally. There are some who tell us that they don't want anyone to touch their text, period. They insist that the way their final draft reads is exactly how they mean it to read. Some have hired private editing before they finalized their manuscript; others contend that they have edited and re-edited it in detail all by themselves, and this is how they want it to look. They ask us to please leave their text alone, and just format and typeset it. We usually give them what they want, but only after familiarizing ourselves with their final draft, which of course might have become different from the initial text that we saw back when they first submitted their book for our acceptance—and after making sure that the author did not exaggerate when he said that the book needed no further intervention.

All books, anywhere in the world, will read differently from how the reader would have written it if they had the will or the ability to write it. This is the beauty of language, of communication. Everyone is free to let the words, the sentences, the chapters come out of his mouth or his pen the way that fits and suits him best, and in most cases, everybody else understands him. Book writing is not much different from storytelling: it is up to the teller to choose a form of expression. And it is up to the listener to decide if he wants to listen.

This is an area where PublishAmerica does not follow the conventions of mainstream publishing, conventions that are relatively new and that for hundreds of years have not existed in the publishing world. In mainstream land, too many books are virtually written by a small handful of practically anonymous editors. They let the authors come up with the story concept, with the characters, and with a first draft—in other words, the leg work—but when this is done, they sink their teeth in it and demand substantial changes. Why? Because they ultimately don't care about the identity of the authors, their individuality and personality, but instead they have determined a highest common denominator somewhere among what they deem to be the niche audience for the book, and they decide what these listeners will listen to. And so they change word choice, storyline, character development—and when all is said and done, the final product of the book barely resembles what the authors initially had in mind. Because their editors told them that there was "a better way of saying this," a.k.a "you write it my way or we will cancel your book."

These developmental editors are often very good at what they do. They take what was a raw steak, cut it in small pieces, kick and mash and hammer them into flat patties, flip and re-flip them like hamburgers, and lo and behold, here's your next chunk of fast food, ready for mass consumption. That's the kind of business they're in, to serve the masses, because if they don't, the boss will fire them before he himself gets fired: too much money is invested in those mega houses; they can't bother thinking about the voice of the author. Everything is played to the ear of the listener. And the author? She invariably writes on the book's acknowledgment page, meekly, that she is so grateful for how her editor took her voice away—and that's assuming that it was actually the author writing the acknowledgment.

It has not always been like that. In fact, it has mostly not been like that. This kind of mutant editing is generally a thing of the past fifty years, and it is limited to a small minority of book publishers, those who are in murderous competition for the megabuck. Throughout most of the history of publishing, a book's style was left alone. The author was seen as the expert, the authority, and the ultimate word artist, and audiences agreed. And let's be realistic about this, among most audiences, those that form a niche, the author is still seen as she traditionally has been seen: as the owner of her voice. PublishAmerica upholds this tradition seamlessly. We leave an author's style alone.

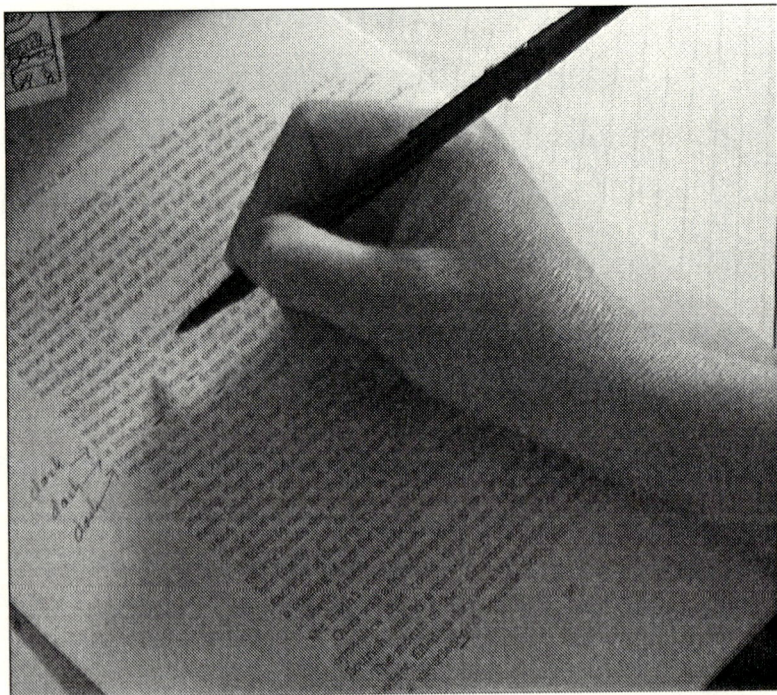

THROUGH HOOPS

Actually, we go through hoops to ensure that our authors are completely satisfied with how the text eventually reads. We give them at least four opportunities to get it right: first when they ask us to read their manuscript and we invite them to send it for our review, next if and after we have accepted the book and we ask them to make any changes and improvements they can think of before they send their final draft. The third time they get a chance to fine-tune the book is when we present them with the page proofs and we ask them to make a final set of corrections. And there is a fourth time after we have implemented those final corrections and we ask them to go once more through the text to see if everything is in place the way they intended.

That, friends, is traditional publishing. That's how they did it in the days of Gutenberg; that's how they have done it ever since. It also is what many authors appreaciate so much about PublishAmerica. We give them a voice that is their own, and that remains their own.

Chapter 13

"I am so proud to be part of the Publish America family."

—Bonnie Block, author of *12 Ways to Hug Yourself*

The Family

The main reason why all these thank you's and expressions of appreciation show up in these chapters is not that it serves to demonstrate how wonderful, how super, or how bigger than life we are. We're not. At PublishAmerica, we are just a team of normal people, and there is nothing special about us. We are in the exact same league as our authors—all of us are someone's brother or sister, son or daughter, father or mother. We have similar job histories as some of the folks who paraded in Chapter 7, we come from all walks of life, and we discuss the same water cooler issues as any other office. We debate *American Idol* and *Desperate Housewives*, and, given the fact that our team counts many more women than men, we also discuss upcoming weddings and wedding gowns. We are just as Norman Rockwell as everybody else.

Since October of 2004 we occupy a very large brownstone in the heart of our town, a building with an unusual interior, thanks to the fact that it once was two adjacent buildings, one of which is said to have been designed for Roger Taney. Frederick, Maryland, has an uneasy relationship with the Honorable Mr. Taney, the Chief Justice of the U.S. Supreme Court during the administrations of no less than ten nineteenth-century presidents, from Andrew Jackson to Abraham Lincoln—a man of many virtues, but also the author of the court's infamous *Dredd Scott* decision, a guy who by and large ended up on the wrong side of history. That's why our town does not advertise its once-favorite son who practiced law here for two decades. Instead, Frederick is bigger on Taney's brother-in-law Frances Scott Key, the author of the national anthem whose gravesite is a few blocks south of our office, next to the baseball stadium where there are fireworks on some game nights, rockets' red glare and all. We're not sure that Taney ever spent time in our office, but it is a grand building anyway.

Until 2004, we were housed first in one downtown office, then two, three, and we even had to add a fourth office in a building outside town. Most people never saw how much office space we were really occupying, because we kept our "headquarters" in the original building, and that's all that visitors would see. That office was also known as The Netcrafters Building, after the name of a successful internet service provider that Larry Clopper owned and operated there before we started PublishAmerica. It was a lovely office, about a century old, with a big wooden staircase and eight rooms that we filled up to capacity in less than no time. Larry and I shared a large office there for four years, a circumstance that we are inclined to credit for a significant part of our early success. It allowed us to work in tandem, to make all decisions together, to weigh and discuss options, and even though we sometimes refer to it as the Room of Indecisions because there was very little that we did not debate back and forth before reaching a conclusion, in reality it made us probably an unusually decisive, forceful, and resolute management duo.

NEVER MISSED A DEADLINE

However, eventually two-thirds of our staff was working in different pieces of real estate, so we knew all along that it was only a matter of time until we'd have to find ourselves more room, preferably under one roof, so that we could bring everyone together. It took us almost a year to find the appropriate location, and then two months to move everyone, every desk, and every piece of equipment in such a way that production would not suffer, and no days would be lost. That worked.

The PublishAmerica building is a mostly quiet place. Most visitors are surprised to find how big it really is and how many people are working there. It's a disciplined place, where everyone knows her tasks and her targets, and where backlogs and slush piles are not allowed to grow. It's a place where deadlines are not permitted to be missed, and one of our proud achievements that has remained practically invisible to the outside world is that we have indeed never exceeded a single one. All of our many thousands of books went into production within the contractually mandated time frame, they were all released on time, and when royalty season comes twice a year, it's all hands on deck because there, too, we have deadlines to meet—and we have never violated one.

Royalties are serious stuff. It is money that is not ours,

despite the fact that we sit on it until payday comes in February and in August. It belongs to the authors, and we must treat it accordingly. Royalty checks are important to our authors, comparable with the advance dollar bill. It has a symbolical value that goes beyond being a token of appreciation from the readers to the writer, beyond the actual dollar amount on the check. It has the worth of a certificate, one that announces yet again that, yes, here is a published author, someone who has achieved something of significance. In fact, ten percent of the authors never deposit their royalty checks—they frame them and make them keepsakes.

Royalty months are hectic months at PublishAmerica, increasingly so as the number of payable authors mushrooms. We have no more than three weeks, or fifteen business days, to get everything right: add up all vendor numbers including the very latest, break down all separate kinds of sales, do careful double-checks, print thousands and thousands of individual statements, print an equal number of checks, match statements and checks, put them in envelopes, don't seal them yet but do cross-checks to make sure that no one will receive somebody else's statement or check, then seal them, stamp them, and get them to the post office in time.

99.8 PERCENT ACCURATE

Because there is so much manual effort involved, it is a process that can be prone to error, and since we are human, we do make an occasional mistake. But they are rare. More precisely, they are very rare. Send out ten thousand royalty checks, and we will receive some three hundred questions from authors, some agitated, but most concerned in an amicable way. That's roughly three percent. Ninety-seven percent of our authors check their statements and find them to be in order.

Of the three hundred questions, maybe twenty leave us with a real question mark; the others are investigated and returned to sender with a, "No, sir, that friend who told you that he had bought your book never bought a copy, that's why it did not show up on your royalty statement," or, "The bookstore that bought your book last month will not pay their bill until two or three months later, so we haven't received your royalty money yet; you will find that on your next statement," or, "We did not send you a statement because you instructed us in your contract to mail it to your agent, and that's what we have done."

All of our authors are always welcome to come and visit us and check their book's records with their own eyes, and those who actually do so invariably go home completely satisfied, without exception. This includes those who are among the twenty or so whose questions leave us scratching our heads. In half of those cases we must admit that apparently we did make a calculation error, so we apologize, correct it, and send an additional check, and in the remaining cases we do acknowledge that there appears to be an inconsistency but we draw a blank and can not find a definitive answer. In such situations the benefit of the doubt rules, and we send those authors an additional check as well.

That's twenty out of ten thousand, two-tenth of a percent. It's not so bad when you do things right 99.8

percent of the time. And the reason why it is limited to such a small fraction of the total is that everyone at PublishAmerica is aware of how vital it is that we do it right. If we were to do a sloppy job on record keeping and royalty paying, as occasionally occurs elsewhere in the publishing world, it would constitute stealing from our authors, and they would never trust us again. This is why February and August are our hectic months; we've got to get it right, and we have only a hundred and twenty hours to get the massive job done. That's how editors, designers, shippers, and also Larry or I may be found sitting at long tables, helping our accounting department matching statements with checks, folding, stuffing, double-checking, sealing. And we have never missed the deadline.

At such crunch times there is this family atmosphere around PublishAmerica, a sense that many of our authors recognize because they, too, feel that they belong to a family of authors. It is not hard to detect that feeling when you read our author message boards on our website, and you notice the friendships that are forged there—in fact, some of our authors met their future spouses there. And when we invited our authors to travel with us, three times, they reacted with the excitement that a family reunion usually triggers. Although our trip to Key West was blown out of the water by an approaching hurricane, we did travel to Iceland with a party of forty for an audience with that country's president and a bunch of gushing geysers, and at home we hosted a party of three hundred to see, among other things, the Gettysburg battlefield. It was great fun.

A MOVEMENT

Now where does that family sense come from? After all, what we're all involved in is primarily business. Signing a publishing contract is sealing a business agreement, selling books is business, writing someone a check is business, money changing hands is business. Yet there is a feeling out there of "we're all in this together," a sense of being related, of sharing a common goal, even a common cause. And that is clearly where the key is.

PublishAmerica is not just a company that publishes

people's books. It is also a movement. It is that iceberg that is in the process of tipping over, people parting the waters. By their sheer number, our authors are bringing about a change—they *are* the change. Together they are shaping a future that will never be the same as the past. PublishAmerica may have opened the gates, but it's the thousands upon thousands of authors who are now occupying the territory that was once reserved for the elite, and they are redesigning it, landscaping it all over again.

They encounter opposition, of course they do. They're not wanted there, there are no open arms, and in the final chapter I will put that in a wider perspective. But this only brings our authors closer together, makes them more acutely aware of their common purpose. Keep in mind, this is not their day job; their bread and butter is not at stake. They have mouths to feed and they will feed them anyway. So they are patient. They are not knocked out by a punching, kicking elite; the future is theirs regardless. They have entered the once forbidden garden, and they are there to stay.

To be sure, it isn't always easy when some blast your book not because of its content but because of how you got it published for free. And not all bookstore managers are equally nice to you when they see that they can not return your book to the publisher if they don't sell it. It means that they would actually have to work on selling it, and that's something that bookstores are generally not very good at. In fact, there is something about the relevancy of bookstores, period, that we'll look a bit closer at in the next chapter, but, yes, it would be nice if some of them would be a little more accommodating. Also, wouldn't it be a tad more comfortable if premium publishing specialist Jerry Jenkins, who gathers such data, had not calculated a few years ago that 81 percent of the population feels that they have a book inside of them? Fortunately, according to Jenkins only six million actually wrote a manuscript. But still, that's a lot of competition. It's crowded.

IRREVERSIBLE CHANGE

Nevertheless, none of these minuses tend to deter the

average PublishAmerica author as an individual or as a group. They are here, and they're not going anywhere. There are pluses galore, as far as the eye can see. They are allies, brothers and sisters—there's a bond. They are walking down Main Street with their shoulders straight and their heads up high. They are recognized in their towns. People tell them, "I've read about you in the paper!" They are what they had wanted to be for a very long time: a published author. Not a spectator, but a participant. Not on the bleachers, but in the arena. They had a dream, they followed it, and they made it come true.

That, and then some, is what they share together. That is what they are proud of. They are grateful—to their families for bearing with them when publication was not yet assured, to themselves for believing when the eye could not yet see anything at all, and also to PublishAmerica for opening a door and taking a risk.

That's where the thank you messages come from, and that's why they are mentioned throughout these chapters. Not so I can self-congratulate PublishAmerica, because we don't need any self-congratulations, or any congratulations for that matter, thank you very much. We are just doing our job; we had our own dream, we are fulfilling it, and our own rewards are manifold and multifaceted. The author thank you messages are mentioned because they serve as a confirmation, an acknowledgment, a recognition of irreversible change. It is a change that PublishAmerica made possible, but that our authors, the real heroes, made come true.

It was about time that someone said it, and that is what this book does.

Chapter 14

"I just got the final cover art... ***YAY*** It's awesome! The cover very much reflects the story inside! It's eye-catching and so far my family and friends love it. But mostly—I LOVE IT!"

—Peg Watts-Cartwright, author of *Chasing Venus*

23 Seconds

One of our least publicly debated departments is our team of cover designers, which is noteworthy since a book's cover is the first impression anyone will get, whether it is in a bookstore, on a coffee table, or in the writer's hands. The cover is a book's business card, its face, its front yard. If the cover looks inviting, it makes all the difference. If it doesn't, it makes the difference as well. But inviting alone is not good enough. A cover must be appealing, warm, welcoming. It must be honest, true. It must do right to the story *and* to the author. A quality cover represents the author; it conveys who he is all about. PublishAmerica's book covers do all of the above.

That's why there is not much of a debate about them. They are simply fantastic. Our cover art is unusual, artsy, top-notch, and put together by a small crowd of professionals who do what they love and love what they do. Ninety-nine point nice percent of our authors would readily agree. If we hear from them at all, it is in the form of thank you letters with a forest of exclamation points, occasionally accompanied by a box of chocolate. A few examples:

"Your cover design exceeded all my expectations," wrote Faith Berlin, author of *The Lion Next Door*. "It is wonderful! I am so proud. Thank you very much. Please go ahead with the book. I can't tell you how delighted I am with this cover. You did it JUST RIGHT!!!" A sentiment that is echoed by her colleague Barbara J. Robinson: "PublishAmerica did a fantastic job with my book cover, and everyone loves it. It is a cover which draws attention, gets noticed and praised. They also did a great job designing the cover to fit the story. I am proud of the great job and proud of my paperback!" The title of that paperback is *Magnolia: A Wilting Flower*.

And Cary E. Smith, of *I Will Bless Them That Bless Thee*: "Oh my! I am so stunned I can scarcely believe my eyes! What a beautiful job on the cover design!!!!! Everything looks perfect... My highest praise to the art department—you have picked up my idea for the book cover and designed something even better than I had envisioned!...You all have been so wonderful! I was a little leery of what all I would encounter as I got further into the development of the book, but everyone at PublishAmerica has been so incredibly helpful and kind. I can not commend you all enough!"

Powerful stuff, and each time it happens, it leaves a

designer very pleased. This is what they come to work for every day; this is why they applied for their jobs. They show up for work every morning so that they can enjoy what they do, and so that they can learn and improve themselves, and, naturally, so that they can earn their bread and butter, but most definitely they also come to work so that they can serve. Each cover designer at PublishAmerica knows that today she will make yet another author a happy camper. It is one of the most gratifying experiences and it's fun; it's what anyone would want to do for a job, knowing at sunrise that you are going to serve someone else well. As one of them wrote in her goodbye letter when she left PublishAmerica for a job outside the publishing world, "I will miss the accolades from the authors who were so thrilled to be able to publish their books."

It is not hard to understand how this comes about. Authors are writers, not illustrators. They knew how to compose their manuscript, how to find the words, where to dig, delve, and probe. While they are also restless when they are waiting for their page proofs to arrive, at least they know more or less what to expect. They authored those proofs, there are no surprises there. But the cover design, that's an altogether different story. They surely had their own ideas about it, back when they wrote their story, but when it comes to putting abstract illustrative ideas into concrete, actual, tangible practice, that's another world, one that they have no passport for. The cover, their book's face, they must leave it to others to give it birth.

8 SECONDS

And to think that all that effort, and all that excitement, has only a 23-second relevancy. There are people who are actually studying that kind of thing, scientists with video cameras who spy on unsuspecting bookstore customers, shopping behavioral experts, specialists who know exactly why we buy, how we shop, and what does and does not get our attention.

Book front covers get our attention for eight seconds. That's not much, though it's approximately forty times more than the amount of time it takes a car driver to decide to make a panic stop, and four times as long as a helicopter pilot has to react to an engine failure. Eight seconds—two opposing basketball teams can easily score a three-pointer each within that time frame, and at the beginning of a baseball game the national anthem singer will get as far as "Oh, say can you see by the dawn's early light, what so proudly we hailed..." That's it, that's all the time a front cover has to communicate something positive. Within that time, the reader has to be willing to pick up the book, adjust her glasses if she has any, look at the title, look at the cover image, and get the message.

The good news is that once the book has been picked up, it will almost certainly be flipped over for a closer look at the back cover. Some books don't need it. One of the smartest cover designs I have seen in a long time is that of the book *Tilt*, about the leaning tower of Pisa. Published by Penguin, it has a hole in the front cover, in the shape of the tower, tilting of course, and on the stepback cover is an actual photo of the tower in sepia tones which jumps at you through the cover opening.

Tilt has a simple but prescription-strength subtitle: *A Skewed History of the Tower of Pisa.* There is no doubt what that book is about, and since no one who has ever been in Pisa can escape wondering what the heck the real story is, I did not hesitate for a second, and bought the book. It was only afterwards that I realized that I had barely given any attention to the back cover. Instead, I had spent at least twice as much time looking at the front, and rightfully so, because the back confirmed the impression of the front: this book was going to answer all questions about why, when, and at how much damage.

15 SECONDS

But that's the exception. The rule is that books need their back covers. Most new books in regular trade publishing are fiction, and it is very rare that their front covers can fully explain, at a glance, what the story will be about, no matter how beautifully they are designed. The average time spent on examining a book back cover is fifteen seconds, almost twice the time spent on studying the front. That's time spent on reading, not looking. Or maybe briefly looking at the author's photo, if one is there, but certainly reading the author's brief bio. Is this an intriguing guy or gal? Is this someone I could relate to? Oh, and what's the story about again?

Back cover texts must be short and very much to the point. If they are the equivalent of *Tilt: A Skewed History of the Tower of Pisa,* which could also have been the one-line back cover text of that very same book, it would make life considerably simpler for the reader. The prospective book buyer wants to see within seconds if this is going to be something for him. If he has to dig his way through the book description, as in "Knockout beauty Maggie Jackson discovers her love for handsome Brian Dorwell when they meet at Dr. Susan Humphrey's Halloween party against the beautiful backdrop of New Hampshire's lake region where clouds gather, winds howl, and lightning strikes, but not until a ghastly crime is committed, and Maggie's life hangs precariously in the balance," you have lost him. Unless the buyer is the author's sister, in which case she doesn't care and she'll buy the book anyway out of loyalty.

At PublishAmerica we give our authors a big say in how the back cover text will read. We ask the author to come up with what they feel is the most effective summary, but we always caution them not to expect to see their version verbatim on the cover. Our back cover texts are the final responsibility of the editor who has worked through the book, and who knows exactly what is and is not material to the story. They edit not only the manuscript, but the back cover text as well, and the author gets a final opportunity to review that text for errors. And that's it, that's the stuff that the potential book buyer spends his fifteen seconds on.

But let's put this whole 23-seconds thing in perspective, because one has to understand some of the odds that rule the book publishing industry. There are currently a little under two million books in print in America. Every year, between 150-175,000 new books are added, more than three percent of which are compliments of PublishAmerica. There is no bookstore in the entire country that is even capable of carrying all those available books, much less willing. For a bookstore to keep up with the more than 450 new books that come off American presses every day, Saturdays and Sundays included, it would have to add nineteen feet of new shelf space each day. And that's if they would only put one copy of each newly released book on their shelves.

That's not happening, obviously. Bookstores do not, and can not, stock every available book. Even Amazon.com, a virtual bookstore with display shelves that exist only in cyberspace but one that owns giant warehouses around the country, does not have the physical shelf space available to carry all books.

AMERICANS AVOID BOOKSTORES

But then again, how much of a help is a bookstore anyway these days? There are roughly 15,000 such stores from sea to shining sea, one bookstore for every 20,000 Americans. But according to publishing guru Dan Poynter, who makes a living studying these kinds of stats, only 6,000 of them have visited a bookstore in the past five years, and 14,000 have not. Only 30 percent of all people go to a bookstore now and then; 70 percent of all Americans can not remember the last time they did. And of the ones who do enter a Barnes & Noble, a Borders, or a Brentano's, 60 percent come in knowing exactly what they want. They won't stop by your book to pick it up and spend 23 seconds with it. They walk in, find the book they are coming for, pay, and leave. Only 40 percent of all bookstore visitors, a meager 2400 per average bookstore, over a period of five or so years, are potential impulse buyers.

Those are stats that our cover art department keeps in mind when they design our books. Only a minority of all books are bought in a bookstore. And of all bookstores, the big chain bookstores—where most books are and where the competition to have a book stand out among the others is by far the fiercest—account for only 25 percent of all book sales. Seventy-five percent of all books are sold elsewhere: almost 18 percent are sold through book clubs, 15 percent go through the dying breed of small and independent bookstores, 7 percent through online stores such as Amazon.com, and the remaining 35 or so percent are sold through a variety of other venues, including hand-delivery by the author—which, by the way, happens a lot more frequently than some may think.

With all of the above in mind, our design team does their work, quietly, professionally, and successfully, using state-of-the-art computer programs, abiding by complicated formatting specs that our various printers require, and proceeding in a highly efficient manner without surrendering a scintilla of quality, while producing up to twenty-five new covers per day, a world record in traditional publishing.

And each day there is this sense of instant gratification, each time thank you messages come in such as this one from the author of *Buttercup Fields*, Laura Belle: "Many thanks to everyone involved with making my dreams a reality. When I saw the cover for the first time, it was just as I had imagined and hoped it would be and more. I have now earned the title of a published author and am proud and blessed to be in the ranks of so many talented and gifted people. Thank you, PublishAmerica, for giving me the gift of a lifetime."

Chapter 15

"Hello, I want to take a moment to thank you all for your patience and support. I've been very impressed by the quick responses to my many questions. You have all done a terrific job and made this first-time author very glad to be a part of PublishAmerica."
—Joe Benarick, author of *Bob the Goblin*

"I am so impressed with your company...I have been treated with extreme respect, and had so much support from your staff."
—Teresa Polychronis, author of *Below Yudaha*

Supporting the Author

All organizations have their unsung heroes, and PublishAmerica does, too. In our case, it is our author support team, internally known by their acronym AST. They are the ones answering the phones, responding to emails, taking orders, handling our authors' questions and insecurities. It is a high-volume, high-pressure job, and work that not everyone is equally capable of doing. In fact, it took us the longest to put that team together and make it a real "team," and if it weren't for the efforts of our executive director, Miranda Prather, who knows where we'd be.

Miranda is at times a magical worker. Young, energetic, and versatile, she can be tough as nails. She is someone who is thoughtful and will never forget your birthday on the one hand, but at the same time she will be your regular bad cop if she feels that the situation calls for it. A college graduate, she joined PublishAmerica early on, applying for and getting a job in our mailroom, and soon we noticed that each task we asked her to perform she took on with an unusual drive and sense of efficiency. She helped build our shipping operation from scratch, then went ahead and took charge, or rather command, of our text department, our acquisitions team, our marketing efforts, the cover designers, our author support team—

and before too long Larry and I decided that Miranda would be our ideal director, one who would run much of the day-to-day operations. Soon enough we made her responsible for all of our departments except text, and one of the challenges we asked her to tackle was to build AST into a real and effective team.

Anyone who has ever worked in a call center knows about the pressure of phones ringing off the hook. Everyone who has ever been part of a telemarketing operation knows how some people can talk back to you, and PublishAmerica is not even involved in telemarketing, never making any cold calls, only taking them—cold, warm, hot, and icy. It's like everywhere else in the world: eighty percent of all mortals are nice and well-behaved. It's the other twenty percent that can give you headaches, and they tend to take up eighty percent of your time.

DIFFICULT PEOPLE

Our author support team was created to do just that: to support our authors. They don't deal with writers who are not yet our contracted authors; they only work with, and for, the ones who are true PublishAmerica authors, and their readers. On average, they answer roughly 50,000 phone calls per year and 75,000 email messages. Most of it is run-of-the-mill material, some of it is hand-holding, and a tiny percentage is difficult people.

Difficult people are people who generally don't listen, don't hear, don't concentrate on what the other person says. They are people with a mental shortcoming. They have made up their mind about an issue before asking questions about it, and they don't hear the response, which makes one wonder why they ask the questions at all. Our AST staff is very polite, not only because we tell them to be but also because they are people persons. It is what we select them on. They possess social skills that others may have to a lesser degree, and they generally flourish in the company of others. They like meeting new people. Our AST staff is good on the phones and good in answering mail. But no matter how good they are, they can not satisfy the difficult people.

"Thank you for taking the time to respond to my letter. As always, it is a pleasure dealing with the staff at PublishAmerica," wrote the author of *Abduction*, Darrel Day, to us. That is the general response that we get after people have dealt with our author support team. It's not that they have to thank us for something that is normal, common, and standard, such as trying to help people find answers to their questions in a polite and expeditious manner. But they often thank us anyway, and it is good for us to keep that in mind, so that the small minority of difficult customers do not get a chance to leave our AST team with an aftertaste as if all people in the world are problematic.

Quite the contrary is true. Most of our authors realize very well where they are coming from, and they don't hesitate to tell us. Author Jake Green, who wrote *Detachment X-Ray* and *Covert Avengers*, reminded us, and himself, that, "I received 184 rejections (those that answered) for Detachment X-Ray. But then it happened, PA come alongside. And then it happened again. I couldn't resist; shortly after Detachment X-Ray was published three of my rejectors asked for a chance at my second book. I wrote them a letter of rejection." Jake is one of those many authors that our AST team loves to work with.

And Robin Gorley, of *A Lifetime of Words*, told us, "For the first time I have a book that is all of my own. After years of searching I finally found a publisher that takes my work seriously. I am grateful to PA for their belief in my work and giving me the chance to really create and work my gift. Like I always say: Whatever the Challenge, Whatever the Goal, Endure to the End." We took that motto to heart as we molded and built our author support team to the strong service providers that today are taking care of the needs of anyone who contacts PublishAmerica. Miranda conducted endless interviews with applicants for the job; she picked the right people, reorganized everyone's primary responsibilities, and put a team together that is all smiles, all action, and all service.

48 HOURS, OR ELSE

To spend a day in the AST office in the back of our building, where a door opens to a patio where one can hear the birds sing, is like an exercise in catching your breath. They handle five hundred questions per day, today, yesterday, and tomorrow they will do it again. That sounds like it is a lot, and it is, but that's what you have a support team for: to answer questions. Miranda put a system in place that aims at answering all questions within 48 hours, not only in the name of good old customer service, but it would quickly create a living hell for all ASTers if we were to allow that many support requests to back up. It would soon logjam our operation, and eventually no one would receive any support whatsoever.

We mostly succeed in getting all questions answered in this timely manner. Occasionally we fall a few days behind, but that is not the norm. Sporadically a question falls through the cracks, but as soon as an author alerts us to her feeling overlooked, we remedy and rectify it, straight away. And as to the scores of authors who find our office closed overnight and leave phone messages: they are the first voices we hear when PublishAmerica's morning breaks.

PublishAmerica is great at tracking information; we must be among the best in the land. There is no question that an author can ask us—whether it is about an individual book's production stages, or about a printing or shipping issue, or about what they asked us three years and seven months and fifteen days ago—that we can not answer within minutes or even seconds. We have everything archived down to the smallest detail and available at our fingertips. Everything about every book is documented every step of the way, and if an author would say, "But you told me last year that...," we can respond within seconds, "Actually, this is what we said, because your question back then was as follows...," and, straightened out, they'd happily move forward down their great and narrow.

There are of course many forms of support that our authors request and receive. Such as, "Hello, how do I obtain a direct link to my book page on the PA website for my website? Thanks, Laurie," to which our response would be, "Dear Laurie: Linking information can be found at www.publishamerica.com/link.htm. Have a good weekend. Thank you, Shawn." Or, "Why do you need the names of the newspapers in the area so early? The editing department said that it may take eight months before I hear anything from them. Thanks, Lee," and we would answer, "Dear Lee, the press release announces that you have signed a contract with PublishAmerica. That is why now is the right moment for us to contact your local media. Thank you, Patrice." Which is true: we always contact an author's local newspapers as soon as that author has signed his contract, send them a news release, and tell them how proud we are to have signed this new author. The only thing the author sometimes needs to do is follow up with a phone call of his own and see if the reporter is interested in doing a story, which is often the case. And if not, then there's always the next news release we send out, when the book has gone to press.

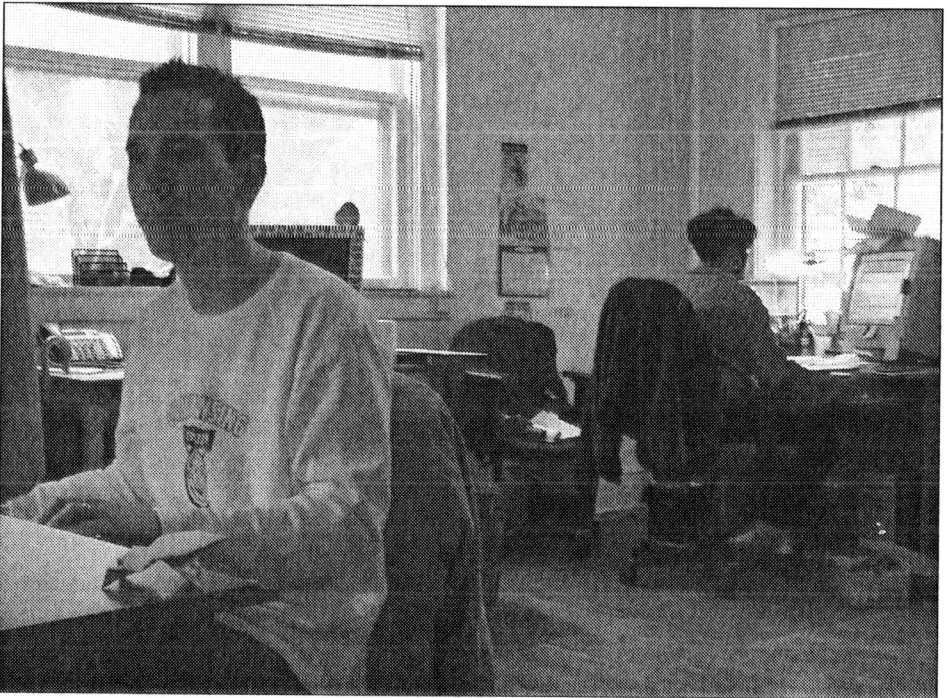

Or someone ordered a book and gets a little nervous. "Gentlemen, I just placed an order, and the wrong zip code got entered in and I couldn't change it before the order was accepted. The right mailing zip code is 59860 and not what went through. I have a concern that if this isn't caught, the book will go to another state somewhere and I will end up paying for it." Our support team answers with, "Dear sir, we have corrected the zip code on your order. Have a good day. Thank you, Mike," knowing that we have a shipping accuracy record of better than 99 percent. Rarely anything goes wrong with our shipping, and if and when it does, we always replace not-arrived books promptly, no questions asked.

THE BIG WAIT

"Greetings, I was just inquiring what stage my book is in. Hope to hear from you soon, Gladys." That's another one. After the excitement of having a book under contract has somewhat subsided, and the active work that is involved with fulfilling the Author Questionnaire has been done, the Big Wait begins. This is the stage that authors typically don't like. Some compare it to a pregnancy period: they have received confirmation that there will be a baby, and now there are seven or eight months to be spent with just waiting. There are those who don't mind the delay—they like the anticipation—but many others get a little fidgety. We are used to it, so we send them a calming response.

Dear Gladys, I hope this email finds you well. Your manuscript is progressing through the publication process without complications, but it is still in the very early stages. Your manuscript has moved to our text production department where it is waiting to be assigned to an editor. The wait time varies, and we understand that this is the hardest part for an author. In the publishing industry, among traditional publishers such as PublishAmerica, the average length of time for this wait is over one year. We are proud to inform you that our timeline, which could be as long as several months, is much shorter!

The editor will do an initial proofing and e-mail you a copy of those proofs for review. You will have two weeks to go over your proofs and make any grammatical or typographical changes. Your editor will then make those changes and finalize the manuscript. You will have another review period of 48 hours to ensure that your requested changes were made. Once you return this second proof, your manuscript will be final, and the book will enter the cover design department.

A cover designer will create and format the cover image of your book. Then, you will have a 48-hour review period to request any changes. Once your cover is finalized, your book is sent to our printers, and your author copies are ordered. Approximately 6-8 weeks later, your book will be released to the industry, which means that it will be available through Ingram, Amazon.com, and Barnes & Noble.com. Also, it will be available through all bookstores nationwide. Have a good day. Thank you, Jessica, Author Support Team.

And so on and on and on. "How much will my book cost ? Looking forward to hearing from you when you have the time. Take care and God bless. Joy." "Dear Joy, The retail price of your book is $19.95. Have a nice day." And, "I would like for someone to send me as soon as possible the information concerning the purchase of [book title]. I have lost my copy of the invoice and need this information to complete my income tax filing. Thank you. Nelson."

"Dear Nelson, Please find a copy of the invoice attached to this email."

Or, priceless: "As I understand your questionnaire, this is to be on a disk which I will do. Question: Do you want the Author Questionnaire, synopsis, biography, etc. on disk also?? Should I use the same disk or do you want the book on a disk alone? Only thing left at this time is for a self-photograph...(which I hate, because the photo always looks like me...ugh). Oh well, we are what we are... If it's not too much trouble, could you send me a brief list of everything needed so I can check it off as it's completed? Sorry to be such trouble, but you are dealing with a granny and I need things simple. Thanks much. Mary."
"Dear Mary: Please put all the material on a disk. You may use the same disk, but please label each section clearly. Our mailing address is [etc.]. The list you need is in your Author Questionnaire. Thank you. Ashley."

GOOD-BYES

There are other requests for support, too. Now and

then an author falls seriously ill and can not finish the book. We always tell them not to worry, and our author support team sends them flowers. Or, worse, an author dies, and the next of kin scramble to correct the page proofs, or they request that we mention the death in our direct mailing letter, in case some may have missed the news. Those are sad moments, hearing that one of our authors died. Some of the last things they did in life was finish their book, sign our contract, and, fortunately, feel happy that now there was a lasting legacy. The sad part is that they did not live to enjoy their readers' reactions.

One example that always stands out in my memory is of a Wyoming author who published two books with us, and who submitted a third. We refused that one because her first two books had sold less than ten copies each, and we had lost a considerable amount of money on them. A year or so later we were told that she had died, and I felt a sense of regret that we had not accepted that third book after all so that at least the legacy of that work would exist for the ages. But I also felt satisfaction that at least we had enabled this woman, at the end of her life, to share no less than two labors of her love with posterity, at no cost to her whatsoever. And that was, and is, as it should be. Nothing was expected of her in return. Period.

Today, her books are still in print.

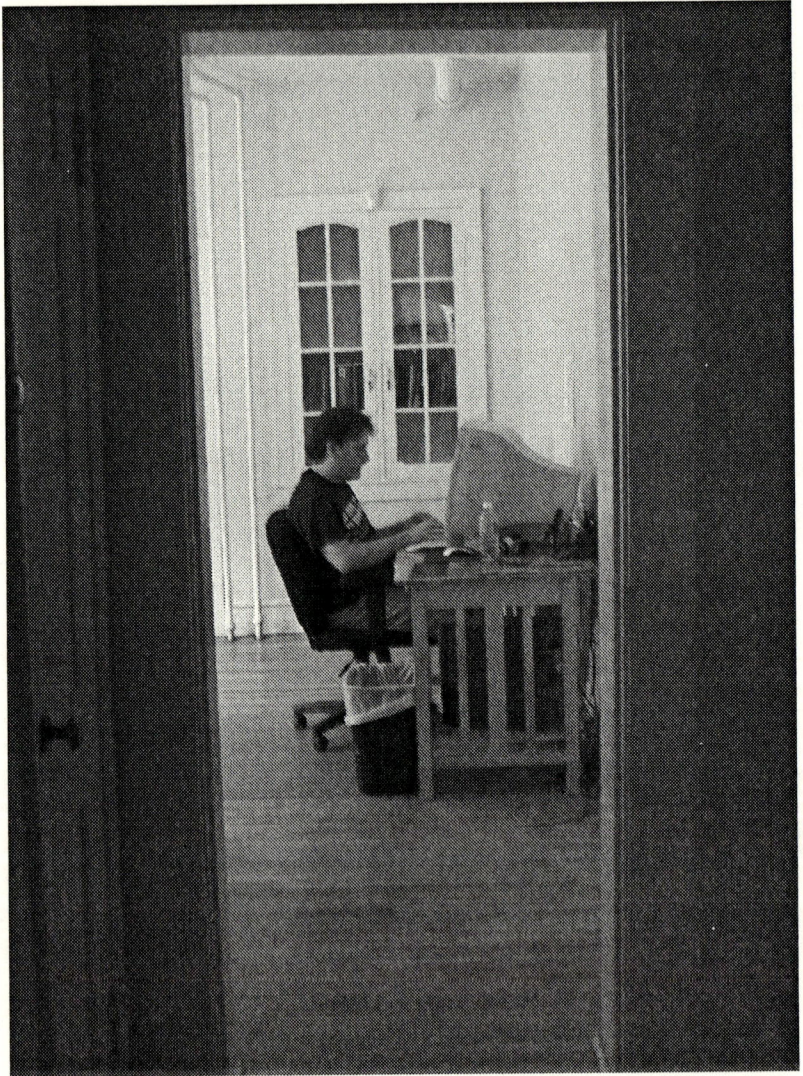

Chapter 16

"My day started with someone hitting my two week-old car. I then came home to find out that my two-month-old computer has to be replaced. When I checked my email using my other computer I found out that PublishAmerica has decided to publish my second book. This goes to show you how you can have a terrible day sometimes, but God sent PublishAmerica to make my day."

—Prince M. Kaywood Jr., author of *Godsight: The Language of God*

Birth of a Salesman

The essence of publishing is that you make the written word public, that you offer it to an audience and share it with anyone who cares to read what the writer has to say. That's how books get out of the basement offices, author's dens, or laptops that they have been written in, or on. You transform them into a physical paper product, you print them black on white, you wrap them in an attractive-looking cover, and you make them available to venues where people typically go to buy books. This, as we discovered on pages [....], is a more complicated matter than at first seems.

Contrary to urban legend, most books are not sold in bookstores, and most people never see the inside of a bookstore. Recent attempts by superstores to change buyers' habits have gone nowhere. Building big, bulky bookstores outside shopping malls, opening café latte corners, selling Clay Aiken CD's—it has made no difference whatsoever. The vast majority of Americans are not attracted to bookstores; they don't like them, bookstores don't appeal to them, and they just won't go there. Barnes & Noble, Borders, Brentano's, Books-a-Million, B. Dalton, and whatever the other chain store names may be that someone once decided should begin with the B of *book*, they are fantastic supermarkets, but three-quarters of all books are not sold there.

Never before in the history of the world have readers been able to go to such superstores and find more than a hundred thousand voices collected, printed, and bound sitting on shelves—the ultimate town hall, or, in the words of historian and writer David McCullough, "the most democratic forum, the most democratic marketplace of ideas imaginable. No civilization has had anything like what we have now," and that's not even counting the reading place that the Internet has added. Borders stores offer a minimum of no less than 120,000 titles to choose from; Barnes & Noble does approximately the same. Together, both chains have more than a thousand of those megastores polka-dotted around the country. But sales remain by and large flat, and if there is any uptick detectable, it's usually because some hypercelebrity wrote a new book, such as J.K. Rowling, or Bill and Hillary Clinton, and people briefly flock to the stores to obtain their own copies.

In other words, while American bookstores do a

fantastic job at making books available to just about everyone, better than anywhere else in the world, it's not where people go for their books. And even if they do, most book titles that are in print can not be found there, simply because even the superest of all superstores can not stock all the books that are in print. Those who believe otherwise have not done their homework. For publishers such as PublishAmerica it is one thing to say, "Our books are available through all bookstores from coast to coast," which is true because every bookstore has full access to all of our titles, but this is not enough. We must do more if we want to live up to the "publi" in publishing.

RETURNS ARE A CURSE

One of the blessings in disguise that we encountered during our early efforts to build PublishAmerica was the fact that we failed to set up our own printing operation. It forced us to work with Ingram, the nation's primary book wholesaler, even though at first we had tried to avoid that. I had worked with Ingram before Larry Clopper and I started PublishAmerica, and I had not always been happy. My foremost experiences with Ingram had been box after box of returned books, while at the same time they kept placing orders of those very same returned titles, which to me made no sense at all.

Book returns are the curse of book publishing, and you will find no publisher who will contradict this. The book world is one of the very few segments of industry where merchandise is routinely distributed on a consignment basis. Again, traditionally this has never been the case. The returnability issue dates back to the early 1930s, during the Great Depression, when book publishers believed that they needed to help booksellers stay afloat, so that they themselves could continue to count on having enough vending outlets available for the books that they would continue to release even in those money-strapped days. They agreed to stock the stores with their books without payment in advance, furthermore to be paid only for books that sold, and to take back any and all unsold copies at no cost to the retailer. It was a move that made sense at the time, even though publishing companies went belly-up left and right anyway, but when Franklin Roosevelt's happy days were back again, that should have been the end of the aid season. It was not. What few other retailers got away with, booksellers did. Intended to be only a temporary bandage, a brief relief measure, the book returns policies stuck, and they have choked many small publishers to death ever since.

Back when we started PublishAmerica, the awareness of what the new on-demand printing technology would mean for book returns was still in the process of taking root, and slowly so. Not everyone in our industry saw it yet, but among the ones that did see it immediately were the nation's largest wholesalers. They never liked this returnability issue either, primarily because they were the middlemen and therefore at the hub of distributing to-be-sold and unsold books back and forth, which at times can be a logistical nightmare, if for no other reason than that returned books require tons of extra space in their warehouses as they transit and await shipment back to the publishers. Both Ingram and their competitor Baker &

Taylor decided to experiment with on-demand printing early on. Ingram established Lightning Source, and Baker & Taylor started Replica Books, digital printing outfits where computers took over the role of shelf space: wholesalers became printers, too.

PublishAmerica's founders at first agreed that it might be a good idea to stay away from Ingram, mainly because of my earlier experiences with book returns. We had decided that we were not going to play by those non-traditional rules of bookstores wanting to ship back books, now that digital printing technology enabled us to determine exactly how many books we wanted to print, and when to print them (after we received a firm order!), and we figured that having Baker & Taylor as our main wholesaler would sufficiently take care of our books' store availability.

UNDERESTIMATING OUR OWN CLOUT

Baker & Taylor accepted non-returnable books, they served virtually all bookstores around the country, plus no less than 90 percent of all libraries, and we were going to escape the curse of that dirty little secret that few people are talking about when they discuss books and bookstores: of all books that are shipped to bookstores, between twenty and eighty percent come back unsold. The twenty percent returns is what the small handful of largest publishers deal with on a good day, and up to eighty percent is what the huge majority of smaller houses frequently must absorb. It is insane, and it does no one any good.

But we miscalculated. We overestimated our ability to force bookstores into working with our wholesaler, and we underestimated Ingram's ability and willingness to work with individual publishers. Most of all, we underestimated our own clout as we were quickly growing into a serious force.

After we had abandoned the idea of printing our own books, we worked for a while with a big printing company in the outskirts of Philadelphia that served all the major players. They rolled out the red carpet for us, in their fancy headquarters, with their fancy PowerPoint presentations and their fancy president who had made the local news by installing a $250,000 kitchen in his fancy home, and they did a pretty decent job—until they caved under their own weight and went bankrupt. So we needed a new printer, and that's when Ingram came back in focus.

Bookstores did not like our avoidance of Ingram. When they go looking for a book title, the first thing they routinely do is checking Ingram's database. Most bookstores prefer ordering through Ingram. We knew this, but we had hoped that we could convince bookstore managers to follow other ordering patterns, and while we were not completely unsuccessful, they generally didn't like it. So we used the occasion of our printer's demise to start uploading all of our titles to other printers, now also including Ingram's printing daughter Lightning Source. This automatically made all of our books available through Ingram, which now also accepted non-returnable titles—and eagerly so, as we found out—which made life for those bookstores easier. The number of bookstore complaints decreased considerably.

Then one day we received a phone call from John

Ingram. John is chairman of a wildly successful operation, one that reportedly ships approximately two-thirds of all books that go through wholesale, or some 125 million books per year, with annual sales that easily exceed a billion dollars. His dad basically invented book wholesaling back in the 1960s when all bookstores still ordered directly from the publishers, and often had to wait six or more weeks before their orders shipped. Bronson Ingram stepped in as the middleman who could cut that waiting time down to just a few days, by just stocking those publishers' books in his own warehouse and springing into action immediately as soon as a bookstore placed an order.

Ingram Senior had no book industry experience—his background was in oil and ships—and at first he refused to stock more than five hundred different titles, because he thought that was more than enough. He was quickly forced to change his mind, though, and today his company makes more than a million and a half different book titles available to bookstores, libraries, and many other places all over the world.

"AMONG OUR TOP CUSTOMERS"

It's the "many other places" that intrigued us, and this was in the back of our minds while we listened to John Ingram as he explained how PublishAmerica had been on his radar screen for a while now. He said that he wanted Lightning Source to earn our business, and that they were going to do whatever it took to convince us that they should be our primary printer. We thanked him, but expressed concern that at Lightning Source, where they dealt with more than 2500 different publishers, we might get lost in the crowd, whereas with our other printers we were among their top customers and we received their top attention. That was an easy one to answer, John said. "With PublishAmerica's volume, you will immediately be among our top customers."

Regardless, we took a full three years to step-by-step move the bulk of our business to Ingram and Lightning Source, allowing other printers to supply us with sizable chunks of volume until we were fully satisfied that we got what we wanted. And we did. Ingram and Lightning Source are good companies to work with, and staffed with good guys. They also ensure that a book is available through many other venues than the nation's brick-and-mortar stores that account for only a minority of all sales. Thanks to Ingram, all PublishAmerica books are available through scores of online vendors, most of which most people have never even heard of, and also through gift stores, libraries, drug stores, grocery stores, home centers, airport shops, toy stores, computer stores, and many other specialty stores, including hobby stores, and places such as Wal-Mart.

They are available in at least twenty foreign countries, for delivery within only a few days, typically through Lightning Source's European plant in Milton Keynes, U.K. There are individuals who take their cue from Ingram's availability lists and offer our books on Ebay, even though those books have yet to be printed, much less bought. Baker & Taylor continues to also distribute our books, but they order through Lightning Source. And anywhere any retailer would like to obtain a PublishAmerica book, in any quantities between one and one million, they can do it.

At the time of this writing, bookstores call or log on to order a PublishAmerica book more than three hundred times a day, each day. Of those, Barnes & Noble alone orders a PublishAmerica book more than a hundred times each day. And Amazon, never one to be outdone if they can possibly hclp it, is quickly catching up, faxing in orders all the time, up to almost half the number that Barnes & Noble orders. Borders, Books-A-Million, Waldenbooks, they are all strong runners-up, and although most store managers are instructed by their own headquarters to place their orders through Ingram or Lightning Source, many consider a headquarters instruction as no more than a suggestion, so they often call our office and get their order processed very quickly. Since this also gives them a better discount deal, everybody is happy.

AIRCRAFT CARRIER

But important as all these retail sales may be, there are still other venues that readers use to buy their books.

We quickly learned to assist people with events in churches, libraries, country clubs, company cafeterias, hospitals, retirement centers, military commissaries, hotels, diners, schools, city halls, fire stations, police barracks, private homes, colleges, universities, local airports, clubhouses, ballparks, public parks, private parks, supermarkets, street festivals, art fiestas, black tie galas, even an aircraft carrier in the Mediterranean, and we have become quite good at it. Wherever folks need books to be for sale, we'll get them there, and we'll get them there on time.

Among a book's best sellers are the authors themselves, as has traditionally been the case. The author is often a book's best pitcher, and the more famous he is, the more likely it is that his publisher actually requires by contract that he go out, give speeches, and do book signings. This is not unlike the movie industry where millionaire actors must agree to a provision in their film contract that obligates them to do rounds of promotional events. This, and this alone, is the reason why you see Richard Gere on *David Letterman*, Julia Roberts on *Good*

Morning America, or Tom Cruise on the *Today Show,* pitching their new movies. It is also the reason why you can actually line up and meet Jon Stewart, General Tommy Franks, Rush Limbaugh, or *My Life So Far's* Jane Fonda in a bookstore, signing your copy of their books.

The not-so-famous have no such clauses in their contracts, for the one and only reason that they are not famous and therefore would not attract a crowd. But they put themselves in the center anyway. Although the majority of all book writers have a tendency to be shy and insecure about their own book—unsure that it will be good enough, unconfident that it will compare positively to what else is out there—many discover to their own surprise that they have a talent to discuss their own book, a natural aptitude to pitch it, the skills to promote it. In reality this is less surprising than it seems, because everyone becomes an expert on anything that comes from within, and of course nobody knows their book better than the author. Ask them any question about it, and they will know the answer.

In fact, they have not only become experts on their

own book, but on the job of writing as well, and many have gone on to teach writing classes. When PublishAmerica organized the largest gathering of its own authors a publisher ever brought together—in February of 2004 in our Maryland hometown where almost three hundred folks came from all over the country and beyond—the key part was not our mass book signing party that filled up a local mall from end to end and that earned us a place in the Guinness Book of World Records. No, it was two days of workshops about the realities of being a writer, and the easiest part was to find moderators who had something to say: we had thousands of experts to pick from. And when our moderators opened their classes, the rooms were too small.

I remember walking into the room that had been assigned to good old Lynn Barry, the ever-energetic author of *Puddles* and *Bjoyfl*: standing room only. Hotel workers were scrambling to find more chairs so that more might sit. The same thing happened during lectures given by *Plumbing in Harlem*'s Joe Benevento, *Journey*'s Robert Amoroso, Linda Alexander of *Until Next Time* and *Dorothy*

From Kansas, or Hattie Halsey and Deborah Rosenkrans who together wrote four books including their *RB* sea adventure trilogy: not enough chairs. And when they spoke, everyone in attendance agreed: there are no better experts than those who speak from experience. The best judges were sitting right there in the audience, they were the moderators' peers, they knew exactly where these speakers were coming from.

ABS: ALWAYS BE SELLING

Expert teachers, expert pitchers. John Charles Cheek, author of *Stay Safe Buddy*, has a motto that he calls ABS: Always Be Selling. Henry Custer says, "I've sold [my books to] the tire salesman at Sears, my optometrist, two dental assistants, the next bed patient in a nursing home with my sister-in-law. We takes 'em where we finds 'em..." He wrote *Dirt Floor, Concept of Justice*, and *Bizarre Justice*. Jake Green, the guy with the 184 rejections from other publishers, adds, "If they have money, I will sell them a book. I sold a house back in October and sold seven books to realtors, three to lawyers, and two to the buyer of my house. Oh yeah, I made it to Sears also—the hearing aid desk bought two. Insurance agents are fair game. I placed seven copies at my agent's office. Oh yeah, two went to my tax accountant. [...] Costco is not tough. I just sold two books over their counter. Bought some new glasses and sold the books to a nice lady who adjusted the new specs." Says John Cheek, "Agree [with] Jess and Henry. I sold two copies in the food court of Costco last November."

And these are folks who had never before sold a book in their entire lives, not until they became published authors. They don't *have* to sell a book, they *want* to. That's how the majority of book buyers never see the inside of a bookstore. Books come to them in myriads of other different ways.

Chapter 17

"I have bragged about your company to everyone I know, and think you all should get a big pat on the back for all the hard work you do to get authors published. You are a true breath of fresh air and I am glad to see you are getting the recognition you so deserve."

—Lynn Reed, author of *The Adrenaline Rush*

Fighting Goliath

So there we have it. This was how PublishAmerica came about, this is what and who we are, and this is what we do. When we entered the publishing world with our company, our concept, and our compassion, we helped our authors change it. We were the first publisher who decided to publish authors on a large scale without having any previous sense at all of their books' market chances, and without expecting anything back from them in return. We just figured that, on average, each book would probably sell enough copies to sustain our enterprise and its concept. And we were absolutely, one hundred percent right. Since PublishAmerica, every writer now stands a normal chance to become a published author at no cost to them, at zero expense, at a price tag of zip, null, nada.

PublishAmerica has its critics, of course we do. We are bringing about a change to the traditional publishing world, a huge change: we have democratized it, for the first time in history. We have opened the gates wide for *we the people*, for the regular folks, for those of us who reside on Main Street. Provided that they wrote a work of reasonable quality, now everyone has an equal opportunity to see it in print and made available to the whole wide world. Not everybody likes that, and among them are the usual suspects.

Who do not like change? Those who benefit from things as they are, the status quo, those who are also known as the elite, or who think that they are an elite, or, worse, who believe that there even ought to be an elite, and that they belong there and nobody else does. They are championing literary Apartheid; they have clubs, guilds, fraternities where elite published authors ballot other published authors and turn them away, not because of the quality of their published work, but because of *how* they got it published. They are like Marie Antoinette who, when told that the poor peasants had no bread to eat, contemptuously said, "Let them eat cake." Translation: if those poor bastards who also wrote a book but can't get themselves accepted by a mainstream publisher really want to see their work in print, well, let them pull their wallet and pay to be published, the vanity way: it's all fine, as long as they don't delude themselves into believing that they are now one of us, the elite.

DAVID WINS

History has always known elites, and it has always dealt with them in only one way: they disappeared, and always under the pressure of irresistable change. Historically, all elites have been replaced by majority rule, and where this has not happened yet, it will over time, inevitably. As soon as an excluded majority senses that empowerment is within reach, they will grab it. Authors who have always been refused and denied the opportunity to see their book in print unless they paid for it now have an equal opportunity to be in the exact same league as the elite, and they will, by their sheer number, bring an end to the elite's existence.

This is why the elite is fighting, kicking, biting. They want it, this literary Apartheid. Their old status is what set them apart from the rest of us; it gave them their legitimacy, their eminence, their authority. They resist change because change will do them in, will take away their special rank, remove part of their prestige, chip away at their prominence. Not that there's anything wrong with prominence—if it is hard-won, well-deserved, and the result of a unique achievement matched only by a very few, who would not want to consider another person prominent? But to keep others out who have matched your achievement because you are afraid that you will not stand out prominently enough among too many peers— that is pitiful. And it is a battle that the elite will lose.

They will lose it because they deserve to lose it, because their time is up, because there is a crowd moving in, and because PublishAmerica opened the floodgates. David is overtaking Goliath, not by exterminating him with a slingshot, but by dwarfing him.

The vast majority of our authors dislike elites, though an occasional one does like the upper class idea and clandestinely aspires to be one of them, then gets disappointed when the elite brotherhood does not want him. Asked why not, the elite respond by saying that they don't judge an aspiring member on the content and quality of his book, but on his publisher, and that they, the elite, are not responsible for the refusal, but the publisher who has the audacity to publish a crowd. Of course there will always be an upper class hopeful or two who get confused by such convoluted dialectics and turn around to speak in tongues to us—with what message, I don't know, because at PublishAmerica we don't understand the language of doom and gloom. But I do know that when elites start saying that what really drives them is that they have the best interests of non-members at heart, at a time when non-members are overrunning the playing field, their days are counted. We wear their criticism of PublishAmerica as a badge of honor.

I once met a guy who knew everything about Apartheid: Nelson Mandela. We both attended the same publishers conference in Kyoto, Japan, and slept in the same hotel. One morning we shared an elevator, and on our way down a hotel employee stepped in on the second floor. "Mr. Mandela," she said, "the hotel management is asking if you would stop by to sign our VIP guestbook." This was the man who had spent twenty-seven years in prison because an elite did not want him to be equal. They did not consider his content, only his cover, and they found its color not of their liking. The year was 1991, one year after the pressure had built up so much that they had to let him walk out free. And now perfect strangers wanted him to sign a VIP guestbook.

"Sure," Nelson Mandela said. "If the VIPs don't mind."

They did not mind. They didn't even have a choice anymore.

WE ARE THE FUTURE

Whether critics like it or not, we are shaping the future of book publishing. We are modelling, fashioning, forging it. PublishAmerica is turning book publishing into a democracy. We are the people's publisher; we are offering representation *without* taxation. This is unstoppable. No reasonable soul can possibly believe that the PublishAmerica model will not determine the landscape of publishing in the future. There will always be a few large mainstream houses with pockets deep enough to publish the celebrities. There will always be writers with such a deep sense of independence that they prefer to self-publish their books—today with the help of a vanity publisher, tomorrow by using small book printers hooked up to their PC or to a computer in a bookstore. But the vast majority of writers and aspiring writers in the next two, three decades will be published by a traditional publisher who charges them nothing and who expects nothing from them in return, and those writers will number in the hundreds of thousands, and eventually millions. Take that, elite.

Today there is no one else who is doing what we are doing. There is no other publisher that gives all of its authors a free website, a free email address, free exposure to book vendors all over the world, free books, free copies for reviewers, free assistance in setting up book signings, readings, or lectures, free press releases, and the production, manufacturing, publishing, and promotion of their books for free, *and* do this for thirteen thousand authors at a time. No one else is doing this, period.

PublishAmerica is offering each of its authors a free website at www.publishedauthors.net, and thousands are using it. In fact, *any* published author is welcome to join the opportunity and put up their own website there, which is in line with our policy of open doors and open arms—we are includers, not excluders. We are giving everyone using that website option a free email address, name@publishedauthors.net, another benefit that many use. Of course we are making their books available, at no cost to them, to book vendors everywhere, primarily at home, but in reality also to at least that many merchants overseas. You can purchase a PublishAmerica book in bookstores as far away as Britain, Spain, France, Germany, Italy, Greece, Israel, Sweden, the Netherlands, Norway, Switzerland, South Africa, the Cayman Islands, or Australia.

And it speaks for itself that we are giving our authors free copies as soon as their book is printed. They love it— it is what they have always been waiting for, and what we receive their most heartfelt thank you letters for. Just as self-evident is that we provide professional reviewers with free books as well, at a rate of thousands of free books per year. A good review is good for a book, and good for the author whose confidence gets a boost each time someone pats her on the shoulder. And, yes, our author support is free as well, as are our efforts to inform the media about our authors and their books. Thousands of positive stories have appeared in the press about PublishAmerica authors. The smaller the newspaper, the closer to an author's home it is, and the more understanding it is of the enormity of the author's achievement. Small newspapers serve the nation's grassroots, and when someone achieves something unusual, they comprehend it, grasp it, get it in a heartbeat.

All these elements that we are offering for free are things that are normal, standard, traditional, one would say. That's correct, that is what it is, or at least should be. But again, PublishAmerica is the only publisher that is providing all of this, and then some, on this large scale. Today, that is. Tomorrow, it will be the norm.

WE TRUST BOOKS

Why do we do this? For all the reasons that I have mentioned throughout this book, but not because

PublishAmerica's founders are saints. We are certainly not. We are also leading the way on this because it makes money sense. "You can not hold a torch to lighting another's path without brightening your own." Few authors serve mega-niches, but many serve micro-niches that, combined, also become a mega-niche. Mainstream publishers serve the nation like interstate highways serve those who use the fast lane. Main Street PublishAmerica serves the nation the way Main Street runs, county by county, and that is where people live their lives.

PublishAmerica's founders never expected anything back from their authors. Larry Clopper and I have never asked them for a dime, and instead have actually refused money when it was offered to us in return for special favors such as an increased production tempo, or past-deadline text changes to a book, or other preferential treatments; whenever we could, we did those favors anyway, and for free. Moneywise, all PublishAmerica authors are treated equally, whether their name is Jamie Farr of *M*A*S*H* fame, or Agathe Von Trapp, whose singing-family life was made immortal by *The Sound of*

Music, or John Doe and Jane Roe from Peoria, Illinois—we accept no money from them, under any circumstances. We never wanted their money, we wanted their books.

Because we trust those books. We trust them to be attractive, appealing, tempting enough for others to want to read them. The readers, those are the people whose money we are interested in, and we don't care how the books reach them—through bookstores, book clubs, cybersellers, Wal-Marts, house parties, or through our authors. We always reasoned that if the book's author was an interesting enough man or woman to spend months and often years to even conceive it, write it, finish it, then the author's book would certainly also be deemed equally interesting both by readers who knew them and by those who were going to get to know them. These books would sell, that we did not doubt for a second. Some might sell dozens, others hundreds, yet others thousands, and there would be some that wouldn't sell anything at all, and some that would sell exceptionally well. Which book would fall into which category we could not predict, and we were not going to do any pre-market research. There were no certainties, no assurances, no guarantees, and there were surely no obligations; there was only the faith we placed in trusting our authors and the fruits of their labor.

Our assumption was correct. After all, this is a country that buys an average of five books per capita per year, babies and great-grandmothers included, regardless of what the experts may tell you about declining readerships. America reads; it buys one-third of all books that are sold *worldwide*. According to recent numbers, the average household of four purchases ten fiction books per year, four romance books, two religion books, two diet books, and three mystery novels, etcetera, which all in all adds up to a total of 1.6 billion books per year. If placed on a bookshelf, spines facing you, they would run the distance from New York to Los Angeles. This is a country of readers, folks who could be persuaded to read what our authors have written.

And that is exactly what happened, to the tune of one million books at the moment of this writing, and counting rapidly. While we were holding the torch for others, our own path was indeed brightened as well, a result we are both very proud of and grateful for. No company can blossom without sufficient revenues, and ours enabled us to continue down the path of self-funded growth at formidable speed. To this day, we owe no one a penny—no bank, no investor, no lending institute. PublishAmerica is funded solely by book sales.

DREAMS COMING FULL CIRCLE

Such is the story of PublishAmerica. Feared by some, rightfully so, and cherished by many. The only publisher with a sense of a large family about them, because family is at the heart of our authors, and it is at the heart of Main Street. We are a young family, a large family, a united family, and occasionally a reunited family.

I mentioned earlier that we never solicit our authors. We don't find them, they find us. When they join us, they do so at their own instigation, their own initiative, voluntarily, spontaneously. But there has been one exception. One morning, I found buried in a low-circulation newsletter the following "lost love" text. It was written by a man in his seventies, and is an excellent example of what Main Street writing is capable of, in a nutshell.

'We have loved more in one brief summer than most people have loved in all their lives. Oh, how I wish you were a simple Icelandic fisherman so that you could stay with me rather than fly away.' It was September 1955 and I received this letter shortly after my departure from Iceland. The deceptively named island in the North Atlantic had been my theatre of operations for a year and I had played the role of Supply Sergeant. At that time, there were over 20,000 military personnel stationed at Keflavík air base, located about 30 miles from the capital city of Reykjavík, but very few like me who took an interest in the country or its people. Her name was Ragnheidur Ingvarsdóttir—Dottie for short. She was a beautiful auburn-haired nurse. She worked in a city hospital and we met at a dance fairly early in my stay, although our lives didn't intertwine until my last three months there. Her semi-fluent English was comparable to my semi-fluent Icelandic, so we were linguistically compatible (aside from other compatibilities). When I was up for some furlough time, I took her to Scotland and England, which provided her with her first experience of the world outside of Iceland. The highlight of her trip was, I imagine, the afternoon spent shopping the big London department stores.

Memory is a funny kind of reservoir. There is sometimes no logical reason why certain things are quickly effaced and others stubbornly stick. Dottie and I parted. The probability of our lives ever crossing again was practically nil. Our stars followed different trajectories in different parts of the universe with no intergalactic communication. And yet 47 years later when my daughter Eve suggested that we take a vacation together in Iceland and I had agreed, the submerged, stubbornly sticking details surfaced. How can one forget a name like Ragnheidur Ingvarsdóttir? Many images of our distant encounter materialized. I was ready to go back to Iceland in June 2003, but the trip had now assumed an unexpected emotional dimension. Not only was I going back geographically, but I was also going back to my past life and I wasn't sure of what I would find.

Icelanders use a patronymic system for naming their children—you are somebody's son or somebody's daughter (dóttir)—but the handy thing is that women do not change their names when married. Phone book white pages list people by their first names first. There are about 275,000 Icelanders on the island and they are all in the national database with name, address, phone number and date of birth. Six Ragnheidur Ingvarsdóttirs popped up on the computer screen at the hotel information desk. Three were quickly eliminated because of their age. I reached two others by phone and verified that they were not the person I was looking for. The last possible woman had an inoperable phone because the number had been put "in storage," a system permitting a person to disconnect her phone, but reserve the number for future use. Well, I had the address, so I decided to make a personal appearance.

It was a neat complex of two-storey apartment buildings and a woman in the parking lot pointed out the correct unit. There were four apartments in each unit and the lit doorbell of one flashed 'Ragnheidur Ingvarsdóttir.' I held my breath and pushed the button. Who would walk through the door? Had she been waiting for my return? Would she even remember me?

There was no answer. I then noticed that her

mailbox was stuffed with letters and papers indicating it had not been emptied for some time. I left a note: 'My name is Ed Chalom. I was a soldier stationed at Keflavík in 1955 and I had a friend named Ragnheidur Ingvarsdóttir. I don't know if you are that same woman. You can reach me at....'

According to a recent census, there are 73,165 horses in Iceland. This horse is a unique breed and Eve was eager to ride. We were planning to go to a large stable for a group ride, but at the last minute I decided it would be preferable to go to a smaller stable on our own. Two lady riders went out with us on the trails through the lava field and in conversation with one I found out that she was the Director of Nurses at the main Reykjavík hospital.

'Is it possible that you know a nurse, probably retired, by the name of Ragnheidur Ingvarsdóttir?'

'No, but I have a complete directory at the hospital of all past and present Icelandic nurses. After our ride, we'll go to the hospital and check it out.'

At the hospital the director drew down the three-volume directory of nurses and there on the bottom of a page of Rs was 'Ragnheidur Ingvarsdóttir' with the same birth date as the woman with the "in storage" telephone. There was a full paragraph outlining her life story, and when we turned the page her serene clear-eyed photo looked out at me. Among the details of her education, work history and lineage was the fact that she had married an American sailor in 1959. They had one son and sometime thereafter had been divorced. She retired as a nurse in 1989. It struck me as somehow sad to see her life summarized in a paragraph as, indeed, my own life similarly could be reduced to a few words and numbers.

Iceland is a volcanic island where hot water for heating and swimming surges out of underground springs. On our next to last day in Reykjavík, we made our daily visit to one of the ubiquitous swimming pools. Then, impelled by my genetic persistence, I decided that since I knew where the right woman lived, I could find out more information about her absence from one of her neighbors.

"Do you speak English?"

"Yes."

"Do you know Ragnhcidur Ingvarsdóttir?"

"She doesn't live here."

"But her name is right there on the doorbell."

"Oh, but she is living in Spain now. Every year

she lives in Spain for six or seven months and then she comes back."

Our days died imperceptibly—day is day and night is day in the Icelandic June.

We arrived at the airport a couple hours before flight time, passed through security, and were waiting at the gate when a voice over the PA system said, "Would passenger Edward Chalom please come to the information desk in the main terminal?"

"Eve, watch the baggage and I'll go see what they want."

As I approached the information desk, a white-haired, graceful lady turned to face me.

"Hello Ed. Long time, no see."

The heart is also a funny reservoir. From the depth of an inexpressible emotion, tears leaped to our eyes. We touched hands and stood there weeping senselessly.

The flight back was silent and uneventful.

After I read Ed's sweet reunion story, I searched the Internet until I had tracked him down, found his phone number, called him, and asked him to turn the story behind that story into a book, and offered him a publishing contract. The only time I ever solicited an author. PublishAmerica published *The Heart is a Funny Reservoir* in 2004. It is co-written by Ed and Ragnheidur.

Dreams coming full circle. That's us. That is what PublishAmerica is all about.

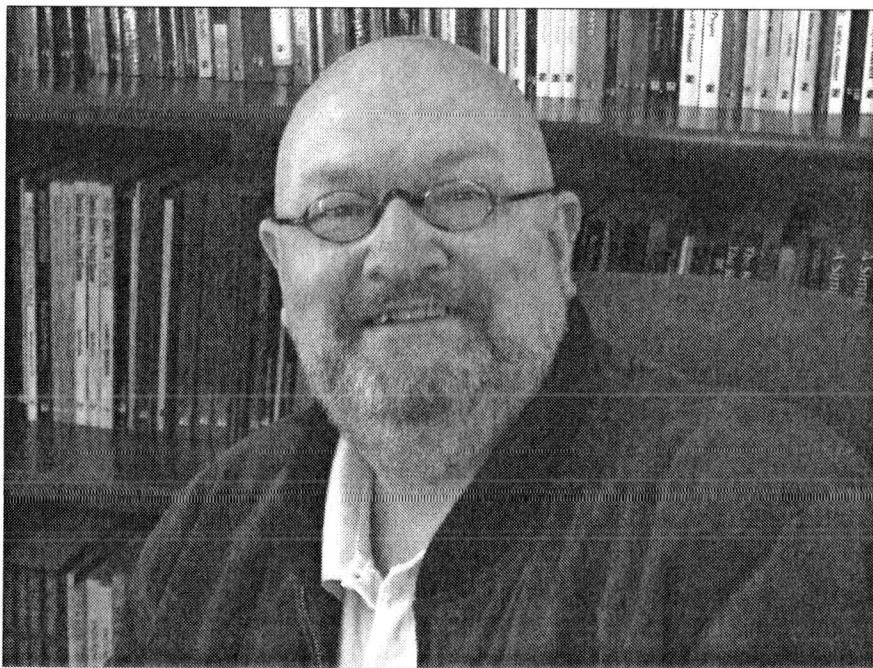

About Willem Meiners

The author is co-founder, co-owner, and CEO of PublishAmerica. Born in Amsterdam, he has spent most of his life in publishing, on both sides of the Atlantic. He was a newspaper executive, has authored twelve books, and his preferred job description is simply, Publisher.

Willem Meiners is a husband, a father, and a grandfather. He is also a helicopter pilot. When away from PublishAmerica's hectic excitement, his Icelandic wife Sigurveig and he consider the majestic surroundings of Reykjavik their true home.

And the big

Thank You

goes to:

Morris Aagard, Joseph Aarntzen, Hugh Aaron, Sherri Abad, Sunday Abakwue, Robert Abbamonte, Raymond Abbott, Walter Abbott, Michelle Abbott, Lumukanda Abdul-Kenyatta, Gamel Abdullah, Frederick Abel, Janice Abel, John Abel, Tabitha Abel, Joanne Aber, Troy Ables, Anthony Aboujaoude, Byron Abrams, Elena Abraszek, Lara AbulHusn, Sean Acker, Gary Ackison, Mary Acton, Beth Adair, Gail Adams, Ronald Adams, Gail Adams, William Adams, Lawrence Adams, Anthony Adams, John Adams, Benge Adams, Chris Adams, William Adams, James Adams, Fred Adams, Stephanie Adams, Stacy Adams, Erica Adams, John Adams, Latanya Adams, Lawrence Adams, Randal Adams, Robin Adams, Rudolph Adams, Carla Adams, Catherine Adams, Gwendolyn Adams-Evans, Margaret Adamson, Rhonda Adamson, Yinka Adebiyi, Dave Adelberg, Olufunmilayo Ademosu, Sunmade Adeyemi, Jeffery Adkins, Belinda Adkins, Vickie Adkins, Jack Adler, Kelly Adolph, Julian Adomako-Gyimah, Patricia Agerston, Allison Agius, Susan Agne, Pearl Ahnen, René Aikens, Robyn Aikin, Donnie Aikins, Ruth Aird, Kari Airgood, Jeffrey Aita, Richard Aites, Jeremy Akers, Saundra Akers, Jeremy Akers, Sharron Akers, Dolores Akey, Josephine Akhagbeme, Nathaniel Alabi, Ron Albea, Randall Albea, LeAndrew Albert, John Albert, George Albitz, Adam Albrecht, James Albrigtsen, Alexter Albury, John Alcamo, Frank Alcock, Lynn Alcock, Frank Alcock, Tommy Alcorn, Georgia Alderink, Artis Alderman, Berta Aldridge, Samuel Alesich, Lisa Alessi, Linda Alexander, Samiko Alexander, Hansen Alexander, Mary Alexander, Emily Alexander, Samiko Alexander, Christopher Alexander, Allyson Alexander, Alberta Alexander, Sandra Alexander, Chris Alexinas, Shaaira Alexis, Michael Alford, Michael Alger, Twila Alger, Roy Algiam, Elliott Alhadeff, Murad Ali, Anthony Aliberti, Julia Alibrando, Rodney Allaway, Thomas Allebach, Codrey Allen, Pauline Allen, Rida Allen, Sir Allen, Teresa Allen, Rosie Allen, Harold Allen, Megan Allen, Tom Allen, Kathleen Allen, DarNella Allen, Lynn Allen, Linda Allen, Joseph Allen, Johnny Allen, John Allen, Joanne Allen, Jim Allen, Gary Allen, Emily Allen, Mary Allen, Maureen Alley, Ariana Allias, Linda Allison, Carol Allman, Donald Alloway, Leighton Allred, William Allred, Effie Allred, Malcolm Allred, Russell Allred, Jonathan Almanzar, Nancy Almodovar, Betty Almond, Theophilus Alozie, James Alten, Paula Alty, Kelley Alunni, Michael Alvarez, Nando Amabile, Lee Amato, David Ambrose, Allen Ambrosino, Janice Amburgey, Ricky Amburgey, Nicolea Ambush, Joseph Amedeo, Melissa Amen, Dudley

Amendola, Vicki Amerault, Matthew Amerling, Christina Amie, Don Amiet, Reine Amodeo, Betty Amorelli, Robert Amoroso, Elizabeth Amos, Jacqueline Amos, Joshua Anchors, William Anders, Steven Andersen, Julie Andersen, Carlette Anderson, Mignon Anderson, Nancy Anderson, Perry Anderson, Richard Anderson, Robert Anderson, Ryan Anderson, Willard Anderson, Luleen Anderson, Jeri Anderson, Nadine Anderson, Donna Anderson, Joyce Anderson, Mike Anderson, Dwayne Anderson, Kenneth Anderson, Stephen Anderson, Harold Anderson, B. Anderson, Charles Anderson, Debera Anderson, Donald Anderson, Dwayne Anderson, Marsha Anderson, Evalyn Anderson, James Anderson, John Anderson, Joyce Anderson, Karen Anderson, Kathleen Anderson, Edward Anderson, Edmund Andracki, Zenon Andracki, Edmund Andracki, Frank Andrade, Christopher Andreae, April Andrews, James Andrews, Robert Andruszko, Billie Angel, Donald Angell, Ralph Angelo, René Angers, Michelle Angers, Charles Angevine, Lisa Angius, Gwen Angstrom, Jude Angus, Juliana Anjos, Luci Anscombe, Peter Anstiss, Kenneth Antaya, Iva Anthony, Robert Anthony, Anna Antonsdottir, George Antoscia, Jack Apostol, Cindy Appel, Shirley Appleby, Richard Applegate, David Aquino, Mary Aquino, Dave Aquino, Shahida Arabi, Lot Arangua, Lise Archambault, Richard Archer, Kathy Archer, Darrin Ard, Victor Arditti, Lucille Ardrey, Stephen Arend, Anne Arenfeld, Sean-Michael Argo, Carolyn Argyle, Luis Arias-Contreras, Andrew Armacost, George Armenia, Antonio Armenteros, James Armentrout, Paula Armes, Robert Armstead, Phyllis Armstrong, Terri Armstrong, James Armstrong, Judith Armstrong, Harold Armstrong, Anthony Armstrong, Cynthia Armstrong, Morris Armstrong, Zaynab Armstrong-Jones, Linda Armstrong-Miller, Faye Arnett, Douglas Arnold, Jeana Arnold, Lois Arnold, Lou Arnold, Charlotte Arnold, Tracy Arnot, Jill Aro, Sarah Aronhalt, Norma Arrambide, Sharmin Arrington, Marliss Arruda, Louis Artalona, Steven Arts, Tristan Arts, Brian Ary, Donna Arz, Emily Asad, Ephrem Asfaw, Cyril Ash, Rebecca Ash, Christopher Ash, Keith Ashby, Elisabeth Ashe, Opal Ashenbrenner, Elizabeth Ashley, Joanne Ashley, Elizabeth Ashley, Damien Ashton, Elizabeth Ashwood, Mark Assi, Harold Aster, Shivraj Asthana, Frank Atanacio, Richard Atencio, Nickolas Athanasatos, David Atherton, John Atkins, Melaine Atkins, Roberta Atkins, Carrie Atkins, Andrew Atkinson, Irene Atkinson, Seth Atkinson, Andrew Atkinson, Adam Atterberry, Richard Atwood, Kimberly Aube, Michael Aubrecht, Glen Aubrey,

Jesse Auchter, Stella Auchterlonie, Adalsteinn Audunsson, Elaine August, Vernadette Augustusel, Becky Auker, Sarah Auld, Jessica Ault, Robert Ault, Jim Ausfahl, Donald Austin, Tamera Austin, Shawn Austin, William Austin, Douglas Austin, Donald Austin, Alexander Austin, Donald Austin, Alice Avery, Melissa Avery, Vikki Avila, Lorraine Avocato, Stacey Awe, Pamela Ayer, John Ayers, Hamilton Ayuk, Rana Ayzeren, Carol Azams, Unoma Azuah, Frederick Babb, Rebecca Babcock, Rick Baber, Penny Babson, Katherine Bachman, Lindsay Bachman, Patricia Backora, Eugenia Bacon, Myrna Badgerow, Robert Badoux, William Baer, Gail Baer, Marsha Bagley, Cathy Bagley, Michael Bagley, Glenn Bagley, Marsha Bagley, Peter Bagnuolo, Nelson Bagsby, Jason Bahre, Michael Bahrich, Howard Bailey, Matthew Bailey, Nichelle Bailey, Kristina Bailey, Joyce Bailey, Jeffrey Bailey, Brenda Bailey, Anthony Bailey, Annette Bailey, Andrea Bailey, Esther Bailey, Bob Bailey, Thomas Bailie, Darrell Bain,

Christopher Bair, Willa Baisden, Andre Baity, Judy Baker, Bernadette Baker, Karla Baker, Phyllis Baker, Karla Baker, Jason Baker, James Baker, Dean Baker, Bernadette Baker, Benjamin Baker, Wayne Baker, JoLynn Baker, Hilda Bakering, Jim Balbirer, Carol Baldwin, Dan Baldwin, Evelyn Baldwin, Ellen Baldy, Mark Bales, Stephen Balga, Lynn Balko, Donald Ball, Kenneth Ball, Nina Ball, Richard Ball, Tracy Ball, Naomi Ball, Gregory Ballan, Teri Ballard, Dana Ballez, Sheryl Ballou, James, Balme, James Balme, Alan Balter, Constance Balukoff, Geoffrey Bamber, Nancy Bane,

Oindrila Banerjee, Olusheyi Banjo, Charles Banks, James Banks, Tyrone Banks, Joycelyn Banks, Neha Bansal, Lisa Baptist, Nicole Baptiste, Joseph Baraba, Ruy Barada, David Barbasso, Willette Barbee, Brenda Barber, Effie Barber, Joanne Barber, Nathan Barber, Paul Barber, Tonitia Barbosa, Bruce Barbre, Sylvia Barchue, MaryLei Barclay, Barry Bardone, Elaine Bardsley, Siegfried Barger, Amy Barham, Suneil Barkat, Richard Barker, Paul Barker, Richard Barker, Barbara Barker, Adrienne Barker, David Barker, Wesley Barkley, Paul Barlin, Terrence Barlow, Linda Barlow-Lockard, Narayan Barman, Isadore Barmash, Roger Barnes, Judy Barnes, Estelle Barnes, Charlotte Barnes, Carey Barnes, Arch Barnes, Patricia Barnes, Arthur Barnes, Richard Barnett, Arthur Barnhart, Patricia Barnhart, Shelby Barnhart, DeQuinda Barnum, Jessica Barone, Molly Barr, Erika Barr, Louise Barr, Kendra Barr, Steven Barraco, John Barradale, April Barrett, Barbara Barrett, Maile Barrett, Somars Barrett, St.John Barrett, Sharon Barrett, Leonard Barrington, Christina Barritt, Richard Barron, Deirdra Barron, Verne Barry, Brent Barry, Lynn Barry, Richard Barry, Teddy Bart, Marvin Bartlett, Isaac Bartley, Giuseppe Bartoli, Anthony Barton, Chester Barton, Jason Barton, Michael Bartosik, Ashok Baruah, Edward Bas, Aysun Basaran-Kuck, Sylvia Basile, Jennie Bass, Joseph Bastian, R. Bateman, Roy Bateman, Alice Bateman, Oliver Bateman, Billie Bates, Elizabeth Bates, William Bates, Lissa Bates, Robert Batey, Tommy Batson, Robert Battaglia, Greg Batte, Lynwood Batts, Krystal Batts, Tera Baty, Monica Baudendistel, Greg Bauder, Henry Baugh, Jennifer Bauman, Ellen Baumgartner, Judy Baus, Michael Bavota, Martha Baxley, Carl Baxter, Deborah Baxter, Rebecca Baxter, Tammy Baxter, Nickolas Bay, Elaine Bazarian, Cheryl Bazzoui, Beverly Beach, Rick Beachy, Ruth Beall, Jason Bean, Tim Beane, Catherine Bear, John Bear, Grover Beard, Jody Beasley, Anne Beattie, Ricky Beaty, Elaine Beaubien, Christine Beaucage, Gerald Beaudet, Dennis Beaudry, James Beauhall, Frances Beavers, James Becher, Lenore Bechtel, Donald Beck, Ottis Beck, Donald Beck, Gina Beck, Mary Becker, Ginny Beckman, Lyndel Beckwith, Bridget Becnel, Charles Bedell, Stewart Bedford, Peggy Bedingfield, George Bedsole, Derrick Beech, Rory Beel, Donna Beeler, Nancy Beeler, Joseph Beer, Gary Beers, George Begault, Jeanne Beggins, Rosa Behn, Matthew Behner, Patricia Behnke, Thomas Behunin, David Belanger, George Belanus, Glynnis Belchers, Wesley Belk, Robin Belknap, Pamela Bell, Thomas

Bell, Christopher Bell, Cathy Bell, Richard Bell, Randell Bell, Celia Bell, Janet Bell, James Bell, Cindy Bell, Janet Bell, Guy Bellaver, Dianne Bellenger, Sarah Bellian, Scott Bellows, Sietske Bellsmith, Sharyn Bellville, Tracey Belton, Chris Belyea, Jane Beman, Latesheia Bembry-Bacchus, Clarence Benage, John Benage, Joseph Benarick, David Ben-Ariel, Leola Bench, Charly Bench, Kathryn Bender, Terry Bender, Joseph Benevento, Robert Benfer, Judy Benge, Brian Bengtson, Jason Bengtson, Daniel Benitez, Scott Bennett, Carol Bennett, Holly Bennett, Judy Bennett, Elsie Bennett, Sandra Bennett, Robert Bennett, Mark Bennett, Marjorie Bennett, Kimberly Bennett, Jeffrey Bennett, James Bennett, Helena Bennett, Elsie Bennett, Eileen Bennett, Diana Bennett, Deborah Bennett, Carolyn Bennett, Gillian Bennetts, Michael Bennitchi, Cecil Benoit, Linda Benoit-Bilodeau, Roberta Benor, Jacqueline Bensaadat, Joe Bensen, Gladys Bensimon, Marvin Bensman, Lauretta Benson, Michael Benson, Patricia Benson, Peter Benson, Lesley Bentley, Toni Bentley, Charles Bentley, Joel Benton, Gary Benton, Douglas Benton, Jason Bentsman, Paul Benvin, David Benz, Carol Benzel-Schmidt, Richard Beougher, Margret Berendes, Steven Berez, Oris Berg, Eliot Berg, Ruth Bergad, Ronald Berger, Lowell Bergeron, Rena Bergeron, Scott Bergin, Bill Berkin, Sonya Berkley, Edwina Berkman, Faith Berlin, E.J. Berlinski, Timothy Berman, Derek Berman, Carl Berman, Anton Bernard, Jerry Bernard, Anne Bernard, Johnny Bernard, John Bernardo, Daniella Bernett, Lisa Bernhard, Noel Bernhardt, Vita Bernhardt, Mona Bernstrom-Gartrell, Brandon Berntson, Elton Berry, James Berry, Jennifer Berry, Kelly Berry, Ronald Berry, Joe Berry, Nellie Berry, Ellis Bert, Andrew Berubee, Gloria Besley, Kathryn Beson, Dennis Bessire, Mary Best, Jessie Best, Estrella Betances de Pujadas, Marian Betancourt, Howard Bethea, Susan Betters, Leslie Bettner, Donna Jeanne Bever, Wojciech Bialkowski, Anthony Bialobryski, Paul Bianchetti, LaTonia Bibbs, Roberta Bible, Robert Bible, Lucia Bibolini, Don Bick, Virginia Bickel, Brenda Biddix, Linda Bielowski, Sara Biesterveld, Naomi Bigelow, Edward Bigger, Lee Biggs, Nicostrato Bignami, Kameelah Bilal, Jeremy Billingsley, Joshua Billow, Robert Bimson, Abby Binder, Logan Bingham, Lori Bingley, Sherry Binkelman, John Binkley, Reginald Birch, Judith Bird, Kelly Birks, Heather Biscoe, LaJuanda Bishop, Charles Bishop, Anne Bishop, Kathleen Bishop, Diane Bisson, Suylayne Bitowt, Joseph Bivins, Vincent Bivona, Barbara Bixon, Kay Bjerke, Sigrun

Bjorgvinsdottir, David Black, Teresa Black, Alexander Black, George Black, Eric Black, Jordan Black, Denise Blackburn, Kenny Blackburn, Henry Blackburn, Robert Blacketer, Brian Blackington, Rodney Blackmon, Monica Black-Saunders, Richard Blackston, Eshe Blackwell, Janette Blackwell, Barry Blackwell, Robert Blackwell, Jern Blahammar, Les Blain, Jerry Blaine, Arlene Blair, Jonathan Blair, Shirley Blair, Paul Blais, David Blake, Heather Blake, Gordon Blake,

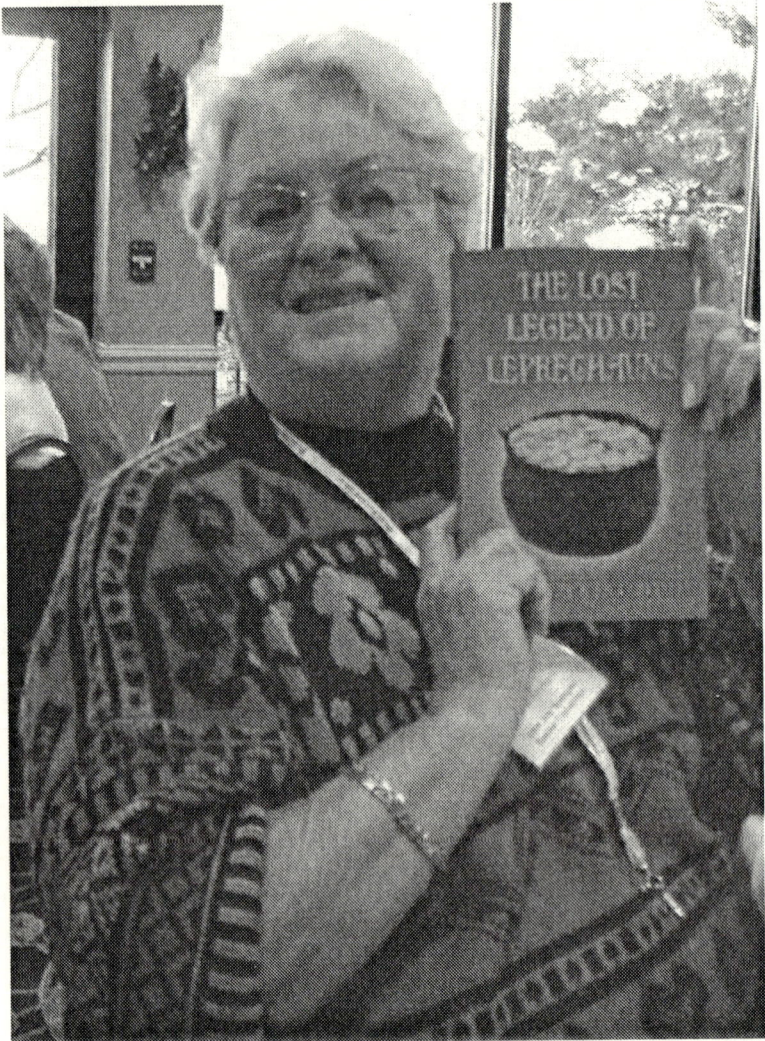

Stephen Blake, Shawn Blakeley, James Blakeney, Cynthia Blalack, John Blanchard, Kristan Blanchard, Ralph Bland, Diane Bland, Naydean Blanding, Terae Blank, James Blasdell, LeTia Blassingame, Kathy Blaylock, Patrycja Blazejewska, Charles Blazek, John Blazewick, Brandi Bleau, LaRon Bledsoe, Doreen Bleich, Nina Bleigh, Rita Bleiman, Paula Blevins, Robert Blevins, Gloria Blier, Bruce Blinzler, Donald Bloch, Bonnie Block, Leslie Blohm, Susannah Blood, Leon Bloom, Minerva Bloom, Susan Blotz, Mark Blount, Letitia Blount, Doyce Blount, Joan Bloyd, James Blue, Elizabeth Blue, Henry Blue, James Blum, John Blum, Robert Bly, William Blythe, Gerard Bodalski, Johnny Bodley, Bernard Bodmer, Patricia Boehm, David Boehmer, Steven Boehnke, Paul Boerger, Eunice Boeve, Tonya Boff, Mike Bogart, Darryl Bogatay, Valerie Boggess, Dallas Boggs, David Boggs, Peter Bohaczyk, Larry Bohall, Christopher Bohannon, Jack Bokholt, John Boland, Naomi Bolden, John Bolduc, Brian Bolitho, Donna Bolk, Richard Bollhorst, Andrew Bolsinger, John Bolton, Mark Bond, William Bond, Jose Bonilla, Jose Bonilla, Melanie Bonnefoux, Alfred Bonnell, Darlene Bonner, Timothy Bonnette, Jeffrey Bonomo, Luis Bonorino, Mathew Bonta, Erik Bonthron, Phillip Book, Maria Booker, David Booker, Michael Bookman, Peggy Boone, John Boor, Steven Boorstein, Crystal Booth, Stacie Booth, Anna Booth, June Booth, Ronald Booth, Gary Boothe, Milton Boothe, Carolyn Borden, Lyle Borders, Adam Bordes, Brian Boren, Yaja Boren, Patricia Borge, Roy Borges, Emily Borgman, David Bornus, Luba Borochok, Jane Boruszewski, Gerald Bosacker, Ivan Bosanko, Michael Bosco, Fredrick Bosco, Katherine Bosley, Patrick Bosold, Philip Bossert, Linda Bostwick, Bess Boswell, Monica Boswell, Richard Boswell, Kathleen Bosworth, Roland Botelho, Janet Bottiglier, Daniel Bottoms, Sharon Bouchard, Wendy Boucher, Troy Boucher, Lisa Boucher, Charles Boucher, Ava Boudouris, Tammy Boulds, Mary Bousquet, Patrica Bousson, Karen Bova, Regina Bovill, Randall Bowden, Dorae Bowen, Ronald Bowen, Kathryn Bowen, Debralee Bowen, Regenia Bowens, Melane Bower, Tonya Bowers, Maz Bowers, Kimberly Bowers, Katherine Bowers, Nancy Bowie, Julie Bowles, John Bowling, Constance Bowman, Leslie Bowman, Todd Bowman, Michael Bowser, Jane Bowyer, Mathew Bowyer, William Boyack, Robert Boyd, Robin Boyd, Stacy Boyd, Eva Boyd, John Boyd, Jaime Boyden, Jefferson Boydston, Patricia Boyer, Robert Boyer, Michael Boyett, Joseph Boyle, Michael Boyle, Tobias Boyle, Debra Boyle, Robert Bozec, Clovis

Bracey, Kirsten Brackney, Alvin Bracy, Alan Bradbury, Martha Bradbury, Stefin Bradbury, Jerry Bradford, John Bradford, Cornelius Bradley, Dari Bradley, John Bradley, Mary Bradley, Sean Bradley, Terry Bradley, Howard Bradshaw, Farral Bradtke, Maurine Bradwell, Jasper Brady, Stephanie Brady, Andrew Bragg, Darlene Braggs, Tandy Braid, Catherine Brakefield, Carlotta Bramlett, Cynthia Bramscher, Frank Brancaccio, Mikall Branch-Lopez, Cheryl Brand, Leonna Brandao, Joseph Brandon, William Brandon, John Brandt, Caroline Brandt, Richard Branham, Barbara Bransfield, Danae Branson, Von Braschler, Michael Brass, Grace Brasure, Johnie Braswell, Eva Braswell, Daniel Bratetic, Jennifer Braun, Karl Braungart, James Brawner, Cheryl Braxton, Iva Bray, James Bray, Vincent Brazauskas, Francis Brazeau, Alice Breaux, Philip Bredahl, Gayle Breding, Loretta Breece, Kristine Breed, Samuel Breeland, Kenneth Bremer, Robert Bremmer, Craig Brenizer, William Brennan, Scott Brennan, James Brennan, Beulah Brenner, Joachim Brenner, Michael Bresciani, Christopher Breslin, Michael Breslin, Robert Bresloff, Lynn Bresnan, Jean Bressler, H. B. Marcus, Linda Bretzer, Josephine Brew, William Brewer, Robert Brewer, Damon Brewer, Audrey Brians, Janie Brians, Craig Bridges, Doyle Bridges, John Brier, Frank Briganti, Eva Briggs, Reginald Briggs, Cheryl Briggs, Benjamin Bright, Michael Bright, Steven Bright-Jordan, Charles Brindley, T.L. Brink, Christine Brinkley, Diane Brinkley, H. Brinkmeyer, Joyce Brinson-Untiet, Donna Brinton, Margaret Brisco, Scott Britner, Roberta Britt, Myrlen Britt, Erica Broach-Stewart, Junius Broadnax, Lydia Brocato, Amelia Brock, Dionne Brock, Eric Brock, Michael Brockbanks, Betty Brockett, Dana Broehl, Betty Brogaard, Patrick Brogan, Michael Brogan, Lawrence Brogan, Bernard Brogan, LeAnne Brogan, Karen Brohn, David Brollier, Cynthia Bromley, Semyon Bronevetsky, Linda Brook, Tammy Brooke, C. Brooks, Doug Brooks, Robin Brooks, Nichelle Brooks, Jacqueline Brooks, Angela Brooks, Lorene Brooks, Monique Brooks-Washington, Gary Brosch, Theresa Brotherton, James Broughton, John Broussard, Michael Broussard, Charmin Broussard, John Broussard, Marian Brovero, Michael Brovold, Sol Browdy, Mark Brower, Sharon Brown, Chasity Brown, Marlon Brown, William Brown, Cynthia Brown, Veronica Brown, Susan Brown, Earma Brown, Shirley Brown, Michael Brown, Roy Brown, Ronald Brown, Rodney Brown, Stephen Brown, Ruth Brown, Roberta Brown, Nadia

Brown, William Brown, Sedric Brown, Daniel Brown, Sandra Brown, Jimmie Brown, Monica Brown, Marcel Brown, Sophia Brown, Joan Brown, Sonja Brown, Joshua Brown, Darnell Brown, Jim Brown, Herb Brown, Alice Brown, Sean Brown, Richard Brown, David Brown, Garnett Brown, Courtney Brown, Candace Brown, Benjamin Brown, Angela Brown, Donna Brown, Morris Brown, Rebecca Brown, Phyllis Brown, Jimmie Brown, Michael Brown, Maryann Brown, Kelly Brown, Katie Brown, Kathryn Brown, Judith Brown, Joshua Brown, Keisha Brown, Cheryl Brown-Avery, Jennifer Brown-Banks, Robert Browning, Inez Browning, Steven Brownlee, David Broyles, Eddie Bruce, Ginger Bruha, Walter Brumbaugh, Dave Brummet, Donald Brundage, David Brundage, Janet Brunette, Sadra Bruney, Elsie Brunk, Celeste Brunner, Albert Bruno, Beatrice Bruno, Thomas Brunswick, Ella Brunt, Jean Brutus, Timothy Bryan, Stephen Bryant, Adam Bryant, Albert Bryant, Glendola Bryant, Tod Bryant, Ruby Bryant, Mark Bryant, Guilda Bryant, Carl Bryant, Julie Bryant, Deborah Bryant-Dudley, John Bryce, Conny Bryceland, Ron Bryson, Cynthia Bucci, Marcine Buchanan, Timothy Buchanan, Jerome Buchanan, James Buchanan, Cynthia Buchanan, Paul Buchheit, Gary Buck, Timothy Buck, Scott Buckingham, Rebecca Buckley, Lowell Buckner, Leonard Budai, Kirk Budhooram, Annettee Budzban, Alexandre Bueno da Silva, Marcia Buffett, Lisa Buffington, Edward Buhrer, Margaret Bulko, Rex Bull, Jennifer Bullard, Deborah Bullas-Rubini, John Bullock, Roberta Bullock, Thomas Bullock, Donna Bumgarner, Gloria Bumpus, Elaine Bunbury, Richard Bunce, John Bunjes, Cullen Bunn, Margo Bunnag, John Burbridge, C. Burch, Muriel Burch, Natashia Burch, Nancy Burchianti, Matthew Burden, Robert Burdick, Robert Burfitt, Betty Burge, Edward Burger, Sharon Burger, LaTosha Burgess, Marjorie Burgess, Charles Burgess, Raynene Burgess, Erick Burgess, Carla Burgess, Lawrence Burgess, William Burgett, Lisa Burgin, Anna Burgin, Steven Burgin, Roger Burgraff, Pearl Burk, Gillian Burke, Patrick Burke, Wayne Burke, Lisa Burke, Sheila Burke, Stephanie Burke, Nancy Burkhard, Eleanor Burks, Rachel Burkum, Bob Burlbaugh, Emilie Burmeister, Ellen Burmeister, Samantha Burnell, Jo Burner, Keith Burnett, Donna Burnham, Davona Burno, Brian Burns, Carolyn Burns, Russell Burns, Annette Burns, David Burns, Susan Burns, John Buro, Marjorie Burr, Charles Burrall, Jason Burrell, J. Burress, DianeMarie Burrier, Ken Burris, Lance Burris, Augusta Burrus,

Vincent Burse, Michael Burt, James Burt, Arthur Burton, Gloria Burton, Richard Burton, Amy Burtt, Danny Burttram, Donald Bush, Clifton Bush, Anthony Bush, James Bush, Todd Bush, Rosetta Bush, Joseph Bush, Wanda Bush, Adam Bushashia, Bruce Bushong, Charles Bushroe, Joseph Buskey, Darlene Busse, Ngwesi Butandu, Humberto Butcher, Kimberly Buteau, Aaron Buterbaugh, Wayne Butineau, Robert Butler, Josie Butler, Anthony Butler, Andrew Butler, Stacy Butler, Joy Butler, Erika Butler, Josie Butler, Peggy Butler, Gary Butterfield, Terry Butters, Ralph Buttner, Phillip Button, James Byers, T. Byers, Donald Byington, Paul Bylin, Eva Byram, Ronald Byrd, Leo Byrne, Frank Byrns, Goodloe Byron, Thomas Byron, Goodloe Byron, Deborah Bystrowski, Daniel Cabrera, Daniel Cacciatore, Cindy Cadelo, Silvio Cadenasso, Dorn Cady, Larry Caffery, Richard Cagan, Teresa Cage, Steven Cagnina, Rochelle Cahoon, Carol Cail, Michael Cain, Donna Cain, Robert Cain, Ivan Cain, Robert Cain, Susan Cain, Andre Cairo, Arnita Caise, Frank Calabretta, Randal Calais, Anne Calamease, Bernie Calaway, Maria Calderon, Alistair Caldicott, Janet Caldon, Leslie Caldwell, Denise Caldwell, Elizabeth Caldwell, Jessica Caldwell, Kathryn Caldwell, Nancy Calenberg, C. Cales, Chester Caling, Anthony Callan, David Callaway, Hoyden Callaway, Anita Callender, Richard Callian, Jeffrey Callico, Stephanie Callicott, Frances Callicutt, Michael Calomino, Floride Calvert, Pamela Calvin, Alan Cambeira, Albert Cambio, Mary Cameron, Kristin Cameron, Dawn Cameron, David Cameron, Yvonne Caminiti, Marie Cammarata, Marie Cammock, Violet Camp, Michele Campanelli, Henry Campbell, Janie Campbell, R. Campbell, Philip Campbell, Linda Campbell, HD Campbell, Geraldine Campbell, Donald Campbell, Deborah Campbell, Dan Campbell, Cornelius Campbell, Claud Campbell, Robert Campbell, Mary Campbell, Albert Campbell, Patrick Campeau, Jacqueline Campos, Thomas Canady, Iloise Canady-Jordan, Jade Canal, Camille Cances, Jean Candee, Lisa Canfield, Elizabeth Canion, Joan Cannon, Rhonda Cannon-Jones, John Canter, Emilee Cantieri, Lon Cantor, Jimmie Cantrell, Keith Cantrell, Jose Cantu, Israel Cantu, Neo Cantu, Lorraine Canty, Anthony Capaci, Dawn Capalongo, Thomas Cappucci, Nicholas Caputo, Phil Caputo, Thomas Caramagno, Michael Carden, Jolene Cardwell, Lawrence Carey, Virginia Carey, Wayne Carey, Tamika Carey, Andrea Carey, Michael Carey, Audrey Carey-Haick, Katherine Cargill-Willis, Theresa Carle, Beverly Carlin, Patricia Carlin, Larry

Carling, David Carling, Kelly Carlisle, Aubrey Carlisle, Nicholas Carlo, Gary Carlson, Richard Carlson, Sandra Carlson, John Carlson, Gerald Carlstein, Jill Carlton, Dick Carmack, Mary Carman, Donald Carmichael, Richard Carmichael, Elayne Carnegie, Jonathan Carnes, Marissa Carney, Jay Carnine, Marlene Caroselli, Felicia Carparelli, Russell Carpenter, John Carpenter, Timothy Carpenter, Jeff Carpenter, Mary Carpenter, Londis Carpenter, Emma Carpenter,

Emanuel Carpenter, Earl Carpenter, Patricia Carpenter, Anne Carpio, William Carr, Larry Carr, Miranda Carr, Charmell Carr, Karen Carr, Arline Carr, Michael Carrel, Julie Carrico, Robin Carrig, Russell Carriker, Joan Carringer, Dawn Carrington, Tracy Carroll, Timothy Carroll, Emily Carroll, Edgar Carroll, Robert Carroll, Ute Carson, Eugene Carson, Tommy Carson, DiAnne Cartee, Jason Carter, Howard Carter, Mary Carter, James Carter, Damian Carter, Michael Carter, Kristin Carter, Royal Carter, Patricia Carter, Linda Carter, Gary Carter, Howard Carter, Earl Carter, Catherine Carter, Richard Carter, Frederick Cartwright, Heather Cartwright, Randall

Cartwright, Robert Carucci, Michele Caruso, Madelyn Caruthers, Donna Carver, Josephine Carver, Wendell Carver, William Carver, Jennifer Cary, John Cary, Charles Case, Mary Case, Thomas Casey, Mervin Casey, Claudia Cashman, Julie Casper, Lucille Cassarino, Grace Casselman, Valerie Casses, Patrick Cassidy, Lee Cassity, Fortunata Cassone, Yvonne Castaneda, Lenny Castellaneta, Alicia Castelli, Cecil Casterline, William Castillo, Maritza Castillo, Sharman Castillo, Grant Castillou, Robert Catalano, Anthony Cataldo, James Catapano, Hollis Cate, Anna Cates, Alicia Cathell, Adam Catlin, Bonnie Cato, Derrick Cato, Lucas Catton, Gregory Causey, Lenny Cavallaro, Robert Cave, Barbara Cavender-Jenkin, Karem Cavit, Rita Cayer, Edgar Cearley, Dr. Alhasan Ceesay, Adam Celaya, Angela Cerda, Donna Certain, Mia Chabral, Thomas Chace, Monica Chaddick, Helen Chadwick, Debi Chadwick, Monica Chafe, Karen Chalfant, Clint Chalk, Kenneth Challacombe, Edward Chalom, Colette Chamberlain, Kimberly Chamberlin, Glenda Chambers, Barbara Chambers, David Chambers, Kenneth Chambers, Nancy Chambers, Pamela Chambers, Gwendolyne Chambliss, Jean Champagne, Betty Chan, Robert Chan, Gloria Chananie, Lee Chance, Charles Chandler, Danielle Chandler, Vicki Chandler, Janvier Chando, Monica Chang, Jill Chapin, Micah Chaplin, Micah Chaplin, John Chapman, Susan Chapman, Teresita Chapman, Robert Chapman, Lisa Chapman, Gregory Chapman, Cheryl Chapman, Chad Chapman, Thomas Chappell, Sherre Chappell, Joseph-Jony Charles, Barbara Charles, Evan Charles, William Chastain, Norman Chastain, Austin Chatman, Vicky Chatten, Peter Chatto, Daniel Chavez, Alex Chavez, Elizabeth Chavis, Mary Cheatham, Alice Cheek, John Cheek, Ayub Chege, Darwin Ch'en, Glenn Cheney, Marta Cheng, Norman Chenoweth, James Chenoweth, Scott Cherney, Theresa Chernosky, Brian Cherry, Charles Cherry, Jason Cherry, Susan Cherry, Roxanne Cherry, John Chesney, Raynee Chesson, Sheryl Chester, Janet Chestnutt, William Chevalier, Josephine Chia, Gerald Chiappetta, David Chidester, Kimberly Chidester, Roy Chikwem, Stacey Chillemi, Michael Chin, Timothy Chism, Simone Chisum, Rachel Chittams, Young Choi, Adam Choi, Antoine Choueifati, Mary Christensen, Dan Christensen, Sharon Christian, Doris Christian-Johnson, Jesper Christiansen, Megan Christianson, Christine Christofis, Ronald Christopher, Keven Christopherson, Ora Chrysler-Stacy, Cynthia Chubboy, Stacy Chudwin, Tiffani Church,

Lisa Church, David Churcher, James Churchill, Marvia Cicchino, Joseph Cicero, Paul Cilwa, Dawn Cincotta, Sonia Cintron, Marie Cipriani, Kristina Circelli, James Ciscell, James Cisneros, James Ciullo, Silverman Civil, Betty Claiborn, Alexandra Clair, Antoinette Clair, Alexandra Clair, Richard Clair, Stella Clancy, Barry Clapsaddle, Laura Clarizio, James Clark, LaTasha Clark, Mark Clark, Michael Clark, Robert Clark, Nancy Clark, Christy Clark, Rosa Clark, Ken Clark, Amanda Clark, Cheryl Clark, Brandi Clark, Arthur Clark, Kathie Clark, Christopher Clark, Deborah Clark, Denise Clark, Gloria Clark, Jamie Clark, Jan Clark, Charles Clark, Anthony Clarke, Beverley Clarke, Jacqueline Clarke, Juanita Clarke, Mary Clarke, Roberta Clausen, Jessica Clauss, Junie Clauther, Cheryl Claxton, Johnnie Clay, Dawn Clay, Lyle Claypool, Ken Clayton, Sean Clayton, Karen Clayton, Joan Clayton, Sheryl Clayton, Sherri Claytor, John Cleary, Kevin Cleary, Valerie Cleary, Joshua Clemens, Sharon Clemens, Glenn Clepper, Donna Cleveland, Ceil Cleveland, Jim Clifford, Mary Clifford, Fred Cline, Robert Clinger, Dominic Clinton, John Clinton, James Clonts, Shirley Clontz, Clydene Clontz, Jay Clontz, Brian Clopper, Charles Clotworthy, Lori Clough, Richard Cloutier, Tameka Cloutier, Paul Clovis, Dawn Clower, LaVerne Coan, Glenn Coates, Michael Coatesworth, Carrie Coats, Rosalind Coats, Susie Cobb, Wendy Coble, Michael Coburn, Debra Cocchio, Fred Cochran, Craig Cochran, Larry Cochran, Jeremy Cochran, John Cochran, Lisa Cocozzella, Julie Coen, Aaron Coffey, Kathy Coffey, LeRoy Coffie, Karen Cogan, Susan Cogan, James Cogdill, Beverley Coghlan, John Cohagen, Winston Cohen, Greg Cohen, Edward Cohen, Brett Coker, John Colantonio, Melinda Cole, Geri Cole, Allan Cole, Michelle Cole, John Cole, James Cole, Chandra Cole, Allan Cole, Carla Cole, Kathryn Cole, James Coleburn, June Coleman, Pansy Coleman, Peg Coleman, Rhonda Coleman, Ryan Coleman, Shauri Coleman, Jane Colhoff, Timothy Colletti, William Colley, Melissa Collier, Thomas Collingwood, Ellen Collins, Audrey Collins, Tina Collins, Kathleen Collins, William Collins, Paul Collins, Wilanu Collins, Michael Collins, Sarah Collins, Jessie Collins, Dennis Collins, Blaine Collins, Reva Collins, Susan Collins, Diana Collura, Doris Colmes, Judith Colombo, Robert Colonna, Stephanie Colsson, Constance Colt, Lacey Colter, Jim Colyer, Jimmy Combs, Patsy Combs, Kenneth Combs, Kevin Comerford, Philip Comfort, Robert Como, Anthony Compagno, David Compton, Vincent Cona, Jorge

Concepcion, Kris Condi-Babich, Robert Condie, Robert Condry, Jana Cone, Deborah Confer, Donna Conger, Michael Coniglio, Debra Conklin, Brian Conklin, Brendan Conlee, Autumn Conley, Bette Conley, Sharon Conley, Autumn Conley, Lynn Connell, Linda Connell, James Connell, Kevin Connelly, David Conner, Edward Conner, Jimmie Conner, Wayne Conner, Jo-Anne Connolly, William Connolly, Wayne Connolly, Sue Connolly, Richard Connolly, Donna Connors, Joseph Conover, James Conroy, Jane Conroy, Kyle Constantinides, Kostakis Constantinou, Stephen Conti, Lucy Conti, Jeanne Converse, John Conway, Rita Cook, Robert Cook, James Cook, Joscelyne Cook, Patricia Cook, David Cook, Roland Cook,

Christina Cooke, James Cooke, Laura Cooke, Tahnee Cooke, Linda Cookingham, Alan Cooksey, Ethel Cook-Wilson, Nancy Cooley, David Cooley, Nancy Cooley, Michelle Coonan, Joseph Cooney, Rebecca Coons, LaDonna Cooper, Vivian Cooper, Tracey Cooper, Jason Cooper, Howard Cooper, Michael Cooper, McKinley Cooper, Lauren Coose, Lorna Cope, Mary Copeland, Thomas Copeland, Wayne Copeland, Donna Copertino, Steven Copling, Raymond Copp, Jeffrey

Copp, Stephen Coppard, Bert Copple, Michael Corbett, Roberta Corbett, Michael Corbett, James Corbin, Wendy Corbine, William Corcoran, Barbara Cordato, Alexia Cordato, Rachel Corday, Charles Cordova, Alan Corkish, Jefferson Corley, Vivian Corll, Robert Cornell, David Cornell, William Coronato, Joe Corrales, Michael Correro, Dawn Corrie, Michael Corrigan, Joan Corser-Gay, George Cortelyou, Dr. Michael Cortson, Sonja Coryat, Jennifer Coscia, Pietro Cosentino, Charles Cosgriff, Liz Cosline, Olga Cossi, Eric Costantino, Tudor Costian, Edward Costikyan, Jennifer Costilla, Thomas Cota, Michael Cotsakos, Karen Cotton, Robert Cotton, Gary Cotton, Margaret Cottrell, Georgia Cottrell, Jimmy Couch, Laura Coulter, Mark Coulter, Hollie Couron, Maxwell Courson, Lisa Coutras, Anthony Covelli, John Covey, Maynard Cowan, Shayne Cowan, Wheaton Coward, Christine Cowden, Sharon Cowhey, Constance Cowing, D. Cowles, Susan Cox, Jermont Cox, Richard Cox, Darrin Cox, Russell Cox, John Cox, Cathy Cox, Tory Cox, Angelia Cox-Sands, Dean Coy, Louise Crabtree, William Cracolice, Billy Craig, Richard Craig, John Craig, Larry Craig, Bryant Craig, Victoria Craig, Angeline Craig, Joanne Craig, Owen Craighead, Sandi Craigue, Jennifer Crain, Thomas Crain, Gary Crandall, Robert Crane, Michael Crane, Tommy Cranford, Tom Cranford, Donny Craven, Sandra Crawford, Robert Crawford, Teresa Crawford, David Crawford, Darla Crawford, Antwian Crawford, Denise Crawford, Peter Crawley, Edna Crenshaw, Ethylene Crenshaw, John Crestwell, Jeffrey Cretan, Betty Crews, Michael Crider, Traci Crigger, Gerald Crisman, Paula Crispin, David Criswell, David Crocco, Elizabeth Crofoot, Christina Croft, Julie Croisetiere, Raymond Crome, Timothy Cromwell, Rodney Cron, Rose Crone, Tonya Crone, Richard Cronin, Charles Cronin, Patrick Cronin, Daniel Cronley, Richard Crook, Julie Croom, Jeffery Crooms, Michael Cropo, Steve Cross, Steven Cross, Virgil Cross, Art Cross, Richard Croucher, Margaret Croulet, Gary Crow, George Crow, Gary Crow, Don Crowley, Irina Cruccanu, Shirley Crum, George Crumpler, Rhonda Crumpton, John Cruse, Lupe Cruz, Christian Cruz, Ana Cruz, Alex Csedrik, Jason Cubberly, Benjamin Cubillos, Paul Cuccolo, Carol Culbert-Johnson, Ted Culbertson, Gerald Culbertson, Wanda Cullen, John Culshaw, Chad Culver, David Cummings, Marvin Cummings, Kathleen Cummings, Mary E. Cummings, Thomas Cummins, James Cummins, Kathleen Cunningham, Ray Cunningham, John Cunningham, Jason Cunningham, Jack

Cunningham, George Cunningham, David Cunningham, Chet Cunningham, Jennifer-Crystal Cunningham, John Cuomo, Tracey Cupp, Karin Cupper, David Cupples, Bernice Curler, Craig Curlette, Timothy Curran, Susan Curran, Vickie Curry, Beatriz Curry, Robert Curry, Rosemary Curtis, Annetta Curtis, Patricia Curtis, Lorina Curtis, Kevin Curtis, Jeff Curtis, Michael Curtis, Letha Curtsinger, Debbie Curwen, Donald Cushenbery, Robin Cushing, Nicholas Cushner, William Custer, Vicki Cutting, Regina Cyr, Susan Cyr, Mark Czaja, Paul Czuchra, Theodore Czukor, Rick Daccardi, Jorge Dacosta, Walter Dacus, James Daddio, Roxie Dadzie, Linda Dagenais, Stanley Daggett, George Dagnall, Lovelee Dagum, LeAnne Dahl, Jenny Dahl, Elwin Dahlberg, Bob Daigle, Paula Dail, Marija Dail, Karl Dailey, Ronald Dailey, Robyn Dalby-Stockwell, Joshua Dale, Robert Dale, Dawn Dale, James D'Alessandro, Arlene D'Alessio, David Daley, John Daley, Alan D'Allessandro, Karen Dalman, Denis Daloisio, Clarence Dalton, Carla Dalton, Kristine Dalton, Jennifer Dalton, Francis Daly, Linda Daly, Marian Daly, Sugirtha Damadram, Janet d'Amboise, William Damerst, Joseph Damiano, Vincent D'Amico, Carl Dana, Sandra Dancey, Susannah D'Angelou, James Daniels, Don Daniels, Laura Daniels, Alla Danishevsky, Filomena Danisi, Daniel Danko, Jeffrey Danowski, Donald D'Anthony, Susan Dantzler, Beverly Daoust, Ken Darby, James Dargon, Gayle Darhower, Phillip Darley, Marcella Darman-King, Alison Darnell, Ronald Darr, Sheila Darragh, Dorian Darroh, Ashley Darrow, Asish Das, John Dascoli, Tanujaa Dash, Rhonda Dash, Paul Dasilva, Farzana Datta, Lohit Datta-Barua, Julie Daube, William Daubney, Lisa Dauscher, Lori Davenport, Kristen Davenport, Chari Davenport, Michael Davey, Charles Davidson, Crystal Davidson, Ellen Davidson, Robert Davidson, Barry Davies, Jay Davies, Neil Davies, Michael Davies, Robert Davies, Shawn Davis, Lucile Davis, Mark Davis, Patricia Davis, Ruth Davis, Lisa Davis, Raymond Davis, Robert Davis, Steve Davis, Susan Davis, Timothy Davis, Tomeka Davis, James Davis, Glenn Davis, Richard Davis, Betty Davis, Kathy Davis, Gwendolyn Davis, Jamesetta Davis, Michael Davis, Leslie Davis, Dr.Diallo Sekou Davis, Josephine Davis, Audrey Davis, Hollis Davis, Ava Davis, Benjamin Davis, Caroline Davis, Chris Davis, Clayton Davis, Dale Davis, David Davis, Edwin Davis, Gerald Davis, Jeffrey Davis, John Davis, Ava Davis, Clayton Davis, Mark Davison, Zolee Davis-Robinson, Grish Davtian, Robert Dawe, Daner Dawson, Douglas Dawson, Harold Dawson, Julia

Dawson, Marcel Dawson, Harold Dawson, Marie Dawson, Darrel Day, Susan Day, Lorelee Day, Kristi Day, Dorothy Dayton, Michael Deakin, Deborah Dean, Rose DeAngelo, Robin Dearring, Karen deBalbian Verster, Francis DeBartolomeo, Vincent DeCampo, Geraldo deCarvalho, Diane deCastro, Lenore DeCerce, Jamie Dech, Donald Decker, Ronald Decker, Christine DeClaire, Jonathan DeCoteau, Daryl Deena, Matthew Dees, Alma Deese, Virginia Defendorf, Kim Deffenbaugh, Richard DeFilippo, Jennifer DeFord, Joyce DeFrance, Sally Defreitas, James DeHart, Diane DeHekker, Hilary Deighton, Kelli Deister, Connie Deitz, Elizabeth DeJesus, Philip DeJulio, Maria DeLaGandara, Rev. Maria DeLaGandara, James Delamater, Michael Delaney, Gary Delaney, Mark DeLap, Troy DeLawrence, Susan DelBianco, Pamela deLeon-Lewis, Gerd deLey, Nicolas DelGiudice, Zenar Delk, William Dell, Michael Dellosso, Scott Delo, Karen DeLoach, Nancy DeLong, Annette DeLore, Riccardo DeLotto, Mark Deloy, Joan DeMarle-Oberlin, Kristofer DeMauro, Michael Demchik, Daniel Demelfi, Alexandra Demenkoff, Tristine Deming, Margaret Deming, Kathleen Dempsey, Vanessa Denha, Lyman DeNiord, William DeNisi, Dennis Denman, Clyde Denney, Shirley Denney, Clyde Denney, Michael Dennis, Howard Denofsky, Jim Denson, Cindy Dent, John Dent, David Denton, Marcia DePalma, Zachery DePauw, Lisa DePetro, Sally Depuy, Peggy DeRita, Mary DeRosa, Raymond DeRycker, Roma Desai, Frank DeSanto, Lawrence Desautels, Egle DeSchooley, Chad Descoteaux, Dorothea Desforges, Deborah DeShields, Frank DeSimone, Maurice DesJardins, Jane Deskis, Timothy Desmond, Janice Desposito, Rose DesRochers, Carmine DeStefano, Jamon Deuel, Patricia Deuson, Genevieve Deutsch, Mark Devane, Randy DeVaul, Marlene deVelasco, Aileen Dever, James DeVita, JoElaine Devlin, Mildred Devlin, Christopher DeVore, Robert deVries, Douglas DeVries, Fernand Dewez, Arlo DeWinter, David DeWitt, Stephen DeWitt, Arthur Dexter, Robert Deyo, Gautam Dhar, Salil Dhawan, Matshona Dhliwayo, Antoinetje Dhooge, Nancy Diaz, Marielena Diaz, Emilio Diaz, Jennifer DiCamillo, Mark DiCarlo, Becky Dice, Joy Dicken, David Dickens, Lori Dickerson, Nan Dickie, Grant Dickinson, Patricia Dickinson, Robert Dicks, Shirley Dicks, Marc Dickson, Lisa DiDio, LaVada Diehl, Lora Dietel, Gaynor Dietz, James DiFonzo, Salvatore DiFrancesca, Robert Digges, Martha Digges, William Dike, Beulah Dilger, Chad DiLillo, Eileen Dillio, Gary Dillman, Mary Dillman, Gina Dillon, John Dillon, Charles Dillon, George

Dillon, Charlene Dilzer, Ramonito Dimaculangan, Anthony DiMarzio, Mike DiMauro, John Dimes, Carl Dimitri, Vickie Dingman, Carson Dingwell, Angela Dion, Faith DiOrio, Philip DiPirro, Diane Dippelhofer, Mark Dirschel, Ryan Discher, Karen Dismore, J Dittbrenner, Kelly Dittmar, Victor DiTusa, Fred Diulus, Thomas DiVerde, Karen Dixon, Robert Dixon, Jeffrey Dixon, Edward Dixon, Kristen Dixon, Nneka Dixon, Corbin Dixon, Ronald Dixon, Rosebud Dixon-Green, Juanita Dixson, William DiYeso, Nancy DiZio, John Dizon, Dolly Dobbs, Carl Dobbs, Dennis Docheff, Aaron Dockery, Jason Dockery, David Doctor, Shirin Doctorsafaie-Brown, Linda Dodd, Mary Dodd, William Dodd, John Dodds, Keshawn Dodds, Edward Dodge, Larry Dodson, Jack Doepke, Melissa Doering, Paul Doerr, Robert Doherty, LeeAnn Doherty, Diane Dole, Nancy Dolejs, Gregory Doll, BilliJo Doll, Glenn Dolphin, Gilberto Dominguez, Jo-Ellen Dominguez, Richard Dominico, Mark Domm, Susan Donahue, Gerald Donais, LuCinda Donato, Seung Dong, Dorothy Donham, Jacqueline Donkerbroek-Jonas, Paige Donnelly, Terrence Donohue, Dana Donovan, John Donovan, Rubina Doobory, Tom Dooley, Sarah Dooley, Sandra Dooley, Julie Doolittle, Lisa Dooreck, Kevin Dopson, Anthony Dorato, Casey Dorman, Karen Dorman, Sheri Dornhecker, Barbara Dorsett, John Dorsey, Lee Dorsey, Angela Dosier, H. Dotson, Linda Doty, Raymond Doucet, Reid Doucette, Brittany Dougherty, Freda Douglas, Joshua Douglas, Connie Douglas, Eric Douglas, George Douglas, Mary Douglass, Brian Douthit, Matthew Dovel, John Dow, Philip Dow, Jack Dowd, Helen Dowd, Tammy Dowden, Derek Dowell, Crystal Dowell, Christine Dowis, Richard Dowis, James Dowling, Brandon Downard, Anthony Downen, Craig Downer, Janice Downer, John Downes, Paul Downhour, Robert Downie, John Downing, Kathryn Downing, Robert Doy, Theodore Doyle, Deborah Doyle, JennaLee Doyle, Rose Doyle, Theodore Doyle, Norbert Doyon, Kenneth Drake, Robert Drake, Charles Dravis, Lee Dravis, Brendaly Drayton, Boris Draznin, Edward Drebitt, Karen Drennen, Mary Dresser, Tascha Dresser, Thomas Drew, Kenneth Drexler, Maurice Driggers, Dean Drinkel, Thomas Driscoll, Thomas Drish, Douglas Driver, Rebecca Drnjevic, David Drown, Diane Druart, Margaret Drucker, Jacqueline Druga-Marchetti, Pauline Drummie, Megan Drummond, Barbara Drummonds, Gary Drury, Tommy Dry, Michelle Drysdale, Jules DuBar, Kathy DuBetz, Gerald DuBois, Edmund DuBois, Ellen DuBois, Sara Dubose, Jean Duckworth, Billie Ducote',

Peter Dudek, Gavin Duff, Samuel Duffy, Kelly Dugan, Tracey Dugan, Lisa Dugan, Daniel Dugas, Mildred Dumas, Naomi Dumont, Melvin Duncan, Lillian Duncan, Cameron Duncan, Carlton Duncan, Leslie Duncan, Jairus Duncan, George Duncan, Ernest Duncan, Sydney Duncombe, Mitchell Dunker, Robert Dunkerly, Kirsty Dunlop, Kathy Dunmire, Valerie Dunn, Andrea Dunn-Bevil, Lisa Dunphy, Clint Dunshee, Joseph Duome, Frederick Duplantier, Lori Dupuis, Ronald Durbin, Barbie Durbin, Andrena Duren, Joseph Durham, Guinevere Durham, Leroy Durkin, Colleen Durning, Florance Durr, James Durrett, Chris Duschik, John Dustin, Melissa Duttlinger, Elaine Duval, Tony Duxbury, Delray Dvoracek, Owen Dwyer, Rebecca Dyar, John Dybvig, Randall Dyck, Aleta Dye, Doris Dyer, Barrington Dyer, Cheryl Dyer, James Dykes, Steven Dykstra, Charmaine Dyson,

Richard Dzurinda, Linda Eadie, Janice Eakle, Melissa Ealey, Natalie Ealy, Michael Eardley, Cynthia Earley, Cambria Earley, Dudley Earlington, Randall Earwood, Malcolm Easler, Edward Easley, Mary Easley, Kenneth Eason, Judith East, Nathaneil East, Tom East,

Richard East, Nic East, Staci Eastin, Peter Eaton, Belinda Eaton, Mark Eatwell, Bonnie Eaver, Darek Eaves, Christine Ebeltoft, David Eberhardt, Christopher Eberle, Gerard Ebert, Charmaine Eccles, Todd Eckard, Wendy Eckel, Robert Eckenroth, James Eckler, Karl Eckstein, Victoria Eckstein, Karl Eckstein, Karl Edberg, Susan Eddy, Thomas Edel, David Edelen, Jerry Eden, Ben Eden, Ernest Edgell, Robert Edgington, David Edmiston, Joan Edmonds, Joyce Edmondson, Mary Edwards, Johnnie Edwards, Nicholas Edwards, Timothy Edwards, Sabrina Edwards, Selina Edwards, Kevin Edwards, Helyn Edwards, Gary Edwards, Deborah Edwards, Christina Edwards, André Edwards, Malinda Edwards, Marion Eggleton, Charles Ehin, George Ehly, Jody Ehrhardt, Genya Ehrlich, Harryet Ehrlich, Jill Ehrlich, Patricia Eichler, Roger Eickmeier, Claire Eide, Mark Eisenberg, Virginia Eisenhower, Melvin Eisenstadt, Antonia Eisenstein, Jill Eisnaugle, Linda Eisnaugle, Onoriode Ekeh, Karl Ekstrom, Thomas Elam, Eugene Elander, Dr. Subhi Eldeiry, Jerry Elder, Keith Elder, Vera Elderkin, James Elders, Tori Eldridge, Hugo Elfinstone, Richard Elkin, Thomas Elkins, James Elledge, Michael Ellefson, Betty Ellenburg, Douglas Ellerbusch, Michael Ellinger, Margo Elliott, Mickey Elliott, John Elliott, Jo Elliott, Debra Elliott, Bill Elliott, Billy Elliott, Terry Ellis, Ryan Ellis, Deborah Ellis, Jim Ellis, Kim Ellis, Sean Ellis, Patricia Ellis, William Ellis, Mark Ellis, Laura Ellis, John Ellis, James Ellis, Doris Ellis, Robert Ellis, John Ellison, Shonett Ellison, John Ellison, Lynette Ellner, Floyd Ells, John Ellstrom, Irving Elman, Diana Elsdon, Jon Elvrum, Justin Elwell, Peter Ely, Terry Ely, Clyde Embling, William Emener, Cyrus Emerson, Doris Emerson-Davis, Eric Emery, Tracy Emery, Ulrike Emigh, Sharon Emmerichs, Mary Emmons, Leon Emo, Eric Enck, Paula Enders-Frye, Susan England-Lord, Christopher Engle, John Engle, Lynda Engler, Robert Engler, Barbara English, Wanda English, Sharon English, Vincent English, Marcus English, Brian Enke, Jim Ennis, Melissa Ennis, Helen Enos, Angela Epps, Richard Epps, Janine Erdahl, Harry Erney, Kathryn Erskine, David Ervin, Randy Ervin, Brenda Ervin, Sharon Ervin, Stephen Ervin, Georgina Erwood, Manuel Escobar, Mechelle Esparza-Harris, Doreen Espinoza, Tracey Esplin, Keisha Esprit, Ronald Esquerra, Pat Estelle, Charles Estep, Lance Estep, George Esterley, Odalys Estevez, Laurant Estey, Duane Ethington, Robin Etter, John Etter, Nancy Ettinger, Eugene Ettlinger, Sandra Eubanks, James Eubanks,

Richard Eubanks, Max Eury, Sandra Eustice, Rachel Evans, Kenneth Evans, Jennifer Evans, Shawna Evans, Sherryl Evans, Lisa Evans, Shawna Evans, Russell Evans, Martin Evans, Jacques Evans, Gary Evans, Dwight Evans, Jeanne Evans, Penny Evans, Kenneth Everett, Louis Everett, Dana Everette, Kelly Evernham, Rebecca Eversole, Richard Every, Todd Ewing, Victoria Ezzo, Craig Faanes, Joseph Fabel, Kataline Fabian, Danuta Fabisiak, Thomas Fagan, Anne Faigen, Catherine Fairbanks, Mary Fairbanks, Estelle Falardeau, Alan Faler, William Falgout, Gregory Faljean, Johanna Fallis, William Fallon, Sandra Fallon, Adrienne Falzon, Olusegun Famoriyo, Wesley Fancher, Bessie Fantl, Steven Farkas, Chad Farley, Linda Farley, Rilla Farley, Sharon Farley, Michelle Farmer, Brian Farmer, Michelle Farmer, Resty Farmer, Teresa Farnell, Craig Farnham, Randy Farnsworth, Terry Farquhar, Jamie Farr, Justin Farrar, Thomas Farrell, Douglas Farren, William Farris, Joseph Fasheh, Betty Fasig, Daniel Fastabend, Asmai Fathelbab, Anthony Fauglid, Barry Faulkner, Harry Faulkner, Donette Faure, Linda Favaza, Joseph Faybish, Mario Fedele, Paul Fedynich, Warren Fee, Marsha Feimster, David Fekay, Rick Feldman, Frances Feldman, Roberta Felici, Jamie Feliciano, Jose Feliciano, Raymond Fell, Sharyn Fellenz, Maxine Feller, Mark Felton, Jesse Felton, Michele Fender, Ronald Fenner, Michelle Fenton, Angela Fenyvesi, Monty Ferbert, Gregory Ferency, Floyd Ferguson, Mark Ferguson, Matthew Ferguson, Nita Ferguson, Scott Ferguson, Walter Ferguson, Michael Ferketic, George Fernandez, Milan Fernando, Stephen Fernbach, Susan Ferrara, Patrick Ferraro, Annie Ferrell, Ean Ferrell, Philip Ferriell, Christina Ferris, Darrel Ferris, Frederick Ferris, James Fershee, Cyndi Few, Bernard Ficarra, Joseph Ficor, Bradford Field, Rhodora Fielding, Uriah Fields, Emily Fields, Rufus Fields, Michael Fields, Uriah Fields, Teresa Figley, Patricio Figueroa, Carolyn Fikes, James Filegar, Marvin Files, Ralph Filicchia, John Filip, Michael Filippello, Peter Filippinetti, Peter Finch, Vivienne Finch, Frederick Finch, Nigel Finch, Shawn Finerty, Joseph Finley, Thomas Finley, William Finley, James Finn, Victoria Finn, Corinne Finnie-Chapin, Leonard Finz, Carmen Fiore, Mercia Fiore, Maria Fiorille, Teresa Firek, Gregory Firely, Russell Fischer, Robert Fischer, Karen Fischer, Tracey Fischer, Steve Fischler, Barbara Fish, Jon Fish, Ruth Fisher, Nancy Fisher, Joseph Fisher, Dave Fisher, Jeffrey Fisher, Douglas Fisher, Sarah Fisher, Michael Fisher, Kevin Fisher, Karl Fisher, Ernest Fisher, Roger

Fisher, Semyon Fishgal, Richard Fitch, Shirley Fitch, Gisela Fitzgerald, Paul Fitzgerald, William Fitzmaurice, Michelle Fitzpatrick, Michael Fitzpatrick, Robert Fitzsimmons, Jennifer Flagg, Ruth Flanagan, Floyd Flanigan, Brandon Flatt, Jerry Flattum, Richard Fleck, Lloyd Fleck, Alicia Fleming, Paul Fleming, Sherrie Fleming-Jones, Charmaine Flemming, Brian Flenniken, Thomas Fletcher, Penny Fletcher, Jan Fletcher, Ernest Fletcher, Donna Flood, Bonnie Florea, Nancy Florence, Amanda Florence-Houk, Stephen Florentz, Achilles Flores, Isabel Flores, Kenneth Floro, Hannah Flory, Robert Flournoy, Kenneth Flowers, Allana Floyd, Julie Floyd, Tonya Floyd,

Henry Floyd, Robert Flux, Amanda Flynn, Arbutus Focht, Jason Fodeman, Timothy Fogg, Todd Fogleman, Claudia Foleng-Achunche, Molly Folken, Sharene Folmsbee, Joanne Folstad, Gail Fonda, Teresa

Fong, Kevin Fontaine, Matthew Fontenot, Kenneth Fontenot, Michelle Foor, Sandy Forbes, Sheila Forbes, Stuart Ford, Homer Ford, Marcus Ford, Marie Ford, Curtis Ford, Mary Ford, Robert Fordham, Marie Fordney, Burton Foreman, Robert Forese, Carl Fork, Marianne Forkin, Larry Fornia, Beverly Forrey, Joyce Forte, Stephen Fortosis, Genevieve Fosa, Bayard Foster, Mary Foster, Feather Foster, Ronnie Foster, Yves Foster, Stephen Foster, Debra Foster, Barbara Foster, Alicia Foster, Tonya Foster, Joseph Foti, Joseph Fotinos, Brigitte Foulke, Edwin Fountain, Myra Fournier, Joan Fowler, Thomas Fowler, Virginia Fox, Charlotte Fox, Michael Fox, Kenneth Fox, Geoffrey Fox, Elsie Fox, Barbara Fox, Barry Fox, Jason Fox, Sally Fradkin, John Fraiser, Vernon Frame, Catherine Frampton, Kendal Franceschi, Kenneth Francis, Diana Francis, Samuel Francis, Christie Francis, Elisa Franco, Carine Francois, Elisa Frank, Eric Franke, Rebecca Franklin, Michael Franklin, Daniel Franklin, Carolyn Franklin, Judy Franklin, Larry Franklin, Donald Frantz, Martha Frantz, Darren Franz, Alvin Franzmeier, Terry Fraser, David Fraser, Adam Frattasio, George Frawley, Dale Fraza, Janice Frazier, Benjamin Frazier, Suprina Frazier, Calvin Frazier, Jeannie Frazier-Goree, Eugene Frechin, Mary Frederick, Sandi Frederick, David Freedman, Sharon Freedman, Monica Freeman, Donald Freeman, Ted Freeman, Ron Freeman, Richard Freeman, Melba Freeman, Marilyn Freeman, Kemberly Freeman, Gary Freeman, Craig Freeman, Barbara Freethy, Susan Freitas, Richard French, Stephen French, Christine French, Luanne French, Suzanne French-Wilson, Lynnette Frenchwood-White, Carol Frenza, Danielle Frerichs, Donald Freshour, Curtis Freund, Lea Frey, Victoria Frey, Michele Frey, Cristina Friar, Patricia Fridgen, Jerry Friedland, Miles Friedman, Gaythel Friend, Gina Fristoe-Rose, Paul Fritz, Roseanna Frost, Robert Frost, Ralph Frost, Donald Froyd, Melody Frye, Linda Frye, Timea Frye, John Frye, Leland Fryer, David Fryson, Mona Fucci, Sherri Fuchs, Alonzo Fugate, Wayne Fujita, Richard Fulgham, Catherine Fuller, Michael Fuller, Sheryl Fuller, John Fullerton, Evalyn Fulmer, Paul Fulton, Charles Fulton, Rocco Fumento, Julie Funke, Patrick Furlong, David Furlotte, Emmitt Furner, Amanda Furness, Mark Fussner, Roothee Gabay, Jillian Gabbriellini, Elizabeth Gaboury, Joe Gadreau, Raina Gaffney, Gemma Gaffney, Matthew Gaffron, Lilian Gafni, Laurie Gage, Eugene Gagliano, Jerry Gaither, Margaret Gaither, Kathleen Galajda, Kathleen Galanos, Zeta Galas, John

Galavan, Trish Galbreath, Michele Galindez, David Gallaway, Delia Gallegos, Reid Galler, Elaine Galliart, Andrew Gallichio, Jean Gallien, Daniel Gallik, Louis Gallio, Adam Galloway, Betsy Gallup, Benjamin Gal-Or, Elizabeth Galyen, Terry Gamble, John Gamboa, Connie Gammon, Samuel Gan, Shirley Gandy, Chanakya Ganguly, Diane Ganzer, Kim Gaona, Brenda Garacci, Karren Garces, Dodie Garcia, Rosabella Garcia, Rodney Garcia, James Garcia, Dawn Garcia, Marita Garcia, David Garcia-Wahl, Tanya Gardepe, Renee Gardner, Terry Gardner, Philip Gardner, Curtis Gardner, Terry Gardner, Theodore Gargiulo, Samir Garib, Douglas Gariepy, Phyllis Garland, Kristina Garlick, Gerald Garner, Ruth Garnes, Earl Garnes, Jane Garrard, Evelyn Garrett, Floyd Garrett, Aimee Garrett, Gregory Garrett, Anne Garrett, Rebekah Garris, Jim Garrison, Victoria Garrison, Gena Garrison, Elise Garrison, Amy Garritson, Laura Garrity, Arthur Garroway, Kimberly Garth-Lewis, Eliot Gartley, Lauro Garza, Leoncio Garza, Gerald Garza, Wanda Gaskin-Smith, Shawn Gaspard, John Gasparich, Lucille Gass, Phylisha Gassaway, Lori Gasser, Jay Gates, Patricia Gates, Dennis Gates, Jay Gates, America Gatria, Michael Gatti, Lynn Gauker, Shannon Gauthier, Kathleen Gavlas, David Gaylor, Lee Gaylord, Glenn Gaynor, Deanna Gearheart, Sandra Gebert-McCann, Carol Gee, Raylond Gee, Mark Gee, Betty Geer, Harold Geesaman, Patricia Gehman, Klaus Gehrig, Linda Gehrt, Lillian Geiger, Mark Geiger, Lorraine Geiger, Yuliya Geikhman, Robert Geis, Almon Geiss, Mark Gelbart, Robert Geller, June Gemberling, Judy Genandt, Ninni Genovese-Lemus, Linda Gentry, Joseph George, Richard George, Tracilyn George, Jack George, Richard Georges, Stelian Georgian, Matthew Geraci, Carolyn Geraci, Matthew Geraci, Robert Gerard, Kathryn Gerbert, Travis Gerdt, Michael Gerenda, William Geringswald, Dianne German, Jolisa German, Richard Gerwolds, Elizabeth Getz, Ann Getzoff, Karen Geyer, Soheila Ghorbani, Jason Giacchino, Vincent Giaco, Cheryl Giandalia, Ryan Gianelloni, Kimberly Giangregorio, Joe Giardina, Louis Giattino, Joyce Gibbons, Michael Gibbs, Bonner Gibbs, Valerie Giberson, Ursula Gibson, Sherry Gibson, Peter Gibson, Kimberly Gibson, John Gibson, Jennifer Gibson, Gerald Gibson, Robin Gibson-Cabot, Robert Gideon, Richard Giedroyc, Richard Giedroyce, Beatrice Giermanski, Hal Gieseking, Margaret Gifford, Victor Gigante-Hueber, Lisa Giglio, Michele Gigliotti, Donna Gilbert, Marjorie Gilbert, Robert Gilbreath, Jill Gildea, Sheila Giles, Charles Gill, Richard Gill, Rebecca

Gillan, Charles Gillenwater, Henry Gillenwater, David Gillespie, Sylvia Gillespie, Dennis Gilliam, Mark Gillies, Tom Gilliland, Marcus Gillings, Eunice Gillion, Jason Gillum, Gayle Gilmore, Shannon Gilreath, Raymond Gilstrap, Robert Gilstrap, Rendell Gines, Richard Gingery, David Ginn, Seth Ginsburg, Jeanette Ginyard, Gregory Giovinco, Rudolph Girandola, Darlenne Girard, Jeremy Girard, Tausha Gittemeier, Cheryl Gittens-Jones, Pamela Gitzendanner, Dale Givens, Stephen Gladish, Debbie Glanz, Sue Glasco, James Glasoe, Keebra Glasper, Maria Glass, Melanie Glass, William Glasser, Jamie Glawson, Michelle Glaze, Beverly Gleason, Ginger Glenn, Willis Glenn, Jessica Glessner, Candy Glidden, David Glivens, Diana Glover, Sarah Gluckman, Thomas Glusaskas, William Gnagie, Marcie Goad, Stanley Gober, Peggy Godden-Smith, Shannon Godfrey, Tyrone Godfrey, Randy Goding, Tony Godley, Sherrie Godley, Audrey Godwin, Gwynell Godwin, John Godwin, Oscar Godwin, Garret Godwin, John Godwin, Shavina Goedar, Dana Goehring, Robert Goerman, Randy Goetz, Diane Goetz, Carol Goff-Wallen, William Goguen, Robert Gohsman, Shawn Goins, Herbert Gold, Raymond Gold, Joel Goldberg, Bruce Golde, John Golden, Valorie Goldenbrook, Adrian Golding, Alfred Golding, Alex Goldman, Richard Goldman, Alan Goldsher, Stephen Goldstein, Lee Goldstein, Lou Goldstein, Christopher Goldthwait, John Goldthwait, George Goldtrap, Lynette Goldy, Jerry Gollihar, Akbar Golrang, Fernanda Gomes, Kenneth Gomes, Eveline Gonsalez, Anthony Gonzales, Jose Gonzalez, Mary Gonzalez, Chris Gonzalez, Pablo Gonzalez-Fernandes, Daniel Goodale, Rosemary Goode, Sylvia Gooden, Ina Goodling, Helen Goodman, Larry Goodman, Mark Goodman, James Goodridge, Glen Goodson, Brian Goodson, Timothy Goodwin, Jeanne Goodwin, Jess Goodwin, Bruce Goodwin, Gregory Goodwin, Rajangam Gopal, Toni Gopee, Preston Gorbett, John Gorby, Wendy Gordon, Charles Gordon, Joe Gordon, Kim Gordon, Lauren Gordon, Lori Gordon, Patricia Gordon, Robert Gordon, Wilhelmena Gordon, Willma Gore, Mary Gorgani, Robin Gorley, Thomas Gorman, Tom Gorman, Thomas Gorman, Elmer Gorrell, Martha Gorris, Johannes Gosen, Kathie Gosnell, Charlotte Gosse, Adam Gottfried, Kathleen Gotts, Herbert Gottshall, Laura Gouker, Robert Gould, Charles Goulet, Joel Goulet, Laurel Gourdin, Bruce Gourley, Barbara Gourley, Maria Gouveia, John Gover, Amanda Govoni, Jill Gowland, Stephen Graban, Elizabeth Grabenkort, Debra Grabow, Vincent Grabowski, Julie

Grace, Paul Gracia, Patricia Grady, Daniel Graffeo, Sai Grafio, Lisa Graham, Dennis Graham, Carolyn Graham, John Graham, Theresa Graham, Susan Graham, Robert Graham, Frank Graham, Dora Graham, Barry Graham, Claudette Graham, Helen Granger, Ed Graning, Ronald Grant, Theresa Grant, Mark Grant, Jacob Grant, Dawn Grant, Gloria Grant, Joseph Grant, Luciena Grant-Fletcher, Elisha Grant-Punska, Dan Grassi, Brandy Grassie, Dawn Grathler, Jay Grauer, Dale Graumann, Alleta Graves, Gloria Graves, David Graves, Berton Graves, Brandi Graves, Mike Gray, Joyce Gray, Cheryl Gray, Lawrence Gray, Tyrone Gray, Theresa Gray, Susan Gray, Robert Gray, Patricia Gray, Michael Gray, Mary Gray, Joyce Gray, James Gray, Jaclyn Gray, David Gray, G. Gray, Kurt Grayer, Gloria Grayson, Michael Greaney, Wesley Greayer, Bruce Grebin, Ethan Green, Alwyn Green, William Green, Trina Green, Tena Green, Keaon Green, Jose Green, Jim Green, Jack Green, Hope Green, Elizabeth Green, David Green, Ronald Green, Devon Greenaway, Carol Greenberg, Richard Greene, Robert Greene, Terra Greene, Ellen Greene, Brenda Greene, Clark Greene, Felicity Greenfields, Dana Greenhoe, Elyse Greenhut, James Greenwald, David Greenwald, Marian Greenwell, Joseph Greer, Bobby Greer, Eileen Gregory, Jillian Gregory, Lawrence Gregory, Edward Gregory, Donald Gregory, Anna Gregory, Graham Greig, Janice Grembowski, David Greske, Thomas Gressler, Margaret Greten, Wilda Gretzinger, Stephen Grider, Carol Grier, John Griffin, Deanna Griffin, Amy Griffin, Weldon Griffin, Doris Griffin, Theresa Griffin, Sylvia Griffin, Stephen Griffin, James Griffin, Elaine Griffin, Dennis Griffin, Debra Griffin, Saundra Griffin, Larry Griffin, J. Griffis, Virgil Griffis, William Griffith, Reginald Griffiths, Russell Grigaitis, Elbert Griggs, Valerie Griggs, John Grimes, Linda Grimes, Misty Grimes, Christopher Grimes, Charles Grimes, Joseph Grimm, Diane Grimmer, Darlene Grimmett, Jeannette Grindele, April Grindrod, Jack Griner, James Grisanti, Beverly Grizzell, Deborah Grizzle, Ricky Groce, Stan Grocki, Leander Grogan, Primwatee Groover, David Grose, Stacey Grosh, Brian Gross, Joseph Gross, Kurt Gross, Victoria Grossack, Merrilyn Grove, William Grover, Lawrence Grover, Lawrence Grover, Matthew Grubaugh, Joseph Gruber, Scott Grueninger, Conrad Grzybowski, Anthony Guagliardo, Ruben Guajardo, Joseph Guardino, Attilio Guardo, Sally Guariglia, Jane Gubelin, Kristrun Gudmundsdottir, William Guerin, Devon Guerra, Dawn Guerrero, Graham Guest, Karen Guffey, Alice Guidry, Karl

Guillen, Raines Guinn, Jimmy Gulle, Arthur Gulley, Veronique Gullick, Cade Gullickson, Gretchen Gundel, Kevin Gunderman, Duane Gundrum, Barbara Gunn, Richard Gunther, Joseph Gurdin, Gail Gurley, James Gurley, Mardel Gustafson, Carol Gustke, Alvin Guthertz, Daniel Guthrie, Kippie Guthrie, Evelyn Gutierrez, Jennifer Gutierrez, Richard Guy, Joe Guy, Michael Gyepes, Sheldon Haas, Maria Habeeb, Rex Haberman, John Hachmann, Connie Hadden,

Chiquita Haddox, Stefan Haderer, Glenn Haertlein, Agnes Hagadus, James Hagarty, Joanne Hagen, John Hagen, Mary Hagen, Florine Hager, John Hagerhorst, James Hagerty, Gaylord Hagescth, James Hagle, Barbara Hahn, Christopher Hahn, Thomas Haigler, Selena Hailey, Samantha Hairston, Thomas Hairston, Russell Hairston, Russel Hairston, Marie Haisan, Charles Haislip, Laurence Hakizimana, Holmgeir Hakonarson, George Hakun, Kimberly Halcomb, Shirley Hale, Scott Hale, Randall Hale, Lynda Hales, Diana Haley-Christian, Randon Hall, Robert Hall, Star Hall, Steve Hall, Yvette Hall, Paula Hall, MaryAnn Hall, James Hall, Danny Hall,

Shawn Hall, Lauri Hall, Donna Hall, Angela Hall, Anthony Hall, Roy Hall, Marcia Hall, Doren Hall, Glenn Hall, John Hall, Karen Hall, Lawrence Hall, Mallory Hall, Byron Hall, William Hallam, Daniel Hallford, Alice Halligan, Lisa Halloran-Glenn, Elvis Hallowell, David Halpert, Hattie Halsey, Debbie Rosenkrans, Charles Halt, Lorie Ham, James Hamblin, Rodney Hambrick, Alfred Hamby, Cynthia Hamby, Jessie Hamel, Teri Hamer, Sarah Hamidi-Sakr, John Hamill, Kathryn Hamilton, Roniele Hamilton, George Hamm, Louise Hamm, Amy Hamm, Timothy Hammell, William Hammersmith, Elizabeth Hammett, Barbara Hammond, Brian Hammond, Jeff Hammond, Sharon Hammonds, Barbara Hammonds, Joseph Hammons, William Hamner, Leola Hamparian, Diana Hampo, John Hampton, Jane Hampton, Braden Hampton, Kirk Hampton, Joy Hampton, Ernest Hams, John Han, Jodi Hanauer, Timothy Hancock, Patricia Hancock, Winton Hancock, Ernest Hancock, Bruce Hancock, John Hand, Janet Haneberg, Deborah Haney, Thomas Haney, Richard Hankey, Sandra Hankey, Harold Hankey, David Hankins, Lorena Hanks, Robert Hanks, Charles Hannah, Robert Hannah, Martin Hannan, Matthew Hansen, Sara Hansen, Carol Hansen, Barry Hanson, Douglas Hanson, Jeffrey Hanson, Sherye Hanson, Alicia Hanson, Paul Harbin, Michael Harbison, Todd Hardage, Kyle Harden, Robert Harder, Sethia Hardesty, Glen Hardgrave, Marilyn Hardigree, Suzanne Hardison, Jeanmarie Hardisty, Colin Hare, Kasey Hargan, Melanie Hargis, Alvin Hargis, Stephanie Hargraves, Jo-Ann Harkleroad, Judy Harkness, Charles Harlan, Lee Harlan, Jeri Harlan, Joe Harless, Andrew Harley, Kathryn Harlin, Rebecca Harlow, David Harm, Justin Harmon, Michael Harmon, Ronald Harmon, Roi Harmon, Sherri Harmon, Patti Harmon-Anderson, Diana Harned, Martha Harnish, John Harper, Wallace Harper, Isabel Harrar, Valerie Harrell, W. Harrell, Owen Harrelson, Michael Harrigan, Chandra Harrilall, Patricia Harrington, Roger Harrington, Kristie Harris, Leonard Harris, Len Harris, Peter Harris, Ruby Harris, Donald Harris, Carl Harris, Tracia Harris, Keshia Harris, Joe Harris, Dorothy Harris, Lorraine Harris, Suzanne Harris, Angela Harris, Daniel Harris, David Harris, Jimi Harris, Knyla Harris, Kristie Harris, Rita Harris, Stephen Harris, Surayyah Harris, Susan Harris, Charles Harrison, James Harrison, Robert Harrison, William Harrison, Steven Harrison, Marriel Harrison, Dexter Harrison, Courtenay Harrold, Billy Hart, Simon Hart, Rochell Hart, Margie Hart, Stan Hart, Semie Hart, Lyle Hart, Louise Hart, Jane Hart, Craig Hart,

Simon Hart, Stan Hart, Deborah Harter, Brian Hartford, Lowell Hartig, Susan Hartley, Joyce Hartman, Wilbert Hartmann, Sandra Hartsell, Raymond Hartung, Luke Hartwick, Lynn Hartz, Shawn Harvey, Marshall Harvey, Eleanor Harvey, Gary Harvey, L. Harvey, Madelyn Harvey-Elliott, Glenn Hascall, Robert Haseltine, Florence Hashem, Dolores Haskins-Meritt, Terri Hasman, Farad Hassan, Dan Hassett, Janet Hastings, Janice Hastings, Kirk Hastings, Vivian Haswell, Randy Hatch, Alden Denison Hatch, Loraine Hatcher, Merlin Hatcher, James Hatcher, Henry Hatcher, Charles Hatfield, John Hatfield, Wendy Hatfield, William Hatfield, John Hatfield, Kendra Hathaway, Michael Hathaway, Robert Hatting, Sandy Hatton, Joseph Haugabrook, Gregg Haugland, Eva Hauksdottir, Laura Haupt, Jeffrey Hauser, Eloise Haven, Karen Havens, LaDonna Hawkins, Ruth Hawkins, Kauthar Hawkins, Felicia Hawkins, LaDonna Hawkins, Kenneth Hawkinson, Donald Hawley, Shahrom Hawley, MaryAnn Hayatian, James Haycraft, Alla Hayden, Angela Hayden, Jessie Hayden, Nicholas Hayden, Lucia Haye de Carezani, Robert Hayes, Cheron Hayes, Tenisha Hayes, Pamela Hayes, John Hayes, Robert Hayes, Juanita Haygan, Leah Hayland, Francis Haynes, William Haynes, Rae-Dawn Haynes, Dianna Haynes, Tammi Haynes, Earnestine Haywood, John Hazlett, Demetria Head, Leslie Head, Loran Head, Russell Head, Jean-Marie Headley, James Headrick, David Healey, Michael Healy, John Healy, Chester Hearn, Robert Hearn, Christopher Heassler, Rollin Heassler, Joseph Heath, Tamela Heath, Julie Heath, Roberta Heath, Marilyn Heavens, Margaret Hebert, Therese Heckenkamp, Theodore Hedden, Paula Hedrick, Susan Hedrick, Shanda Hedrick, Grace Heemstra, Karl Heffelfinger, Janice Heffernan, Patrick Heffernan, Amelia Heffner, Marvin Heffner, Shane Hefty, Ibrahim Hefzallah, Carol Hegberg, Phyllis Hegland, Rebecca Heidemann, Judy Heinly, Edith Heisler, Walter Heiss, Michael Heitkemper, James Heitmeyer, Newell Helle, Paulafaith Heller, Nadine Hellman, Gary Helm, Carolyn Helmbrecht, Amanda Helmecy, John Helmke, Elizabeth Helms, Mark Helms, Todd Hemming, Michael Hemmingson, Gregory Hemphill, Curtis Hendel, Jennifer Hendershot, Karima Henderson, Diana Henderson, Michael Henderson, Sheila Henderson, Gina Henderson, Dianne Henderson, Cecil Henderson, Debra Henderson, Cecil Henderson, Brenda Hendricks, Aline Hendricks, Nadine Hendricks, Eric Hendricks, William Hendrickson, Steven Hendrix, James Hendry, Mildred Henk,

Mike Henle, Matthew Henley, Clifton Henly, Joseph Hennessy, Lisa Hennessy, Robert Hennessy, Ann Henning, Clifford Henning, Dennis Henry, Julia Henry, Philip Henry-Dean, Farolyn Hensley, Exie Henson, Debra Henson, Ricky Henson, Wesley Henson, Debra Henson, Wesley Henson, Jeania Henton, Donna Henzel, Duane Heppner, Theresa Herbert, Santino Herbert, Brittany Herbert, Debora Herdlick, Jodi Herdt, James Herman, John Herman, Margeaux Herman, Mark Herman, Betty Herman, Lisa Hermansen, Julio Hernandez, Mildred Hernandez, Joshua Hernandez, Ana Hernandez, Arturo Hernandez, Eryk-Antonio Hernandez, Elena Herndon, Scott Herndon, Michael Herr, Carla Herrera, Gilda Herrera, Robert Herring, Derek Herring, Cheryl Herrington, Joseph Herrington, Rebecca Herrington, David Herrle, Robert Herron, Barry Hersh, John Hertel, Margaret Hertel, Lillian Herzberg, Therese Heskamp, Jettie Hess, Mark Hess, Jettie Hess, Harley Hess, Rita Hestand, Elmer Hester, Marianna Heusler, Carol Hewett-Holmond, Warren Heydenberk, Marquis Heyer, Nicholas Heyne, Peter Heyrman, James Hibbard,

Joan Hibbs, Franklyn Hibbs, Karl Hicken, Lynn Hickerson, Cynthia Hickey, Cecil Hickman, James Hickman, Pamela Hickman, Betty Hickman, Jim Hickman, Frank Hicks, George Hicks, Laura Hicks, Roxanne Hicks, Scott Hicks, Lisa Hiestand, Bryan Higby, Andrew Higgins, Donald Higgins, John Higgins, Kristie Higgins, Bob High, Gracia High, Harry Highstreet, Barbara Highton, Monique Hightower, Lisa Hildwine, Donald Hiles, Roy Hill, Brian Hill, John Hill, Amalie Hill, A. Hill, Tameka Hill, Robert Hill, Randall Hill, LaTanya Hill, James Hill, Gary Hill, Faith Hill, David Hill, Curtis Hill, Clare Hill, Cheryl Hill, Carolyn Hill, Bart Hill, Joseph Hill, Thomas Hill, Alfonso Hilliard, Lester Hills, Peter Hills, Howard Hilton, Robert Himpfen, Danielle Hiner, Armenta Hines, John Hines, Kyla Hines, Angela Hinkle, Jane Hinrichs, Randy Hinson, Charvella Hinson-Campbell, Charles Hinton, Lonie Hinton, Michael Hinzman, Ryuichi Hirata, Gary Hirdning, Annette Hitchcock, William Hjorten, Jaroslav Hlava, Jessica Ho, Eric Hobbs, Debra Hobbs, Cynthia Hobson, Heather Hobson, Robert Hochstein, Patricia Hock, Margaret Hodapp, Elaine Hodge, Howard Hodge, Ronda Hodge, Norma Hodges, Guinn Hodgson, Noel Hodson, Frank Hoehlein, Ursula Hoehne, Glenn Hoepfner, Pamela Hof, Geoffrey Hoffman, Scott Hoffman, Mallory Hoffman, John Hoffman, George Hoffman, Cheryl Hoffman, David Hoffman, Norah Hofford, Reba Hogan, Lauren Hogan, Lawrence Hogan, Harry Hoge, Matthew Hogsett, Guy Hogue, Molly Hoh, Ruth Hohberg, Richard Holcomb, David Holcomb, Terry Holden, William Holden, Orion Holder, Allen Hole, Angela Holko, David Holland, Maryjo Holland, Ray Holland, Barbara Hollander, James Hollar, Gary Hollen, Dave Hollenbeck, Alisa Holley, Sandy Holley, Anne Holliday, Patrick Holliday, Ralphel Holloman, Janie Holloway, Antoine Holloway, Raymond Holm, Laura Holman, Donna Holmes, Donald Holmes, Suzon Holmes, Bryan Holmes, Stephen Holmes, Michael Holmes, Megan Holmes, John Holmes, Laura Holmes, Kai Holmgren, Kevin Holochwost, Charles Holowell, Sara Holowell, Scott Holstad, John Holt, Charlotte Holt, Ellen Holt, Mark Holt, Michael Holt, Rochelle Holt, Michael Holt, Angela Holton, Mary Holzer, Dominic Homan, Daniel Homeres, Vith Homsombath, Daniel Homstad, Shannon Honea, Leland Honeybuss, Peter Honig, Saul Honigsberg, Raymond Hood, Paul Hood, Raymond Hood, Adele Hooker, Angela Hooks-Batchelor, Eleanor Hoomes, William Hooper, Keisha Hoople, Suzanne Hoos, Donniel Hooter, Dane Hoover, John Hoover, A.T. Hope, Scott

Hopkins, Mark Hopkins, John Hopkins, Dene' Hopkins, Sara Hopp, Keith Hoppe, Delbert Hoppe, Gary Hopper, Joel Hopper, Jewel Hopson, Evelyn Horan-McDaniel, Dana Horbach, Sheryl Horn, Mary Hornback, Robert Hornbeck, Kathryn Horne, Geoffrey Horne, Katherine Horning, Richard Horowitz, Marilyn Horsley, Juanita Horton, Billy Horton, Richard Horwitz, Lana Ho-Shing, John Hoskins, Joyce Hoskins, Will Hostetler, Gerald Hotopp, Lewis Houde, Paula Hough, Ruby Houldson, Janet Hounsell, Stephen Houp, Matthew Housch, Desiree House, Mark Householder, Amelia Houser, Emanuel Houser, Ben Houser, Jerry Houston, Alva Houston, Jessica Houze, Tony Hovis, John Howard, Teresa Howard, Thomas Howard, Ronald Howard, Joseph Howard, Joanne Howard, Janice Howard, Gregory Howard, Anne Howard, Mary Howard, Carolyn Howard-Johnson, James Howell, Dolores Howell, Chad Howell, Keitha Howerton, Diane Howerton, Miloslava Hrbek, Jason Hubal, Cynthia Hubbard, April Huber, Roland Huber, Kelly Huchro, David Huckett, Manissa Huddleston, Andrew Huddleston, Vera Huddleston, Clinton Hudgins, Paul Hudon, Rondha Hudson, Melissa Hudson, Mark Hudson, Loren Hudson, John Hudson, James Hudson, Zach Hudson, Benjamin Huelskamp, Jon Huer, Theodore Hueter, Rick Huff, Lonnie Huff, Kimberly Huff, Stephen Huff, Lonnie Huff, Stephen Huff, Melanie Huggett, Kimberly Hughes, Anthony Hughes, Martha Hughes, David Hughes, Carole Hughes, Tim Hughes, Richard Hughes, Glyn Hughes, Bettye Hughes, Susan Hughes, Nikki Hughes, Michael Hughes, Marylou Hughes, Lorraine Hughes, John Hughes, Esther Hughes, Diane Hughes, Heather Huisinga, Karen Hukill, Brian Hulbert, Rodney Hull, Kevin Hull, Angela Hulme, John Hulse, Geneva Hulsey, Edmund Hulton, Gloria Humes, Michelle Hummel, Loren Humphrey, John Humphrey, Raymond Humphrey, Douglas Humphrey, Francis Humphries, Christy Humphry, John Hundley, Richard Hundley, James Hungerford, August Hunt, Sharlett Hunt, Julie Hunt, Dru Hunt, Margaret Hunt, Terry Hunter, Tammy Hunter, Melanie Hunter, Larry Hunter, Jocelyn Hunter, Jessica Hunter, Darren Hunter, Srunny Huong, Jay Hurd, Cleo Hurley, Dawn Hurley, Kristi Hurley, Cleo Hurley, Paul Hurley, Peter Hurrey, Cory Hurst, Rebekah Hurth, Michael Hurtt, Kimberly Husband, Dorothy Huseth, Megan Hussey, Shanda Huston, Annette Hutchens, Kenneth Hutcheson, Roy Hutchinson, Stephan Hutchinson, Robert Hutchinson, Richard Hutchinson, John Hutchinson, Alex Hutchinson, Stanley Hutchison,

Laurence Hutner, William Hutson, Mildred Hutton, William Hwang, Ritchey Hyatt, John Hyde, Randy Hyde, Tom Hyland, Joan Hyland, Mollie Hyman, Richard Hynes, Renald Iacovelli, Thomas Iannucci, Ekhosuehi Ibie-Eriyo, Joyce Ibrahim, Rosalie Icenhower, Juli Idleman, Veronica Idris, Samuel Ifejika, Edward Ifkovic, Chidozie Ihebereme, Edward Ihejirika, Janice Imbach, Jayne Imler, Marion Immerman, Morris Inch, Daylan Ingersoll, Catherine Inglesby, Mark Inglis, Anthony Ingoglia, Danny Ingram, Gay Ingram, Kristen Ingram, Marion Ingram, Jimmy Inman, Emil Innocenti, Dennis Inns, Richard Ippolito, John Ireland, Barbara Irgens, Sampson Iruoha, Mary Iruoha-Uma, Charlene Irvin, Jacqueline Irwin, Daniel Irwin, Albert Isaac, Di'onne Isaac-Arceneaux, Terry Isaacson, Doyle Isch, Kevin Isenberg, Jonathan Isenor, Gary Ishler, Anthony Ismael, Leah Isom, Judith Issette, Lisa Ivester, Shirley Ivey, Tracie Ivey, Stevie Ivey, Brenda Ivie, Sara Izzell, Carol Jackman, Lura Jackowski, Ronald Jackson, Teresa Jackson, Phillip Jackson, Walter Jackson, Stacy Jackson, Angela Jackson, Mark Jackson, Bridgett Jackson, Melissa Jackson, Rayma Jackson, William Jackson, David Jackson, Unique Jackson, Christine Jackson, Patricia Jackson, Dianne Jackson, George Jackson, Jack Jackson, James Jackson, Karla Jackson, Kattie Jackson, Linda Jackson, Michael Jackson, Milton Jackson, Howard Jacob, Linda Jacobs, Rickie Jacobs, Marc Jacobs, William Jacobs, Mona Jacobsen, Mark Jacoby, Taryn Jacques, Roy Jacques, Steven Jaffe, Alan Jaffey, Phyllis Jager, Bradley Jahn, Allan Jahsmann, John Jakob, Joel Jakubowski, Worood Jallad, Roberta Jam, Portionte' Jamerson, Venita James, Gillian James, William James, Sheryl James, Earlie James, Elvira James, Dennis James, Christy James, Andrea James, Phyllis Jamison, George Jan, Emily Janiak, Jeannie Janis, Phyllis Jankowiak, Timothy Jankowski, Anthony Jannotta, Jo Janoski, Steven Janowiak, Tonya Janowski, Lori Jansen, John Jansen in de Wal, Elizabeth Janssen, Paula Jara, David Jardine, Joe Jared, John Jarocki, Laura Jaster, John Joubert, Corbett Jaubert, Shalom Javaid, John Jaynes, Marlene Jeanrenaud, Carl Jech, Marshall Jefcoat, Hannah Jeffers, Roy Jeffords, Freda Jeffreys, Denise Jeffries, John Jeffries, Teresa Jeffris, Daniel Jeffs, Gordon Jemeyson, Melody Jemison, Joel Jenkins, Douglas Jenkins, Randall Jenkins, Tina Jenkins, Jessica Jenness, Janie Jennings, Jeanelle Jennings, Kathryn Jennings-Hancock, Barbara Jensen, Cheri Jensen, Joanne Jensen, Roberta Jensen, Bernice Jepson, Chris

Jesse, Dennis Jesseph, Onica Jessie, Jerold Jessop, Roger Jetter, Jennifer Jevit, Roger Jewell, Britt Jewell, Charlie Jewett, Rafael Jimenez, Beverli Jinn, Joia Jitahidi, Andrew John, Michael D. Johns, Shirley Johnson, Glenn Johnson, Geraldine Johnson, Erin Johnson, Edward Johnson, William Johnson, Tim Johnson, Sondra Johnson, Rachel Johnson, Willie Johnson, Shelli Johnson, Shawn Johnson, Sharon Johnson, Ramona Johnson, Jay Johnson, John Johnson, Rachael Johnson, Douglas Johnson, Sallyann Johnson, Paul Johnson, Aundrea Johnson, Shanita Johnson, Norma Johnson, Maxon Johnson, Robert Johnson, Glen Johnson, Francesco Johnson, Nicol Johnson, Jean Johnson, Johnnie Johnson, James Johnson, Walter Johnson, Cindy Johnson, Portia Johnson, Adria Johnson, Edward Johnson, Erica Johnson, Debra Johnson, Davy Johnson, Ingrid Johnson, Dale Johnson, Jacob Johnson, Christina Johnson, Carrie Johnson, Angela Johnson, Angel Johnson, Andrew Johnson, Agnes Johnson, Agatha Johnson, David Johnson, Margaret Johnson, Polly Johnson, Penny Johnson, Patrick Johnson, Nathan Johnson, Naomi Johnson, Matthew Johnson, Glen Johnson, Mary Johnson, Margaret Johnson, Linda Johnson, Lewis Johnson, Leslie Johnson, Laurel Johnson, Kevin Johnson, Kelly Johnson, Joyce Johnson, Mary Johnson, Kelly Johnson-Moran, Thelma Johnson-Morris, LeeEva Johnston, Patricia Johnston, Patrick Johnston, Rory Johnston, Howard Johnston, Gary Joice, Claire Joliat, Sandra Jones, Virgil Jones, Tracy Jones, Timothy Jones, Terrance Jones, Stacey Jones, Wayne Jones, De'Shani Jones, Ronald Jones, Robin Jones, Robert Jones, Shirley Jones, Adrienne Jones, Philippa Jones, Richard Jones, Linda Jones, Thomas Jones, Jace Jones, Weyman Jones, Steven Jones, Bret Jones, Benjamin Jones, John Jones, Ronald Jones, Marty Jones, Ardel Jones, Henry Jones, Rex Jones, Aubrey Jones, Bret Jones, Christina Jones, Curtis Jones, Deena Jones, Dennis Jones, Digby Jones, Donna Jones, Dorothy Jones, Ferris Jones, Harvey Jones, Hollis Jones, Lila Jones, Renae Jones, Nancy Jones, Michael Jones, Melissa Jones, Marian Jones, Gary Jones, Lucille Jones, John Jones, Kenneth Jones, Katrina Jones, Karin Jones, John Jones, Luke Jones, Apostle Jones-Harris, Anitco Jones-Readdy, Christopher Jonnes, Alisha JonOde, Dion Jordan, Joann Jordan, Lee Jordan, Walter Jordan, Robert Jordan, Annie Jordan, James Jorgensen, Richard Jorgensen, Matthew Jose, Twanda Joseph, Timothy Joseph, Marjorie Joseph, Gregory Joseph, Estelle Joseph, Timothy Joseph,

Larry Jowah, Samuel Joy, Robbin Juanico, Leslie Judd, Roger Judkins, Theodore Judson, Matthew Juergens, Adam Julian, Saundra Julian, Pierre Julien, Donald Julin, Karilea Jungel, Paul Jungnitsch, Doug Jungquist, Tammy Juola, Tamyra Juola, Edward Juskus, Paul Justad, Karamoh Kabba, Dennis Kabelka, Ana Kaderi, David Kadlec, Robert Kahn, Hooshmand Kalayeh, Oladipo Kalejaiye, Naida Kalloo, Philip Kaloustian, Shilpa Kamat, Duran Kamgar-Parsi,

Maurice Kamhi, Kam Kaminske, Alexander Kaminski, Lowell Kammer, Ray Kampa, Tjisse Kampstra, James Kane, Lehuaokalani Kane, James Kane, Jenny Kanevsky, Robert Kanzig, Judy Kaplan, Kathleen Kappler, Edward Karalis, John Karasch, Edward Kareklas, Pamela Karges, Ian Kari, ChristinaLyn Kari, Lee Kariuki, Lorianne Karney, Anthony Karnowski, James Karns, Krystn Karolinska, Michael Karpovage, Debra Karr, Susan Karr, Victoria Kash, Alexander Kassah, David Kastner, Gerald Katen, Steven Katonka, Siddharth Katragadda, Aron Katsenelinboigen, Cheryl Kaufman, Danny Kaufman, Pete Kaufman, Sandra Kaufmann, Mabel Kaufmann, Anandam Kavoori, Iman Kawaja, Adrienne Kawamura, Keith Kawasaki, Robert Kay, Martin Kaynan, Richard Kaynan, Prince Kaywood, Carolyn Kazmierczak, Zhaojin Ke, Lorraine Kean, Thomas

Kean, Robert Keating, Michael Kechula, Richard Keck, Carolyn Keefer, William Keefer, Michael Keegan, Rudolph Keehn, David Keele, Beulah Keen, Geoffrey Keen, Karl Keen, Carolyn Keenan, Charles Keeney, Sara Keet, Eve Keever, Jeanine Keeys, Stephen Kehoe, Julie Kehoe, James Keil, Burton Keimach, Janet Keith, Krista Keith, Danita Keith, Cole Kekelis, Keith Kekic, Moriamo Kelani, W. Kellegrew, Robert Keller, Veronica Keller, Amanda Keller, Gloria Kelley, Joan Kelley, Robin Kelley, Bradley Kelley, Charmane Kelley, James Kelly, Kevin Kelly, Rebecca Kelly, Veronica Kelly, Sandra Kelly, Leon Kelly, Charles Kelly, Anna Kelly, Patricia Kelly, William Kelsall, Aaron Kelsay, Connie Kelsey, Lawrence Kelter, William Kendall, Stephen Kendig, Charlotte Kendrick, Robert Kendrick, Ruby Kennard, Firestorm Kennedy, Vickie Kennedy, Tanya Kennedy, Richard Kennedy, Christine Kennedy, Vickie Kennedy, Richard Kennedy, Bill Kennedy, Amber Kennedy, Ronald Kennedy, David Kenney, Thomas Kenney, John Kenny, Edmund Kent, Darlton Kenton, Mary Kenworthy, Michael Kenworthy, Sukalaya Kenworthy, John Keohane, Joseph Kerker, Mary Kerl, Sandra Kerley, Amber Kerns, Jeannie Kerns, Berley Kerr, David Kerr, Karen Kerr, Troy Kerry, Nadine Kershner, Ron Kervin, Joanne Kerzmann, James Kesler, Robert Kessler, Harman Keys, Davood Khalili, Dianne Khan, Dennis Khan, Aftab Khan, Kundan Khera, Bhekuzulu Khumalo, Bill Kidd, Michellé Kidwell, Mildred Kidwell, Leigh Kidwell, Connie Kidwell, Michelle Kidwell, Jim Kilcoyne, Colleen Kildow, James Kilpatrick, Mark Kim, Barbara Kimball, Edmond Kimball, Margaret Kimble, Michael Kimery, Ronald Kinard, Cynthia Kinard, Terence Kincaid, Christopher Kinch, Richard Kindel, Jonathan Kindred, LaKetra King, Pamela King, Bernard King, Vicki King, Steven King, Thomas King, Dora King, Tammy King, Stephen King, Sheena King, Sharon King, Kevin King, Betty King, Anthony King, Douglas King, Kristin King, Colleen King, Darrell King, Dora King, Heath King, Jason King, Karen King, Anthony King, Willy Kinghorn, David Kingsbury, Shirley Kingsolver, John Kington, June King-Wilbur, Marcela Kinkead, Robert Kinney, Sandra Kinslow, Jeffery Kipi, Nathan Kipner, Bobby Kirby, Shellie Kirby, Jemal Kiria, Cameron Kirk, Constance Kirk, Larry Kirk, Teresa Kirkham, William Kirkham, Gwendolyn Kirkland, Dagny Kirkland, Douglas Kirkland, Chris Kirkpatrick, Keith Kirkwood, Deborah Kirsch, Michael Kirshenbaum, Donna Kirven, Ginni Kiser, Shannon Kish, Richard Kisielewski, Ronald Kisner,

Mildred Kisor, Tim Kissman, James Kistler, Joy Kita, Lesa Kitching, Charles Kittle, Caroline Kiyabu, Todd Kjelland, Kimberly Kjelland, Daniel Klabunde, Bert Klamkin, Samantha Klash, Raymond Klass, Heather Klassen, Bob Klaus, Frank Kleager, Melissa Klearman-Cooper, John Klein, Edward Kleinschmidt, William Klemm, Lorene Klett, Ross Kleypas, Lydia Klima, Emanuel Klimis, Maureen Kline, John Kline, Karl Kline, James Klingenberg, Caissa Klingesmith, Joseph Klingman, Paul Klobusicky, Amanda Kloppers, Emil Klosinski, Laura Klotz, Ronald Klueh, Charlene Knadle, Cassandra Knapp, Orvis Knarr, Judy Knauer, Travis Kniep, Carey Knifong, Max Knight, Mary Knight, William Knight, Patricia Knight, Marilyn Knight, Luther Knight, Genia Knight, Thomas Knight, Steven Knight, Laurence Knighton, Brenda Knighton, Kenneth Knipple, Edelgard Knoob, Tennille Knoop, Steven Knopfer, Margaret Knorr, Daniel Knotts, Eileen Knowles, Judi Knowles, Margaret Knowles, Lorna Knox, Amy Knox, Karl Knutson, Cliff Knutson, Gerald Kobernick, Irene Koch, James Kochanoff, Tom Kochansky, Gregg Kocher, W.B. Koehler, Deborah Koehler, James Koepke, Maureen Koerner, Janine Koffler, Joe Koger, Kathleen Kohl, Norman Kohn, Diana Kokel, Ruth Kolarik, Joseph Kolb, Diane Kolb, Stan Kolodziej, Pierrette Komarek, Joseph Komatz, George Kondos, Thomas Konkol, Nadine Konopski, Corey Konrad, Ed Konstant, Chuck Koopman, Paul Kopal, Terrence Kopet, Kellie Kopinski, Steven Kopor, Kathleen Koppang, Eli Koppel, Donna Koppelman, Beate Korchak, Penny Koren, Oleg Korenfeld, Nikolai Korolev, Barbara Korsness, Victoria Korson, Mark Kortepeter, Jeffrey Kosakow, Anita Kosik-Roden, Miriam Koskela, Edward Kostro, Elaine Kotler, Alexander Koudlai, Michael Kovitz, Elinor Kowalski, Lilia Kozlova, Debra Kraft, Lucille Kraiman, George Kramer, Rosalie Kramer, Mary Kratzer, Janann Krauel, Deborah Kraus, Daniel Kraus, Robert Krause, Kim Krawczyk, Kenneth Kreckel, Brenda Kreczmer, Richard Krejcir, Mary Kreps, Karl Kretser, Daniel Kreymer, Norman Krick, Nirmala Krishnamoorthy, Perumal Krishnan, John Krismer, Deborah Kristeller-Moed, Bjorn Kristjansson, John Kristopik, Alex Kroll, Sidney Krome, Kenneth Kron, Avery Krouse, Linda Krueger, Ronald Kruger, Margaret Kruse, Andrew Kryah, Leora Krygier, Clark Krystek, Thomas Kubizek, Dennis Kucera, Patricia Kucera, Karen Kuehl, Anna Kuehn, Dale Kueter, Corinne Kugelmann, Deborah Kuhn, Shirley Kuhn, John Kuhn, Melia Kuhna, Theresa Kulis, Ivy Kuperberg, Michael Kurtz, Christopher Kuschel, Daniel Kussart,

Merry Kusz, Diana Kuzlik, Dragana Kvajic, Leah Kyaio, Olivia Lab, Charles Labee, Frederick LaBounty, Michael Lacasse, David Lace, David Lacer, Richard Lacey, Romanzo Lacey, Ella Lackey, Sharon LaCouture, Guy Lacroix, Nellie Lafferty, Joseph LaFountaine, Lisa Lahey, Wayne Laib, George Laidlaw, Felt Lair, Donna Laird, Andre Laird, Robert Laird, Markus Laitinen, Farnaz Lak, David Lake, John Lakeland, Whitney Lakin, Geraldine LaMarche, Garth Lambert, Jeanne-Marie Lambert, ReNae Lamberth, Sylvester Lamin, Frank Lamonea, Veronica Lamont, Nancy Lamoureux, Diane Lampert, Victor Lana, Michael Lancaster, John Lance, Lloyd Lance, Stuart Land, Catherine Lander, Joseph Lando, Christina Landreth, Kenneth Landry, Jacob Landry, Judith Lane, Nicholas Lane, Travis Lane, Adam Lang, Louise Lang, Michael Lang, Victoria Lang, MaryLaFleur Langdon, Walter Lange, Kimberly Langley, Lance Langlois, Cheryl Langmesser, Denise-Annette Langner-Urso, Lewis Langness, Majken Lanier, Charity Lanier, AnnieLaurie Lanier Samuels, Bobbie Laningham, Mark Lanio, Arthur Lanoie, Andrew Lansdale, Porter Lansing, Wayne Lanter, Angela Lantzy, Mark Lanz, Richard Lanzara,

Michael Lapajenko, Cosette Laperruque, Dori LaPlant, Lissa Larer, Jeanne Larimer-Adams, Marie Larkie, Neil Larkins, Keith Larocque, Pamela Larry, Lillian Larry, Pamela Larry, Laura Larsen, Laurie Larsen, Talmage Larson, Rustin Larson, Robert Larson, Kenneth Larson, Aaron Larson, Stephanie Lassitter, David Last, George Lastnick, Jude LaStrapes, Andrew Laszlo, Malcolm Latham, Marilyn Lathrop, Ronald Latondress, Lisa LaTourette-Pershan, Nancy Lattif, Donna Latvis, Russell Laudenberger, Frederick Laug, Richard Lavall, Marianne LaValle-Vincent, David LaValley, Ricky LaVaughn, Sidney Laverents, Carl LaVerghetta, Lionel LaVergne, Allan LaViers, Paul Lavin, Lawrence Law, Pamela Law, Twana Lawler, David Lawrence, Richard Lawrence, Catrina Lawrence, Paul Lawrence, Darren Laws, Isaac Laws, Patricia Lawson, Tracy Lawson, Pamela Lawson, Lesa Lawson, Christopher Lawson, John Lawson, Douglas Lawver, Cherilyn Laymance, Aaron Lazar, Andrew Lazris, Jeanne Leach, John Leach, Calvin Leach, Janet Leahy, Arch Leake, Robert Leary, Lee Leary, Donald Leas, Jack Leavitt, Autumn LeBeau, Richard Lebherz, Garry LeBlanc, Joyce Lebra, Anne Lebrecht, Marcel Lebrun, Claude LeCesne, Raymond Leclair, Victor LeClair, Alvin Leder, Margaret Ledger, Talsop Lee, David Lee, Janette Lee, Robin Lee, Valerie Lee, Chris Lee, Solola Lee, James Lee, Hauton Lee, Grace Lee, Chad Lee, Betty Lee, Barbara Lee, Charlotte Lee, Michelle Lee, Edward Leech, Charles Leeper, Corinne Lee-Robinson, Carmen Lees, Melvin Lees, Jennifer Leese, Barbara LeFevre-Smith, Steven Leff, Rita Lefko, Cara Lege, Frank Legge, Jean LeGro, Christopher Lehman, Chris Leibig, Bruce Leigh, Kimbra Leigh, Everett Leigh, Allen Leigh, Gregory Leis, Steven Leiva, George Lemacks, Matthew Lemaster, Brian Lemmond, John Lemon, Mary Lenahan, Lloyd Lenard, Ruth Lengerich, Wayne Lennon, Patrick Lennon, Christine Lennox, Matthew Lenton, Beverly Lentz, Christopher Lenz, Mabel Leo, Jacey Leo, Mabel Leo, Howard Leonard, Geoffrey Leonard, Paul Leonard, Melvyn Leonard, Howard Leonard, Leon Leonard, Keith Leonard, Jerry Leonard, Janet Leonardi, Onnwah Leong-Scanlan, Anne Leonie, Anne Leonie, Michael LePage, Alice Lepovetsky, Caren Lerman, Jennifer Leroux, John Leroux, Eileen LeRoux, Charlotte Leslie, Nathan Leslie, Pauline Leslie, Wendyl Leslie, Chelsea Lessard, Donna Lessard, Robin Lessord, Alexandria Lestat, Margaret Lester, Alex LeSueur, Ed Leszczynski, Helen Leung, John Leunissen, Paul LeValley, Daniel Leversen, Charles Levi, Sarah Levin, Melissa Levine, Stanley Levine,

Murray Levine, Walter Levis, Crystal Levis, Gordon Levy, Vicki Levy, Barbara Levy, Farrell Lewallen, Reginald Lewis, Toby Lewis, William Lewis, Willie Lewis, Norma Lewis, Edward Lewis, Janet Lewis, Robert Lewis, Thomas Lewis, James Lewis, Gloria Lewis, Benjamin Lewis, Bernard Lewis, Brian Lewis, Shanty Lewis, David Lewis, Willie Lewis, Jeffrey Lewis, Jonathan Lewis, Phyllis Lewis, Christopher Lewis, Richard Lewis, Joni Lewis, Paul Lewis, Patsy Lewis, Nolan Lewis, Nicholas Lewis, Jel Lewis-Jones, Mark L'Hommedieu, JoeAnn Lias, Jerry Libonati, Lisa Lichtenstein, Kate Lickey, Lynette Liddell, Freda Lieb, Herbert Liebman, David Liebowitz, Joline Lieck, Edward Liggitt, Jason Light, Jan Lightfoot, Melvin Lightford, Lugenia Lightle, Karen Ligon, James Lilley, Nola Lillie, Kenneth Lilly, Linda Lilly, Nile Limbaugh, Sandra Liming, Aaron LiMuti, Huey-Jia Lin, Michelle Lindberg, Laine Linden, Judy Linder, Patricia Lindner, Edmund Lindop, Hans Lindor, Alexander Lindsay, Carol Lindsay, Sonia Lindsey, Trisha Lindsey, Ernestine Lindsey-Burnett, Lorna Line, Danielle Linhart, Gary Link, April Linz, Gary Linz, Colin Liotta, Leslie Lipman, Jennifer Lippold, Rob Lipsey, Roy Lipton, Francisco Liquido, Jonah Lissner, Janet Litherland, Neal Litherland, Erin Litteken, Kerbit Little, Marsha Little, Kerbit Little, Johnny Little, Berta Little, Christopher Little, Shu-Chun Liu, Dean Livelsberger, Michel Liverpool, Robert Livingston, David Lloret, David Lloyd, Priscilla Loba, Steven Lobel, Richard Lobes, Don LoCicero, Vanessa Locke, Denise Locke-Knight, Tom Locker, Betty Lockey, Sharon Lockwood, Stephen Lodge, Thomas Loeber, Eunice Loecher, Hellmut Loetzerich, Walton Loevy, Richard Loewe, Anna Loffman, Synnika Lofton, Janet Lofy, Steve Logan, Roy Logan, Leah Lollar, Kelly Lomas, Brian Lombard, Oreste Lombardi, Denise Lombardo, Suzanna Lonchar, Boyd London, Hiliary London, Richard Long, Peron Long, Lena Long, Theresa Long, Stephen Long, Sanford Long, Sherry Long, Sharon Long, Kathy Long, Jane Long, Elektra Long, Cynthia Long, Christopher Long, Chris Long, Albert Long, Lydia Long, Patricia Long-Eleby, Evelyn Longenecker, Betty Longpre, Graham Longstaff, Barbara Longstreet, Elissa Lonsdale, Laurie Lonsdale, George Looney, Robert Lopez, Jennifer Lopez, Normand Lopez, Christine Lopez, David Lopp, Frank LoProto, Nick Lorance, David Lord, Albert Loren, Russell Lorenzini, Gabrielle Lorino, John Lory, Toni LoTempio, Darlene Loter, Coretta Louis, Ibhaze Louisa, Kimberly Lounder, Randall Louvier, Donna Loux, Henry Love, Rachel Love, Charles Love, Joy Love, Billy Lovell,

Richard Lovell, George Lovett, Darren Lovin, Mark Lowder, Kathy Lowe, Mary Lowe, Mitzi Lowe, Susan Lowe, James Lowe, Cliff Lowe, James Lowe, Scott Lowell, Rae Lowery, Evanna Lowery, Andrea Lowne, Rebecca Lowrey, Beverly Lowry, Randall Loyall, Ryan Loyd, Constance Lubbert, Lorna Luben, Joseph Lucania, Robyn Lucas, Gary Lucas, Woodrow Lucas, Leslie Lucas, Brenda Lucas, Dale Lucas, Willie Ludden, Cynthia Lueddecke, Vicki Luibrand, Nancy Luisi, Thresa Lukacena, Norman Luke, Jack Lukes, Jimmy Lumpkin, John Lundholm, Michael Lupo, Gary Lusby, R. Lusk, Gerald Lusteg, Gerald Lute, Kevin Lyday, Daniel Lyga, Carolyn Lyles, Ve.Ester Lyles, Dan Lynch, J. Lynn, Harriet Lynton, Eric Lyon, Patricia Lyon, Richard Lyon, Tiffanie Lyon, Linda Lyons, Kati Lyon-Villiger, Donna Lysek, Shawna Lytle, Eugene Lyttle, Lois Maag, Toni Mabry, Colin Macanulty, Elaine MacArthur-Apt, Susan Macatee, Alhassan Macaulay, Sheila MacDonald, Donna MacDonald, Mark MacDonald, Louise MacDonald, Chere MacDonald, Christopher Mace, Daniel Mace, Nicholas Macenas, Solomon Machardson, Portia Machonisa, Ellen Macieiski, Erika Mack, Samuel Mack, Wesley Mack, Gordon Mackay, Patricia Mackenzie, Stuart Mackenzie, Lori Mackey, Timothy Mackin, Bernard MacKinnon, Patricia Mackintosh, William Macklin, Donald MacLaren, Sharlene MacLaren, Judith Maclean, Milton MacLean, Reid MacLean, Roni MacLean, Paul MacNeill, Denny Macomber, Steven Macon, Maxwell MacPherson, David MacRae, Mattea Macri, Shawn MacSwan, Gloria Madden, Sonya Madden, George Maddison, James Maddux, Darren Madigan, Maura Madigan, Barbara Madison, Carole Madrzak, Philip Madsen, Christian Madsen, Robert Magaletti, Jarlon Magee, Michael Mager, Robert Mager, Alicia Maggio, Theresa Magliano, Andrew Magnus, Merilyn Maguire, Shandra Magwire, Renu Mahajan, Tammy Mahan, Donald Mahanay, Mary Maher, Iftekhar Mahmood, John Mahnke, Michael Mahon, Aaron Mai, Kitty Maiden, Ron Maier, Lawrence Maisner, Lucille Maistros, Gail Majcher, Jaclyn Majer, Mark Major, Francine Maklary, Katy Makropoulos, Laura Malcom, Patricia Malemes, Ron Malfi, Sharie Malik, Sally Malkowski, Willie Mallard, Vernon Mallow, Thomas Maloney, Sharon Maloney, Jennifer Malpass, Michelle Malsbury, Paul Maltzer, Cathy Malven, Shirley Mamou, Annette Manaclay, Ricardo Mancebo, Steven Manchester, Richard Mancini, Gilbert Manda, Barry Mandel, Frederick Mandell, Basil Mandy, Robert Maniscalco, Robert Mann, Andrew Mann, William Mann, Bert

Mann, Phyllis Manning, Kenneth Manning, Oreste Manno, Motesem Mansur, Petros Mantarakis, Billy Manus, Nancy Manus, Eron Manusov, John Manz, Luiz Manzolillo, Cecil Maranville, Joyce Marbury, Lisa Marcelletti, Christopher Marceron, Gerard Marchal, Richard Marco, Gerry Marcotte, Gerald Marcotte, Nicole Marcum, Kyla Marden, Daniel Marder, Mary Marelli, Donald Margetson, Becky Margrave, Katwesige Margret, Manuel Marin, R. Marino, Amy Marion, Melody Marion, Peter Marise, Alice Marise, Edna Mark, Mary Mark, Roland Marke, Janet Markey, Paul Markezich, Melanie Marklein, Steven Markman, Elizabeth Markman, Elaine Markowicz, Edith Marks, Mary Marks, David Marks, Henry Marksbury, Philip Marlin, Marc Marlow, Steven Marlowe, Elmira Maroutian, Roderick Marquardt, Ann Marquette, Francis Marquette, John Marquez, Margaret Marr, Luis Marrero, Jonathan Marriage, Jack P. Marschall, Michael Marsden, Peter Marsden, Erifilie Marsh, Daniel Marsh, Karen Marsh, Joanne Marsh, Mark Marshall, Stephen Marshall, Clarence Marshall, Wayne Marshall, Martie Marshall, Jo Marshall, Georgetta Marshall, Gary Marshall, Dennis Marshall, Kenneth Marshall, Anita Marshall-Harris, Therese Marszalek, Jackie Marten-Bevand, Olga Martens, Sharon Martin, Jeffrey Martin, Stephen Martin, Scott Martin, Theresa Martin, James Martin, Sharene Martin, Doris Martin, Jacqueline Martin, Sheila Martin, Kevin Martin, Shelly Martin, Muriel Martin, Richard Martin, Troy Martin, Jon Martin, Carl Martin, Clara Martin, Denis Martin, Don Martin, Hosea Martin, Olivia Martin, John Martin, Jonathan Martin, Kathleen Martin, Kevin Martin, Lena Martin, Lisa Martin, Marceline Martin, Patricia Martin, Brett Martin, John Martin, William Martinez, Daniel Martinez, Mary Martinez, Michael Martinez, Dinorah Martinez-Piney, David Martino, Marianne Marullo, Kathleen Marushack, Joshua Marvit, Arthur Marx, Richard Mascara, Marlene Mascoll, Nicholas Masesso, Ashley Mason, Phyllis Mason, Joseph Mason, John Mason, Eva Mason, Gracia Mason, Victoria Mason-DeBruhl, Patricia Masoni, Deborah Masse, Tiffany Massey, Howard Massey, Roy Massie, Valarie Massie, Linda Massucci, Lon Mast, Rachelle Mast, Dale Masters, Marcus Mastin, Nikolas Mastropavlos, David Matchick, Eric Matheny, Bobby Matherly, Anna Mathers, Betty Mathews, Brad Mathews, Mary Mathews, M. Mathiesen, Peggy Mathis, Tina Mathis, Darwin Mathison, Sharon Matias, Richard Matlick, Anthony Mator, John Matsis, John Matson, Randall Matson, Amber Matthews, Dana

Matthews, Donna Matthews, Bruce Matthews, Louis Mattia, Desmond Mattocks, Ivar Mattson, John Mattys, Carman Mauceri, Rommel Mauma, Sherry Mauro, Robert Mauro, William Mauro, Henrietta Maus, Nini Mawasi, Gizella Mawbey, Charles Mawhinney, Joshua Maxey, Alfred Maxey, John Maxfield, Michael Maxim, Tammy Maxson, Lenna Maxwell, Leona Maxwell, Richard May, Terry May,

Melinda Maycock, Munayem Mayenin, Timothy Mayer, Ryan Mayers, Leslie Mayes, Mandy Mayling, Charles Mayo, Raymond Mayotte, Stedman Mays, Vance Mays, Francis Mazur, Joseph Mazzenga, Timothe Mboule, Sharon McAlister, Barbara McArthur, Kevin

McArthur, Betty McBee, Charity McBride, Robin McBride, William McBride, Raymond McBride, Patricia McBride, Greg McBride, Gordon McBride, Janet McBride-Holt, Mel McCabe, Robbie-Lee McCambridge, James McCann, Clare McCann, Peggy McCardle, William McCarter, Ingrid McCarthy, Robert McCarthy, Elaine McCarthy, Debra McCarty, Barbara McCarty, Robert McCauley, Allen McClain, Brian McClain, Wayne McClain, James McClellan, Juanita McClellan, Tasi McClellan, Douglas McClelland, James McClelland, Nan McClellon, Todd McClimans, Mercedes McClure, Candace McClure, Darlene McClure, Jeffrey McCluskey, Martha McClymonds, Ryan McConkey, John McCorkle, Martin McCorkle, Monica McCormack-Sheehan, Patrick McCormick, John McCormick, Angela McCormick, Charles McCorvey, Angenita McCoy, Dora McCoy, James McCoy, Byron McCoy, Monique McCracken, Greta McCrary, Larry Mccrea, Charlene McCree, Polly McCrillis, William McCullars, William McCullars, Joseph McCullough, Patricia McCullough, Jessica McCullough, Mona McCune, Fawn McCurdy, Alice McCurdy, Richard McCurry, Lynn McCutcheon, Eldon McDaniel, Priscilla McDaniel, Kevin McDermott, Patrick McDermott, Brandy McDevitt, John McDonald, Brandi McDonald, Robert McDonald, James McDonald, Raymond McDonald, Kelly McDonald, Donna McDonald, Kelly McDonough, Bruce McDougal, Valerie McDowell, Anna McDowell, Delinda McDowell, Felita McElroy, Edward McEntire, Lois McEwen, Maggie McEwen, Elspeth McFadden, Paul McFain, Sandra McFarland, Thomas McFarland, Sandra McGarrity, Robert McGeary, James McGee, Philip McGee, Laurie McGinn, Thomas McGoldrick, Catherine McGough, Paula McGovern, Joby McGowan, David McGrath, Ronald McGraw, Robert McGregor, Patricia McGuinn, Daniel McGuire, Rhonda McGuire, Janette McGuire, Tiffany McHam, Kathy McInnis, Caroline McIntosh, Karline McIntosh, Kevin McIntosh, John McIntosh, Chris McIntosh, John McIntosh, Shirley McJunkin, Amabel McKay-Omar, Michael McKee, Margaret McKee, Michael McKenzie, James McKenzie, Robert McKenzie, Joseph McKeown, Mark McKinney, Gertrude McKinney, Linda McKinney, Lynette McKinney, Mary McKinney, Peter McKinnon, Nicole McKnight, Ian McLachlan, George McLaren, Lauren McLaren, Deborah McLaughlin, Joseph McLaughlin, Claire McLean, Lionel McLean, Marc McLemore, David McLeod, William McLeod, Carol McLoud, Ellen McMahill, Brandon McMahon, Jamie McMahon, William McMahon, Robert McMakin, Jay McMartin,

Jane McMaster-Conroy, Jackie McMillan, Larry McMillan, Winton McMillen, Theresa McMiller, Alan McMillin, Raleigh McMillon, James McMorris, Edyth McNair, Francis McNamara, Paula McNeal, Marilyn McNeal, Shannon McNeice, Dorothi McNerney, Marjorie McNutt, Douglas McNutt, Keith McPherson, Ruby McPherson, Henry McQuade, Kimberly McRitchie, Martin McShea, Tameka McSpadden, Jerry McSwain, Patrick McTiernan, Megan McTigue, Douglas McVey, Theresa McWilliams, Shavon McWilliams, Matt Meacham, Edith Meacham, Shaneek Meachum, Charles Meade, Barton Meaders, Claudberta Meador, Kristin Meador, Donna Meagher, Arnold Meagher, Amber Meagher, George Mears, Cletis Mebane, Bendetta Medina-Natal, Florence Mee, Kevin Meehan, David Meek, Jerry Meeks, Frank Megna, Ngadhenjim Mehmeti, James Mehrle, Sharad Mehta, Lars Meiners, Brian Meiser, Jason Melby, Melania Melcer-Lievaart, Alfred Melchiorre, Frederick Melden, Kirsten Meldrum, Renaldo Meli, William Mellas, Mary Mellen, Clyde Melton, Harvey Melton, Elizabeth Melton, Michelle Meltzer, Donald Melville, Dan Membiela, Cynthia Memmolo, Carole Menard, Michael Mendoza, Eliane Menetrier, Joanne Mengel, Michael Mennenga, Adwoa Mensah, Shannon Menssen, Vivian Menzies, Frank Mercado, Earnest Mercer, Gary Mercer, Tammara Mercer, Paul Meredith, Ann Merenda, Akindotun Ogunduyile Merino, Sara Merlene, Nicholas Merolesi, Brian Merrick, Amanda Merrick-Issa, Gail Merrill, Joan Merrill, LaLeita Merrill, Richard Merriman, Keith Merritt, Suzanne Merritt, Sallie Merritt, Keith Merritt, Roy Merritt, Kevin Merritt, Randall Mesler, Noreen Messina, Michael Messineo, Jennifer Messing, Roger Meyer, Ronald Meyer, Dawn Meyer, Eileen Meyers, Margaret Meyers, Sandra Michael, Nicholas Michael, Alfred Michaud, David Michener, Charles Mickles, Sallie Middlebrook, Donna Middlestadt, James Middleton, Michael Middleton, Sharon Middleton, Michael Middleton, Vikki Middleton-Blake, Gary Midge, Sharon Mierke, Nancy Mierzwik, Jill Migchels, Gerald Migliarisi, Ruth Migliore, Paul Mihalak, Crystal Mihalich, Milos Mijatovic, Sheila Milam, Sherly Milaninia, Rosemary Mild, Harry Mileaf, Stanley Miles, William Miles, Jackie Millane, Hudson Millar, Larry Millard, Tekla Miller, Melba Miller, Jon Miller, Dorothy Miller, Kim Miller, Tracy Miller, Donald Miller, Tammie Miller, Mervin Miller, William Miller, Harold Miller, Jeffrey Miller, Stephen Miller, Connie Miller, Constance Miller, Jim Miller, Wilbert Miller, Don Miller, Alan Miller, Betsy Miller, Bobby Miller, Charles

Miller, Janice Miller, Craig Miller, Marie Miller, Debra Miller, Dinah Miller, Gregg Miller, Margaret Miller, Joe Miller, John Miller, Jon Miller, Kelsie Miller, Kenneth Miller, Kevin Miller, Larry Miller, Henry Miller, Cora Miller, Calynne Millien, Misty Milligan, Edward Millis, Mark Millman, Andrea Millon-Jones, Tim Mills, Michael Mills, Richard Mills, Dennis Mills, Barjeana Mills, Mark Mills, Bruce Milne, Claudette Milner, Jennifer Milo, Neil Milofsky, Ronald Milos, Kendell Milton, Dale Milton, Brooke Mimier, Pilar Minaca, Anthony Minadeo, Jerry Minchew, Sabrina Minder, David Miner, Stacee Miner, Ralph Miner, Allen Minor, Brenda Minor, Solomon Minta, James Minter,

Jerry Minton, Hialeah Miranda, Liliana Miranda, Jason Miranda-Levi, Denise Misencik, Scott Misko, Joseph Misrasi, Goslaw Misztal, Malinda Mitchell, Pearl Mitchell, Tonya Mitchell, Susan Mitchell, Phillip Mitchell, Major Mitchell, Katherine Mitchell, Janet Mitchell, Christopher Mitchell, Candis Mitchell, Michael Mitchell, Lois Mitchell-Lane, Raghu Mitra, Edward Mixon, Mary Mizell, Anton

Mkrtychev, William Moake, Ryan Moats, Thomasrael Modden, Sherrel Moeller, Nicole Moens, Michael Moffett, Teresa Mogdics, Sanat Mohanty, Kurt Mohney, Jerry Mohrlang, Carolyn Moir, Stan Mojsich, Ryan Molde, Lynda Moldrem, Joslyn Moldstad, Graham Mole, Linda Moller, Neil Moloney, Robin Molsberry, Stefan Molyneux, Melinda Monaghan, Edward Mondich, Patricia Mondore, Mary Mongiovi, Larry Monkelban, Anthony Monochello, Marlene Monroy, Howard Monta, Shaela Montague-Phillips, Kayli Monteleone, John Montgomery, Kathy Montgomery, Susan Montgomery, William Montgomery, Gary Montgomery, Charles Montgomery, Diane Monti-Catania, James Montondo, Ermila Moodley, Vernon Moody, Robert Mooney, Keshawna Mooney, Keenan Moore, Robert Moore, Sarah Moore, Sherry Moore, Theodis Moore, Adam Moore, Aaron Moore, Ramona Moore, Matthew Moore, Brian Moore, Richard Moore, Thomas Moore, Charles Moore, Merl Moore, Catherine Moore, Christiana Moore, Commie Moore, Erin Moore, Greggory Moore, Kendrick Moore, Billy Moore, Kendrick Moore, Linda Moore, Diane Moore, Cynthia Moorefield, Sherri Moorer, Ritchie Moorhead, Paul Morabito, Luis Morales, Thomas Moran, Johnny Moran, Dawn Moran, Karen Moran, Michael Morash, Rosalie More, Randolph Moreau, Elizabeth Morehouse, Winifred Moreland, Elizabeth Moreno-Urquiza, Patricia Moreton, Christopher Morey, Debra Morgan, Debby Morgan, Kenneth Morgan, John Morgan, Dedra Morgan, Charles Morgan, Aundria Morgan, Addis Morgan, Dedra Morgan, Dorothy Morgan-Maddox, Geraldine Morganti, Joan Morgret, Paul Morin, Evaldas Morkunas, Katy Morlas, Jonathan Morlock, James Morrell, Joan Morris, Aldon Morris, Marilyn Morris, Daniel Morris, Karen Morris, Paul Morris, Vaughan Morris, Timothy Morris, Rosalind Morris, Jeanna Morris, Raymond Morris, Barbara Morris, Elizabeth Morris, Karen Morris, Kerry Morris, Marlene Morris, Jacqueline Morrisey, Daniel Morrison, Timothy Morrison, Candice Morrison, Gwen Morrison, Grady Morrison, Kevin Morrison, Eugene Morrisroe, Scott Morro, Patricia Morrone, Brenda Morrow, Jack Morrow, Thomas Morrow, Bridget Morrow-Cogshell, Mary Morse, Donald Morse, George Mortensen, Denis Mortenson, Robert Mortier, Jermaine Morton, Lloyd Morton, Nancy Morton, Harry Morton, Markos Moschos, Tabitha Moseley, Michael Moseley, John Moser, Eugene Moser, Don Moser, Eugene Moser, Brian Moses, Cherrie' Moses, Barbara Mosher, Spyridon Moshonas, Tim Mosier, Yirael Moskovits, Jack Moskovitz, Ira

Moskowitz, Denise Mosley, Rickie Mosley, Thomas Mosley, Sharon Moss, Bill Moss, Patricia Moss, Cleve Moten, John Motta, Lee Motteler, Bobby Moulder, Shirley Mounsey, Rasma Mount, Joseph Mourek, Dona Moyer, William Moyer, Mary Moynan, Courtney Mroch, Barbara Mrowiec-Michalska, David Muchai, Chenai Muchemwa, Julia Mudembei, Doris Mueller, Robert Mueri, Gabrielle Muftic, King Muhammad, Michelle Muhlhausen`, Sabine Muir, Harriet Muirhead, Barbara Mulkey, Jason Mull, Thomas Mullane, Patrick Mullen, Olevia Mullen, Patrick Mullen, Amy Mullenix, Reto Muller, Kenneth Mullican, Elizabeth Mulligan, Neil Mullin, Jerry Mullinax, Cathleen Mullins, Antoinette Mullins, Allison Mullins, Vanessa Mullins, Tanya Mullins, Lila Mullins, Christopher Mulrooney, Adam Muncy, David Muncy, Kirk Munsch, Simon Muntner, Samia Muqueem, Bryan Murawski, Kenneth Murdock, Jeffrey Murfield, Tracy Murillo, Nester Murira, Nina Murphy, Patrick Murphy, Patricia Murphy, Daniel Murphy, Mary Murphy, Joshua Murphy, Matthew Murphy, Monica Murphy, Gerard Murphy, April Murphy, Lisa Murphy, Antoinette Murphy, April Murphy, Christine Murphy, Danah Murphy, James Murphy, Joseph Murphy, Andrew Murphy, Janice Murra, Victoria Murray, Aloha Murray, Thomas Murray, Donna Murray, Renee Murray, Janice Murrell, Larry Muse, Mark Muse, Ann Musico, Rudolph Muska, Ilham Muslimov, Raymond Musselwhite, Richard Mussler, Lynda Mustain, Michael Muters, Rosemary Mwenja, Maureen Mydlo, Eric Myers, Patricia Myers, Sandra Myers, Teena Myers, Eric Myers, Michael Mykytok, David Myland, Edna Myles, Niki Mylonas, Erik Myran, Murray Nabors, Nitza Nachmias, Barathy Nadarajah, Lorraine Nadeau, Tyson Nafus, Danielle Naibert, Clara Nail, Roze Nalbandian, Lindsay Nall, Lance Nalley, Lauri Nally, Mary Nally, James Nance, Sherre Nance, Charles Napier, Linda Napolitano, Sherry Nardo, Ben Nargi, Sarwain Narine, Aubrey Nash, James Nash, Janice Nash, Bobby Nash, Thomas Nastek, Michael Natale, Benjamin Nathe, Brian Naveken, Cathy Naylor, Tracy Naylor, Scotch Ndlovu, George Ndonga, Wayne Neal, James Neal, Brooke Neal, Robert Neal, Elaine Neel, Stephen Neely, Roger Neetz, Rhonda Neihart, Leslie Neilson, Sherri Neilson, Leslie Neilson, Ginger Nelson, Joan Nelson, Karrieann Nelson, Linda Nelson, Sean Nelson, W. Nelson, Arthur Nelson, Gloria Nelson-Martinez, Frank Nemecek, Karen Nesbit, Anthony Nesbitt, Shannon NeSmith, Kathy Nesselroad, Lynda Nester, Roger Neth, Dale Netherton, Sean Nettles, Wolfgang Neudorfer,

Jeffrey Neugroschel, Edith Neumaier, Carol Neumann, Paul Neumann, David Neuschafer, Barbara Neveau, Ronnie Newberry, Betty Newbold, James Newburry, Tammie Newby, Karen Newcomb, Robert Newcombe, Patricia Newcombe, Frank Newkirk, John Newlon, Raymond Newman, Kurt Newman, Robert Newman, Elsie Newman, William Newman, Lucinda Newsome, William Newton, Steven Newton, Oliver Neyen, Veronica Nguyen, Thoi Nguyen, Drew Nicastro, Kelly Niccolini, Jacqueline Nichol, George Nicholas, Mildred Nicholas, G. Nicholls, Ronald Nichols, Eric Nichols, Lisa Nichols, Patricia Nichols, Rod Nichols, Nancy Nicholson, Michael Nicholson, Deborah Nicholson, Michael Nicholson, Laura Nickel, Lynn Nickens, Kathleen Nickerson, Harold Nickolds, Andrew Nicol, Robbin Nicola, Pat Nicolette, Christine Nielsen, Julie Nielsen, Shannon Nielson, Keitha Nielson, Karl Niemiec, John Nienstedt, Elaura Niles, Kathryn Niles, Paul Nilsen, Thomas Nilsen, Deborah Nilson-Kerrigan, Madathilparampil Ninan, Jean Nipaver, Mark Nippoldt, Robert Nisbet, Balraj Nischal, Terry Niver, Nicky Nixon, Laura Nixon, Racheal Njoroge, Eusebio Noblefranca, Howard Nobles, Victor Noel, Jeffrey Noguchi, Tyisha Noise, John Nolan, Margaret Nolan-Williams, Noble Nolcox, Meagan Noles, Troy Nooe, Mark Noon, Joseph Noona, Steven Norby, Kevin Nordbrock, Elra Norris, Mark Norris, Melissa Norris, Marco North, Patricia Northup, Sharon Norton, Paul Norwood, Marjut Nousiainen, Darlene Novick, Victoria Noxon, Christian Nseka, Nick Nteireho, Walter Nugent, Millie Nunnelee, James Nuovo, Abdel Nuriddin, Ann Nurse, Sue Nussbaum, Hedda Nussbaum, Ronald Nussbeck, David Nussenblatt, Campbell Nutbrown, Anthony Nutter, David Oakford, Elizabeth Oakley, Marilyn Oakley, Steve Oakley, Marilyn Oakley, Marie Oates, Meghan Oates, James Ober, Alida Oberlin, Kathleen Oblich, Eric Obmann, J. O'Brien, William O'Brien, Thomas O'Brien, John O'Brien, Michael O'Brien, Andrew O'Bryan, John O'Bryan, Eruvwuoghene Obuaya, George Oby, Cleve Ochs, Fabian O'Connell, David O'Connell, Bonnie O'Conner, Gudmundur Oddsson, Mary O'Dell, Heather Odle, Scott Odom, John O'Dwyer, Michael Oelke, Charles Oestreich, Jo Offen, Godson Offoaro, Charles Ofoji, Ubaka Ogbogu, Cynthia Ogbuji, Deborah Ogg, Gillian Ogilvie, Bryce O'Guinn, YemiD. Ogunyemi, Goziam Ogwu, Shane O'Halloran, Diarmuid O'Hara, Janet O'Hare, Alvin Oickle, Christine Ojeda, Michael Oka, Ryan Okerlund, Dawn O'Kieff, Clara Oklu, Oladipupo Ola, Johanna Oladottir, Olajumoke Olagbemi, Elizabeth Olagunju,

Somefun Olakunle, Stephen Olar, Olufemi Olawole, Richard O'Leary, Walter Oleksy, Matthew Olerio, Inge-Lisa Olesen, Sheila Olins, Georgina Oliver, Jennifer Oliver, Thomas Oliver, Richard Oliver, James Oller, Catherine Ols, Charles Olsen, Elizabeth Olsen, Cynthia Olson, Karen Olson, Patrick Olson, Rachel Olson, Molly Olson, Peter Olsson, Eniola Oluwaseun, Jillann Olvera, Jerry Olynyk, Paul Olzak, Patricia O'Mara, Paul Omeziri, Helen Omofoma, Tari Omoro, Greg O'Neal, Richard O'Neal, Marlane O'Neill, John O'Neon, Linda Oness, Eugene Onofrio, Christopher Onwiler, Samuel O'Prey, Patricia O'Quin, Angela Oramasionwu, David Orange, Paul Oranika, Clipper Ordiway, Olivia Orfield, Emily-Jane Orford, Shawn Orgain, Carol Orgeron, Samson Orion, Vince Orlando, Terry Orlikoski, Kevin O'Rourke, Betty Orr, Peter Orr, Zelma Orr, Barbara Ortega, Kerri Ortiz, Jacki Ortiz, Kerri Ortiz, Michael Ortiz, Neil Orts, Stephen Orwat, Emily Osborn, Michael Osborne, Donald Osgood, Hashemi Osman, Joey Osmena, Anastasia Osorio, K. Ostahowski, Nickolas Ostdick, Ray Ostenberg, Marcia Oster, Bert Osterberg, Jennifer Ostrander, Barbara O'Sullivan, William Ott, Nelson Ottenhausen, Jerry Ousley, William Overby, LaTonya Overstreet, Eric Owen, Kimberly Owen, Richard Owens, George Owens, Peter Owens, Steven Owens, Carl Owings, Fasehun Oyewole, Patrick Pacalo, Joyce Pace, Eugene Pace, Marie Pacha, Isabelle Pacheco, Theresa Pachesny, Michelle Pack, Andrew Paczkowski, Dorothy Paddon, Robert Padget, JoEllen Padilla, Nilsa Pagan, Michelina Pagano, Alan Page, Michael Page, Kevin Paglia, Cynthia Pagliolo, Cynthia Pagliolo, Angelo Pagnotti, Maria Paige, Julie Painter, Mike Palecek, Henry Palek, Julie Palella, Gail Pallotta, Amy Palmer, Darlene Palmer, Edward Palmer, Mary Palmer, Ann Palmer, Adam Palmer, Brian Palmer, Gary Palmer, Nicolina Palmiotto, Nicki Palmiotto, Richard Paloma, Marie Palumbo, Joseph Palumbo, Keith Panaro, Renee Pangrazzi-Trudeau, Daniel Pann, Leigh Pannell, Linda Pannett, Robert Pannone, Chris Panos, Cynthia Panton, Clara Papa, Richard Papale, Paula Papapetrou, Karin Paparelli, Wayne Papp, Jack Pappas, Ray Paprocki, Susan Paquin, Dorothea Parault, Kerry Pardue, Shirley Parent, Randell Parent, Lori Paris, Christopher Paris, Herschel Parker, Darian Parker, John Parker, Nathaniel Parker, Melvin Parker, Larry Parker, Jesse Parker, Herbert Parker, Carol Parker, Allen Parker, Jesse Parker, Charles Parkinson, Abby Parks, Louise Parks, Sherrie Parnell, Anna Parrish, Katrina Parrish, Anna Parrish, Rusty Parrott, Dian Parrotta,

Arthur Parry, Pamela Parsons, Georgia Parsons, David Partelow, Catherine Pascale, Hallie Paschal, Joseph Pasculli, Beverly Pasden, Dorothea Pasquariello, Colleen Passard, Mary Passaro, Michelle Pastore, Savanna Patch, Johnnye Pate, Lynden Pater, Peter Paton, Cathy Patrenos, Claudia Patrick, Benjamin Patt, Stephanne Patten, Thomas Patten, Stacie Patterson, Christopher Patterson, Jeanne Patterson, Teresa Patterson, Duane Patterson, Tom Patterson, Stacie Patterson, Lori Patterson, Jeanne Patterson, Cindy Patterson, William Patterson, Peggy Pattison, Bill Patton, Lee Patton, Mirella Patzer, Eric Paul, David Paul, Adrienne Paulin, Gary Paulsen, Steven Pavelsky, Stephen Pavey, Marsha Pavlovsky, Yolonda Pawielski,

327

Ralph Paxson, Gregory Paxton, Brent Paxton, Tomitchell Payden, John Payne, Eduardo Paz-Martinez, Jackye Peacock, Shelley Peaks-Waters, Anthony Pearson, Kirk Pearson, Leonard Pearson, Peggy Pearson, Brent Pearson, Thomas Pearson, Amanda Pearson, Fayeshawn Peavy, Lisa Pecchia, Mariella Pechero-Loewen, Paul Peck, Justine Peck, Elizabeth Peck, Paul Peck, Bryan Pedas, Birgitte Pedersen, Laura Pedowitz, Richard Pelc, Terry Pellant, Erica Pelletier, Joyce Pelletier, Peter Pellissier, Terry Pellman, Gertrude Pellrine, Eunice Pender, Gary Pendleton, Debra Penner, Tracey Penney, Joseph Penning, Billy Pennington, Shanna Pennington, Martin Penny, Pamela Penrod, Gary Penton, Anthony Pepe, Monica Pepo, Jason Peppers, Bradley Peraino, Yvonne Peramaki, Harold Perdue, Mary Pereault, David Pereda, Monica Pereira, Saralee Perel, Trihan Perera, Marcela Perez, Christopher Perez, Cesar Perez, Christie Perfetti, Denis Perigord, Carmelina Perillo, Tammy Perkins, Eric Perkins, Perry Perkins, Jacqueline Perkins, Tammy Perkins, Jennie Perkins-Fellows, Henry Perkinson, John Perricone, Rupert Perrin, Patricia Perrotti, Marilyn Perry, Patricia Perry, Stephanie Perry, Fred Perry, Rory Perry, Cedric Perry, Joshua Perry, John Perry, Jessica Perry, Devie Perry, David Perry, Caroline Perry, Marilyn Perry, Gary Persinger, Christine Peryea, Laura Peters, Ramona Peters, Alison Peters, Gary Peters, Holly Petersen, Steven Petersen, Cynthia Peterson, Dawn Peterson, Derek Peterson, James Peterson, Lawrence Peterson, Robert Peterson, Ruth Peterson, Elissa Peterson, Blake Petit, Maria Petre, Christopher Petree, Donald Petrich, David Pettee, Sandra Pettee, Michael Petti, Lafayette Pettiford, Patria Pettingell, Albert Petty, Mark Pewtress, Banafsheh Pezeshk, Elizabeth Pezold, Laura Pfalz, Kathryn Pfeffer, Sara Pfoutz, Mark Phelps, Barbara Philbrook, Joe Philip, Chere Philip, Leslie Philippi, Jennifer Phillips, Patrick Phillips, Frank Phillips, Donald Phillips, Jeffrey Phillips, Robbie Phillips, Erma Phillips, Deborah Phillips, Cindy Phillips, Christopher Phillips, Brendanne Phillips, Anthony Phillips, Tyrone Phillips, Angelia Phillips-Buihner, Summer Philo, Sharon Philpot, Reginald Philpott, Elsie Phipps, Kris Piazza, Alice Pick, Thomas Pickenpaugh, Lori Pielak, Rhona Pienaar, Rebecca Pierce, Jacqueline Pierce, Lola Pierce, Duane Pierre, Arthur Pierson, Ronald Pies, Angela Pike, Jill Pike, Jennifer Pilcher, Michelle Pilkerton, Carole Piller, Peter Pilot, Mary Pinch, Thomas Pine, Douglas Pinegar, Ray Pinion, George Pinkerton, Linda Pinkham, Noel Pinnock, Lila Pinord, David Piper,

Gary Piper, Richard Pirodsky, Julie Pisacane, Thomas Pisano, Samuel Pisciotta, Emile Piscitelli, Rich Pitcock, Richard Pitcock, Dalton Pitt, Gary Pittenger, Howard Pitterson, Anita Pittman, Joseph Pitts, Jerry Pivec, Kathryn Place, Michelle Plank, Jennifer Plant, Trilby Plants, Ida Plassay, Tiffany Plath, Connie Platt, Amy Platt, Julie Platz, Stefanie Plaud, Sarah Playle, John Plewa, Brigitte Pliska, Andy Plotkin, Rebecca Plourde, Amber Plowman, Carol Poe, Judith Poe, Louis Poessel, Virginia Point, Loretta Poisson, Stephanie Pokorzynski, Tim Poland, Sylvia Polanski, William Polden, Nathan Polinsky, Tiffany Polisoto, Michael Polizzi, Carol Polk, Gary Pollard, Edith Pollitz, Gregory Pollock, Cody Polston, Teresa Polychronis, Paola Pomponi, Clarence Pontius, Jan Pope, Diane Popek-Jones, Anna Popescu, Suzanne Popke, Judith Poplawski, Connie Popovits, Lawrence Popp, Barbara Popyach, Laura Porras, Thomas Porrecca, Jean Porro, Kenneth Porter, Kimberly Porter, Judith Porter, Christopher Porter, Christina Porter, Cassy Ashton Porter, Donald Porter, Rachel Porto, Michael Post, Philip Potter, James Potter, Karla Potter, Linda Potter, Marlyse Poulaille, Nick Poulos, David Powell, Eileen Powell, Penelope Powell, William Powell, Neia Powell, Toyanda Powell, Gloria Powers, Robert Powers, Debra Powers, Paul Powers, Julienne Poyerd, Birgit Pratcher, Roger Pratcher, Melissa Prater, Kathryn Pratt, Duncan Prescott, Wayne Pressley, Harry Preston, James Preston, Harry Preston, Renee Preston, Fenton Prewitt, Heidi Price, Darline Price, Barbara Price, John Price, Dawn Price, William Price, Vincent Price, Linda Price, Cynthia Price, Ruth Price, Dianne Price, Frederick Price, Jackson Price, M.J. Price, Dana Pride, Elizabeth Pride, Dana Pride, George Priest, Kenneth Prince, Matthew Prince, Othealor Prince, Linda Principe, Angelo Prisco, Ann Pritchard, Christopher Pritchard, William Pritchard, Audrey Privett, Adam Probert, Brad Prochnow, Bradford Proctor, Lisa Proulx, Jeffrey Provine, Angela Pruitt, Florence Prusmack, Jampa Pryor, Anthony Pryor, Thomas Pryor, Maria Psanis, Susan Puett, Donald Puff, Sarah Pugsley, Deborah Pujoue, George Pullen, Michael Purfield, Emma Purington, Falisha Purkiss, Catherine Puro, Tricia Pursell, Stewart Purvis, Scott Puryear, Leslie Puryear, David Putnam, Randy Putnam, Huw Pyatt, Sylvia Pye, Allen Pyle, Stephen Pytak, Jennifer Quaile, Alvan Quamina, Chris Quarles, Richard Quarles, Damita Quashie, Thadine Quick, Vincent Quick, Debra Quick, Mary Quigley, Mary Quijano, Barbara Quinn, Linda Quinn, Freddie Quinn, Michal Quinn, Timothy Quinton, Angie Rabb,

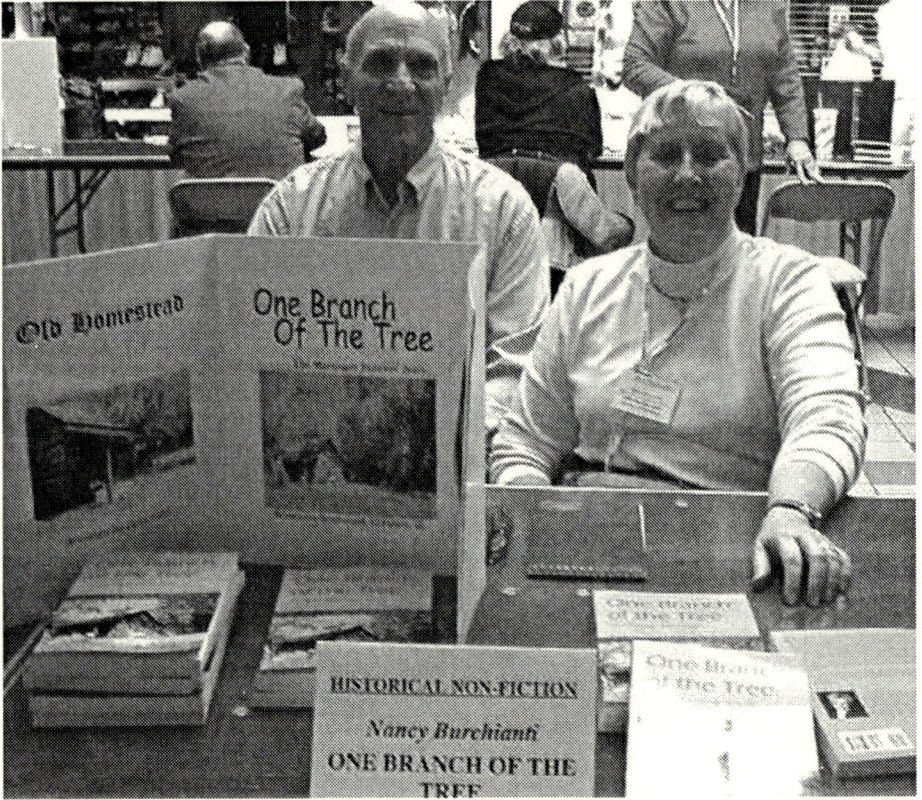

Tamika Raby, Joseph Racioppi, Ray Racobs, Stefan Racz, Alexander Racz, Mike Rader, Kiamran Radjabli, Anita Radney, Marina Radovanovic, Catalina Radu, Alan Raeside, Eric Raeuber, Beverly Raffaele, Stephen Rafferty, Carol Ragab, Michael Lynn Ragsdale I, Boyd Rahier, James Rahm, Janene Rahm, Oliver Rahman, Mohammad Rahman, Edwin Rainey, James Rainey, Jason Rains, Carl Ralls, Tonya Ramagos, Raman Ramakrishnaiyer, Rekha Raman, Thomas Rameaka, Ken Ramirez, Sharon Ramkhelawan, Charles Rammelkamp, Benedict Ramos, Ian Ramos, John Ramos, Vassell Ramsay, Judy Ramsook, Gary Randall, Janet Randall, Carmine Randazzo, Deborah Raney, Christianne Ranger, Thomas Rankin, Diana Ranquist, Theodore Ransaw, Samira Rao, Karanam Rao, Joyce Rapier, Richard Rapp, Marsha Rappaport, Helen Rapson, Anne Rasic, Crystal Ratcliff, Jonna Rathbun, Mary Ratliff, Susan Ratliff, Johnny Ratliff, Susan Ratliff, Sivaprakasam Ratnam, Victor Ratner, Virginia

Rauch, Marc Rauch, Donald Ravenscroft, Melody Ravert, Shirley Rawlins, Francis Rawls, Douglas Ray, Tushar Ray, James Ray, Carol Ray, James Razzi, Rosemary Rš, Diana Read, Oscar Reagan, Dean Ream, Hal Reames, Harold Reames, William Reardon, Laura Rearick, Heather Reaume, James Reaves, Nancy Rechtman, Jeani Rector, MichalAnn Red Eagle, Micki Red Eagle, Carolyn Redford, Lynne Redlin, William Redstreake, Maya Redwood, Bernadette Reece, Reba Reece, Michael Reece, Vanessa Reed, Andrew Reed, Harold Reed, Vanessa Reed, Taryn Reed, Nat Reed, Harold Reed, George Reed, Dalean Reed, Angie Reed, David Reed, Mark Reeder, Pamela Reed-Wallinger, Timothy Reedy, Kathryn Reel, Thomas Rees, Tim Rees, Carolyn Reese, Hazel Reese, Jacob Reese, Deborah Reeves, Michael Reeves, Amy Regeti, Kathy Regini, Richard Regnier, David Rehak, Angela Rehms, Joseph Reich, Lonny Reichard, Herbert Reichlin, Marvin Reid, Lesia Reid, William Reid, Tonya Reid, James Reid, DeAngela Reid, Amy Reid, Ronda Reid, Beverley Reid-Jackson, Elaine Reidy, Catherine Reiker, David Reilly, Edith Reimers, Starr Reina, Karl Reiner, Mark Reinhart, Barbara Reis, Tressa Reisetter, William Reisman, Arthur Reitemeier, Douglas Reiter, Robert Reldan, Shirley Remore, Jerry Rempp, Joe Rendace, Frank Renick, Jackie Rennick, Belita Rennicks, Mike Renquist, Harold Renshaw, Deane Renshaw, Cecil Replogle, Ronald Repp, Mark Reps, Jeffrey Resnick, Dianne Reum, Chris Rexrode, Michael Reyes, Renaldo Reyes, Angelo Reynolds, Donald Reynolds, Lisa Reynolds, John Reynolds, Billie Reynolds, William Reynolds, Sheila Reynolds, Michael Reynolds, Lisa Reynolds, Billie Reynolds, Scott Rezendes, Lynn Rhoderick, Roy Rhodes, Alex Rhodes, Larry Rhodes, Catherine Ricchetti, Christopher Ricci, Ottone Riccio, Dolores Riccio, Patricia Riccobono, Brian Rice, Iris Rice, Karen Rice, Sheila Rice, James Rice, Marc Rice, Sidney Rich, Clara Rich, Sidney Rich, Jon Richard, Paul Richard, Sarah Richard, David Richards, Dan Richards, Hyrum Richards, Layton Richards, Arthur Richards, Yvonne Richards, Dan Richards, Jonnie Richardson, Ernest Richardson, Randal Richardson, Charlie Richardson, Ruth Richardson, Roy Richardson, Patricia Richardson, Joubert Richardson, John Richardson, Dorthea Richardson, Angela Richardson, Karin Richardson, Robert Riche, Steven Richey, Clark Richey, Eric Richie, Daniel Richmond, James Richmond, Martin Richmond, Rhonda Richmond, Susan Richmond, Jeffrey Richmond, Martha Richter, Michael Rickett, Jackie Rickett, Marlene Ricketts,

Andrew Rickis, Michael Ricksecker, Alessandra Rico, Peter Riddle, Laura Riddle, Donna Riddlebarger, Sharon Riddley-D'Entremont, James Ridgway, Melanie Ridner, Ann Riedling, Alan Riehl, William Rieser, Bryan Riess, Michael Rietzel, William Rigby, Christopher Rigby, Robert Riggs, Robbie Riley, Jose Riley, Robbie Riley, David Riley, John Riley, Thomas Riley, Jennifer Rinas, David Rineberg, Karen Rinehart, Sherry Riner, Frank Rinker, Donald Ripley, Kimberly Ripley, Donald Ripley, Kimberly Ripley, Edwin Risberg, Tilak Rishi, Scott Ristau, Otis Ritch, Wilma Ritt, Timothy Ritter, Marlene Ritter, Janet Ritter, Gerald Ritter, Joyce Ritz, Mark Rivard, Louise Riveiro-Mitchell, Carmen Rivera, Jason Rivera, Gwendolyn Rivers, Sherman Rivers, Tammie Rizan, Cynthia Rizzo, John Rizzo, Philip Rizzo, Carol Roach, Joe Roady, Philip Roane, Jackie Roark, Louise Roarty, Martha Robach, James Robar, Wilford Robbins, David Robbins, Wilford Robbins, Michael Robbins, Fred Robbins, Dorothy Robbins, Dean Robbins, Thomas Robbs, Katrina Roberson, Patrice Robert, Theresa Robert, Mervyn Roberts, Glenn Roberts, Thomas Roberts, Clifford Roberts, Sharon Roberts, Kelly Roberts, Jack Roberts, Gwynn Roberts, Susan Roberts, Joan Robertson, Martha Robertson, Susanne Robertson, Lucinda Robertson, David Robertson, Cindee Robertson, Christopher Robertson, Marion Robertson, Michael Robey, James Robinette, Hugh Robinson, John Robinson, Laureen Robinson, Patricia Robinson, Janice Robinson, Emery Robinson, Barbara Robinson, James Robinson, William Robison, Jerry Robson, Richard Roby, Brian Rochester, Elvy Rochester, George Rockwell, Paul Rockwell, William Roddey, Clyde Rodgers, Edwin Rodgers, Janet Rodgers, Clyde Rodgers, Audrey Rodriguez, Rene Rodriguez, Virginia Rodriguez, Zachary Rodriguez, Thea Rodriguez, Juan Rodriguez, Felix Rodriguez, Lauren Rodriguez, Juan Rodriguez, Gerald Roe, Shirley Roe, Dawn Roeder, Mary Roelkey, James Rogers, Michelle Rogers, William Rogers, Kathleen Rogers, Joseph Rogers, Bryan Rogers, Michel Rogers, Willie Rogers, Gary Rogers, Esther Rogers, Elizabeth Rogers, Beth Rogers, Anthony Rogers, Angela Rogers, Jim Rogers, Melodie Rogers, Charles Rohde, Robert Rohloff, Christine Rohmeyer, Jerry Rohr, Thomas Rohrer, Susan Rojas, Louie Rojas, Susan Rojas, Lorenda Rojas, George Roland, Martha Roland, Matthew Roland, Norella Rolek, Susan Roller, Lynna Roller, Christopher Rollier, Anne Rollins, April Rollins, David Rollins, Javier Roman, Gilbert Roman, Bill Romanelli, Michelle Romano, Marilynn Romano, Danielle Romao,

Maria Romero, Rachel Romero, Justin Romine, John Romine, Gregory Romines, John Rommel, Lorenzo Romney, Craig Rondinone, Edmund Rondo, Ela Ronen, Shirley Roney, Debi Ronholt, Janie Rood, Peggy Rooney, Maureen Rooseboom, Robert Rootes, James Roper, Violet Roper, Elizabeth Rorke, DeAnna Rorrer, Roberto Rosas, Remo Rosati, Corinna Rose, Emma Rose, Mary Rose, Phyllis Rose, Robert Rose, Wesley Rose, Steven Rose, Bruce Roseberry, Dinah Roseberry, Joshua Roseman, David Rosenberg, John Rosenberger, Carl Rosenfeld, Gregory Rosenquist, Janet Rosenquist, Katherine Rosenthal, Ben Rosenthal, Dorothy Rosenthal, Jeffrey Rosin, Hannah Rosner, John Ross, Barry Ross, Robert Ross, Barbra Ross, Ross Ross, Mary Ross, Jeffrey Ross, David Ross, Angela Ross, Dennis Ross, Frank Ross, Jeanie Ross, Lionel Ross, Rachel Rossano, Sherry Rossier-Watson, Judith Roswell, Katie Roten, Robert Roth, Katrina Rothra, Clifford Rothwell, Anthony Rotondi, Jessica Roubal, Maisha Rounds, Wendy Rountree, Jeanette Roupe, Norman Rourke, Katherine Rouse, Richard Roush, John Roush, Peter Rousseau, Barbara Rowan, Miriam Rowan, Christopher Rowan, Carrie Rowe, Jamie Rowe, Patricia Rowe, Harley Rowe, Jamie Rowe-VanDyke, Norma Rowland, Tim Rowland, Kaththea Rowland, Cecil Rowlett, Richard Rowlett, Seth Rowley, Charlotte Roy, Marina Roy, Thomas Roy, Sara Roy, Dennis Royer, Summer Royston, Eric Ruark, Margaret Ruben, Patrick Ruberti, Fred Rubino, Carlos Rubio, Webster Ruble, Linda Rucker, Gregory Rudd, Walter Rudd, Ronald Rude, Joseph Ruder, Roger Rudesill, Shelia Rudesill, Grace Rudolph, Catherine Rudy, Sarah Rudy, Thomas Ruffin, Sara Ruffini, Matthew Rugoyi, Shirley Ruh-Booker, Catherine Ruhfel, Kathryn Ruiz, Cliff Ruminer, Clifton Ruminer, Patrick Rummery, Barbara Rumson, Irene Rundell, David Rundle, Ricky Runnels, Gary Runyan, Peggy Rupe, Stephanie Rupp, Joanne Ruscella, Terry Ruscin, Charles Rush, Derek Rush, Betty Rushford, Jesse Rushton, Linda Rusmisel, Monica Russell, Sandra Russell, Stuart Russell, Angelina Russell, Sherry Russell, Mildred Russell, Louie Russell, Joel Russell, James Russell, Jack Russell, Deborah Russell, David Russell, Sandra Russell, Matthew Russo, William Russo, Anthony Russo, Daniel Rustin, Melanie Rutan, Jody Rutherford, Paul Rutherford, Angie Rutherford, Joe Rutland, Kelli Rutledge, Gregory Rutledge, Jason Rutledge, Shirley Rutter, Joy Rutter, Field Ruwe, Danielle Ryan, Joachim Ryan, Thomas Ryan, Michael Ryan, Kristan Ryan, Joachim Ryan, Henry Ryan, Helena

Ryan, Marie Ryba, Rick Rzeszewski, Barbara Saber, Ponn Sabra, Vincent Saccardi, Cornelia Saceanu, Angela Sachs, John Sackman, Irwin Sadetsky, Micah Sadigh, Louise Saenz, Larry Sager, Amy Saiauski, Ella Sailor, Dixie Sain, Maurice Saint-Amand, Raymond Saint-Fort, Susan Sakelos, Diane Saks, Stephen Salamon, Jacobo Salazar, Michael Salazar, Jose Salazar, John Sales, Michael Sales, Marie Salik, Stephanie Salisbury, Nicole Sallad, Steven Salmon, Ronald Salter, Linda Salter, Elizabeth Salton, Wilhelmina Salvatore, Adam Salviani, Charlotte Salyer, Evette Samaan, Sally Samczyk, Timothy Sammet, Gordon Sammon, James Samples, Leslie Sampson, Donald Samsel, Robin Samuel, Elizabeth Sanchez, Martin Sanchez, Michelle Sanchez, Jose Sanchez, Deon Sanders, Douglas Sanders, Judith Sanders, Carol Sanders, Teresa Sanders, Brenda Sandoval, Bre Sandoval, Charles Sands, Vincent Sandstoe, Sigurd Sandstrom, Roger Sanford, Claudia SanLuis, Dorothy Sannes, James Sansing, Eva Santamaria, Raymond Santi, Angel Santiago, Edwin Santiago, Cinsearae Santiago, Pamela Santini, Vito Santoro, Pauline Santos, Raul Santoyo, Oladayo Sanusi, Samantha Sarandos, Robert Sargeant, Anna Sargent, Charles Sasser, Sandra Sasser, Janet Saugstad, Nicole Saunders, Robert Saunders, Linda Saunders, Judith Saurel, Michel Sauret, Margaret Savage, Mark Savage, Myrtice Savage, Anthony Savageau, Angelo Saverino, Mary Savidge, Elmer Savilla, Naim Sawaged, Karen Sawchuk, Ian Sawicki, Ann Sawyer, Flora Sawyer, Stephanie Sawyer, Eddy Sawyers, Mary Saxe, David Saxon, Charles Sayers, Joseph Scalia, Nancy Scandlen, David Scarborough, Damein Scarborough, Rodolfo Scarfalloto, Peter Scariano, Howard Schack, KarenAnn Schaefer, Teresa Schaeffer, Tom Schafer, Sean Schaffer, CindyLou Schaffer, Randi Schalet, James Schanne, Andrew Scharr, John Schasny, Carolyn Scheidies, Dona Schell, Crystal Schelle, Helen Schenning, Joseph Scherffius, N. Schey, Daniel Schiappa, Jared Schickling, Sarah Schiess, John Schiller, Linda Schillig, Lisa Schilling, Kay Schlagel, Robert Schlegel, Kenneth Schlehuber, Boris Schleinkofer, Mary Schlemmer, Donald Schliep, Claudia Schloemp, Chaya Schlussel, Beverly Schmeler, Robert Schmid, Dorothy Schmidt, Duane Schmidt, Sheila Schmidt, Donna Schmidt, Scott Schmidt, Jodi Schmitt, Mark Schmitz, Dante Schmoeker, Christie Schmutzler, Nathan Schnaper, Harry Schneider, Edward Schneider, Alfred Schneider, Timothy Schneider, Richard Schneider, Merry Schneider, Lori Schneider, Janet

Schneider, Arthur Schneider, Lester Schoen, Jean Schoenmaker, Paula Schofield, Patrick Scholes, Ronald Scholze, Amanda Schomas, David Schonfelder, Shirley Schooler, Brian Schooley, John Schooley, Kenneth Schott, Barbara Schrachta, Linda Schramm, Marvin Schrebe, Carol Schriver, Barbara Schrodt, Jane Schroeder, Jarrod Schrunk, Richard Schubert, Catherine Schuett, Jo Schuh, Lawrence Schulenberg, Kathy Schultz, Jacqueline Schumacher, Benjamin Schumaker, August Schupp, Steven Schusler, Allen Schut, Orrin Schwab, Benjamin Schwalb, Donna Schwalbe, Michael Schwartz, Jonathan Schwartz, Thomas Schwartz, Nancy Schwartz, Leonard Schwartz, Kimberly Schwartzmiller, George Schwarz, Robert Schweitzer, Sarah Schwersenska, Bob Schwinger, Vincent Scirocco, William Sciuti, Damon Scobey, David Scott, Doug Scott, Rafael Scott, Leslie Scott, Robert Scott, Roger Scott, Teresa Scott, William Scott, Bill Scott, Kathy Scott, Nicole Scott, Rafael Scott, Justin Scott,

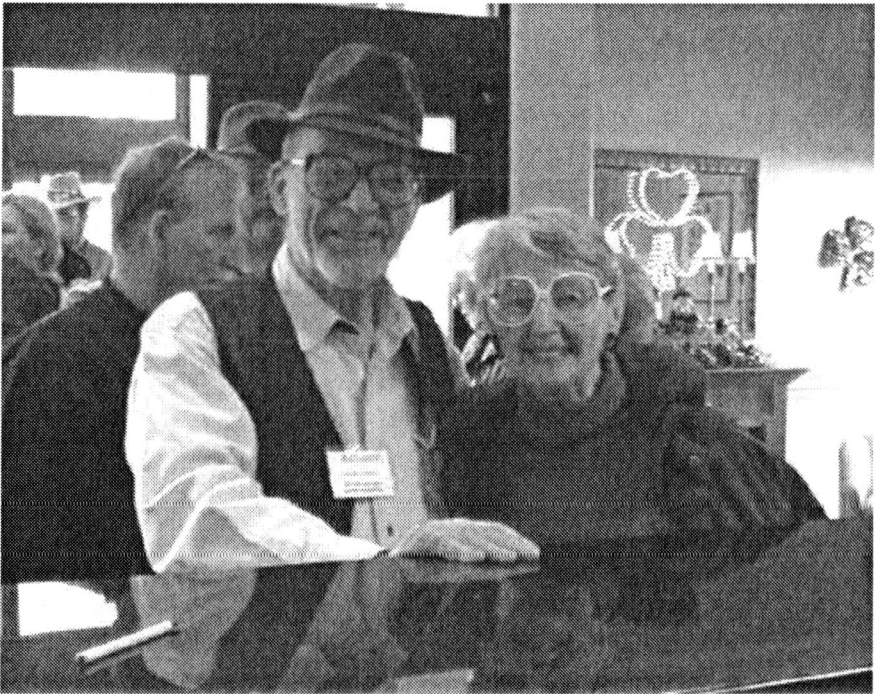

Patricia Scott, Odell Scott, Alan Scott, Andrea Scott, Azalea Scott, Barbara Scott, Beverly Scott, Michael Scott, Billy Scott, Donna Scott, Doug Scott, Gerald Scott, Isaac Scott, Jeremy Scott, Kevin Scott, Matthew Scott, Ray Scraggs, Fred Scribner, Catherine Scudder, Jeffrey Scudder, Brian Scully, David Seaburn, Claude Sealey, James Seaman, Terri Searcy, Veronica Searles, Robert Sears, Don Costa Seawell, Joe Seay, Timothy Sebastian, Marlene Sebastian, Mitch Sebourn, Mitchell Sebourn, Kemal Sedick, Jennifer Seest, Michaela Sefler, Justin Segal, Michael Segedy, Nancy Segovia, Derrell Seguine, Hilary Seher, Tim Seidl, Tina Seigley, Michael Seiler, Edward Seiler, Ehud Sela, Debra Self, James Seligman, Cheryl Sellers, Steven Sellers, Azri-el Sellers, Janiesha Sellers, Fawn Sells, Maryann Selway, James Selwood, Jeremiah Semien, Raymond Semlow, Jolie Semper, Audrey Sennett, Johnny Senter, Rod Senter, Michael Serafin, Pamela Serrilla, Anthony Session, Richard Sestili, Joyce Settle, Cozette Sevier, George Sewell, Ken Sewell, Edward Seyforth, Ashley Seymon, David Seymon, Francis Seymour, Dina Seymour, Vanessa Sgroi, Dewey Shaak, Rahim Shabazz, Alexis Shabazz-Fentress, Hilmer Shackelford, Mary Shackelford, Melissa Shaffer, Mark Shaffer, Richard Shaffer, Tsoltim Shakabpa, Patrick Shanahan, Kathryn Shanahan, Mindy Shank, Charles Shanks, Ronnie Shanks, Danny Shanks, Paul Shanley, David Shannon, Faye Shannon, Elizabeth Shannon, Barbara Shannon, Brigette Shapiro, Brian Sharkey, Raj Sharma, Thomas Sharon, Gaylen Sharp, Penny Sharp, Jennifer Sharp, Bonnie Sharpe, Alexander Shaumyan, Cheryl Shaver, Brianna Shaver, Rachel Shaw, Charmone Shaw, Jesse Shaw, Sharon Shaw, Gregory Shaw, Scott Shaw, Ronald Shaw, Keith Shaw, Jean Shaw, Jasa Shaw, Denise Shaw, Donna Shaw, Kevin Shawda, Marilyn Shea, Deanne Shead, Laurie Shear, Robert Shearer, Stephen Shearer, John Shearer, Wendy Sheedy, Daniel Sheehan, Tom Sheehan, Thomas Sheehan, Eileen Sheehan, Kevin Sheehan, Jason Sheets, John Sheirer, Anna Shekhtman, Melissa Sheldon, Valerie Shelleby, Joseph Shelton, Mack Shelton, Stacy Shelton, Charles Shelton, Kathleen Shelton, Carolyn Shelton, Ronald Shepherd, Aaron Shepherd, Ronald Shepherd, Susan Sheppard, Jacqueline Shepperson, Sue Shepple, Michael Sherer, Daniel Sheridan, Debra Sherman, Joy Sherman, Carl Sherman, Bradley Sherman, Joseph Sherman, Richard Sherrer, Michael Sherriff, Ronda Sherrill, Jura Sherwood, Donald Sherwood, Jura Sherwood, Andrew Shields,

Kathleen Shields, Lewis Shields, Raymond Shields, John Shiffert, Alvin Shifflett, Michael Shinavier, Paul Shine, Gary Shipley, Yelizaveta Shipovskiy, Saeed Shirazi, Gloria Shirley, Melissa Shirley, Patricia Shirley, Ted Shiskin, Dmitry Shlapentokh, Jeannette Shockley, Judith Shoemaker-Hill, Laila Sholtz-Ames, Donna Shook, Jacqueline Shor, Amy Shore, Clara Shore, Larry Short, Michael Short, Jeanette Short, David Shortess, Retha Shortridge, Eron Shosteck, Charles Showell, Della Showunmi, Meghann Shrader, Nancy Shrader, Marvin Shreve, Steven Shrewsbury, Gordon Shriver, Ernest Shubird, Sylvia Shults, Trixie Shults, Mary Shumaker, George Shuman, Georgia Shurr, Lydia Shutter, Christina Shyver-Plank, Michelle Sibiga, Christina Siders, Donald Siegel, Carl Siemon, Nancy Siemsen, Derek Signore, Kristinn Sigtryggsson, Meghan Sirila, Anita Sikes, Nathan Sikes, Abhishek Sikhwal, John Silberman, Jamie Silcox, Richard Silk, Scott Siller, Carlos Silva, Howard Silverberg, Esther Silverman, Jacqueline Silvestri, John Silvi, Robert Silviera, Donahue Silvis, Penny Silvius, Alastair Sim, Keegan Simeral, Charles Simeral, Octavia Simien, Harry Simmons, Bill Simmons, Gloria Simmons, Roger Simmons, Cynthia Simmons, Jewel Simmons, Mark Simmons, Derek Simmons, Chester Simmons, C. Simmons, Donald Simmons, Harold Simmons, Robert Simms, Ernesto Simon, Sheila Simon, Lynn Simon, Alan Simon, Jacquelyn Simon, David Simonson, Tony Simpson, Sue Simpson, Julian Simpson, Yvonne Simpson, Ginger Simpson, Scott Simpson, Molly Simpson, Roz'L Simpson, Carolie Simpson, Taryn Simpson, Larry Sims, Barbara Sims, Calvin Sims, Abdul Sinaid, Aaron Sinay, Michael Sinclair, William Sinclair, Linda Sine, Jesse Singer, Jonathan Singer, Kelly Singer, Jagdish Singh, Sarina Singhi, Ralph Singleton, Kenneth Singleton, Harry Singleton, Margaret Sink, Denise Sinn, Larry Sinnott, Tracy Sipp, John Sippel, Louis Sisk, Jan-Roger Sitaric, George Sites, Evgeny Sjubin, Pamela Skaggs, Ruth Skaggs, Jennifer Skandarsky, Kevin Skelley, Philip Skelton, Donald Skillin, Peter Skillman, Scott Skinner, Amanda Skinner, Cynthia Skinner, Sidney Skipper-Blomquist, AJ Skirboll, Ana Skopec, Quentin Skrabec, David Skramstad, Daniel Skudstad, Nancy Slaff, George Slagley, Keith Slater, Brian Slater, Elaine Slater, Christopher Slates, Stephen Slattery, Guy Slaughter, Netfa Slaughter, Bryan Slaughter, Gary Slavin, Linda Slebodnik, Carole Sletta, Charles Sloan, David Sloan, Karel Sloane, Jerzyna Slomczynska, William Slykas, Robert Smart, Marie Smart, Judith

Sment, Joanne Smet, Ephraim Smiley, William Smillie, Jacob Smit, Sheldon Smith, Sherrie Smith, Stephen Smith, Susan Smith, Troy Smith, Shannon Smith, Ronald Smith, Meighan Smith, David Smith, Richard Smith, William Smith, Russell Smith, Diane Smith, Penni Smith, Patsy Smith, Pamela Smith, Natalie Smith, Misty Smith, Mellie Smith, Melanie Smith, Mark Smith, Marilyn Smith, Marcia Smith, Russell Smith, Stephen Smith, Yolanda Smith, Steven Smith, Patricia Smith, Barbara Smith, Roger Smith, Ron Smith, Nancye Smith, Charity Smith, Virginia Smith, Michele Smith, Thomas Smith, Warren Smith, Marc Smith, Lori Smith, Ralph Smith, Letha Smith, Leslie Smith, Judy Smith, Jeffrey Smith, Jeanne Smith, James Smith, Horane Smith, Douglas Smith, Donald Smith, Tim Smith, Judy Smith, Cheryl Smith, Francis Smith, Eric Smith, Elaine Smith, Dr.Howard Smith, Douglas Smith, Doris Smith, Diane Smith, David Smith, Darryl Smith, Darlene Smith, Damien Smith, Gene Smith, Christopher Smith, Blair Smith, Charlotte Smith, Charles Smith,

Carolyn Smith, Brian Smith, Brad Smith, Lori Smith, Billy Smith, Walter Smith, Alvie Smith, Alton Smith, Alison Smith, Courtney Smith, Joy Smith, Annie Smith, Lisa Smith, Leslie Smith, Lee Smith, Laura Smith, K.W. Smith, George Smith, Juanita Smith, John Smith, Hilda Smith, Harriet Smith, Judy Smith, Henry Smith, John Smith, Hollie Smith, Horane Smith, Irish Smith, Jacquelyn Smith, James Smith, Henry Smith, James Smith, Jeanne Smith, Jennifer Smith, Jacqueline Smith, Quinton Smithers, Marsha Smolev, Gary Smothers, Emilie Smyth, Amy Sneeden, George Snell, David Snell, Christine Snider, Judith Snider, Richard Snider, Elmer Snow, Tina Snowdon, James Snyder, Kathi Snyder, Douglas Soat, Tammy Sobeck, John Sobiek, Tanya Sodders, Sophie Soil, Janeen Solberg, Lyle Solland, Leonard Solo, Nathan Solomon, Frank Solorzano, Lynn Solte, Von Soltwedel, Laura Somers, Alicia Sommer, Steven Sommers, Albert Som-Pimpong, Chuanzhe Song, Nancy Sonneman, Marcia Sonnier, William Sorg, Virgil Sorge, Peter Soszek, Peter Soteres, John Souppa, Glenn South, Marvin Southcott, Callan Souza, Cary Sove, Elizabeth Sowa, Yutaka Sowa, Lori Sowell, Malcolm Sowells, Ned Spake, John Spalding, Patricia Spanedda, John Spanek, Daniel Spangenberg, Gary Spangler, Christopher Spanke, William Spann, Ronald Spano, Bianca Sparks, Delores Sparks, Joanne Sparks, Nancy Sparks, Matthew Sparks, Leslie Speakes, David Spear, Barbara Speers, Robert Spelleri, George Spence, Kevin Spencer, John Spencer, Andrew Spencer, Robert Spencer, Patsy Spencer, Marcella Spencer, Treva Spencer-Dupree, Raymond Spendley, Jacob Spiegelhauer, Jason Spielman, Sander Spin, Mary Spink, Matthew Spitzmueller, Mark Spivey, Jessica Spray, Scott Sprecher, Barbara Spring, Kenneth Spring, Patricia Springer, Dan Sproul, Eric Sproull, William Spruell, George Squires, Larry Squires, Timothy Squires, Kavita Sriram, Robert Ssebugwawo, Lise St.Amant, Mary St.John, Robert St.Thomas, Elizabeth Staadt, Richard Stabile, Kathleen Stacey, Roseann Stachowiak, Rosemarie Stadler, Evan Stafford, Shannon Stafford, William Stage, David Stahl, Debbie Stahl, Jeffrey Stahlman, Cynthia Stahrr, Harold Stall, Linda Stallworth, Kenneth Stalnaker, Alexis Stamatikos, Steve Stamatis, Crystal Stanczak, Mary Standard, Dolores Stanfield, Shirley Stanford, Teresa Stanisha, Helen Stanphill, Ginger Stanwick, Darlene Stapp, Emerald Stara, Jason Starinieri, Kenneth Stark, Thomas Stark, Terry Starker, Teresa Starkey, Kimberly Starks, Robert Starkson, Janet Starling, Edward

Starr, Alexis Starr, Melle Starsen, Martin States, Ryan Stattelman, Kevin Staul, Carolyn Stearns, James Stearns, Kelly Steed, Nancy Steedle, Jeanne Steele, Vageehe Steele, Jeanne Steele, Vageehe Steele, Edvald Stef nsson, Petur Stefansson, Kimberly Steffek, Darla Stege, Christine Steger, Erika Steiger, Allan Stein, Ellen Stein, William Stein, Ryan Steinbeck, John Steinbrook, Sandra Steiner, Emil Steiner, Carl Stekelenburg, Timothy Stelly, Rainulf Stelzmann, Nicholas Stember, Steven Stender, Karen Stensland, T. Stenzelbarton, Charles Stephens, Donald Stephens, William Stephens, Donald Stephens, Diane Stephenson, Leigh Stephenson, T.Matthew Stepp, Bruce Steringer, Martha Sterling, Jack Sterling, Milton Stern, Sandra Stern, Demetria Sternberg, Thomas Sterner Howe, John Steslow, James Stevens, Kim Stevens, Judith Stevens, Joan Stevens, Regina Stevens, Michael Stevens, Larry Stevens, Henry Stevens, Daniel Stevens, Anthony Stevens, Judy Stevens, Paul Stevenson, Peggy Stevenson, Shaun Stevenson, Francis Stevich, Jimmy Stewart, Anthony Stewart, Charlotte Stewart, Shirlund Stewart, Virgina Stewart, Paulette Stewart, Robert Stewart, James Stewart, Cathy Stewart, Margaret Stewart, L. Stewart, Kathleen Stewart, Katherine Stewart, Edna Stewart, Christy Stewart, Cherry Stewart, Charlotte Stewart, Robert Stewart, William Stewart, Ralph Stidham, Bob Stidham, Michael Stidmon, Lucie Stigler, Daniel Stiles, Lisa Stiles, Ron Stiles, Timothy Stiles, Pauline Stillman, Janice Stillwell, Norma Stilwell, Kristi Stingley, Margaret Stitely, Tiffany Stitt-Herbert, Kevin Stockton, Nicholas Stockton, Peter Stockwell, Scot Stockwell, Jeffrey Stoddard, Shirley Stoeff, Dolores Stohler, Angela Stokes, Toby Stolar, Michael Stoller, Sally Stoltzenburg, Kathleen Stone, William Stone, Adrian Stone, Thomas Stone, David Stone, Charlene Stone, Scot Stone, Linda Stone, Brian Stoner, Alexander Stoops, Ryan Store, Rebecca Storey, Stephanie Storey-Morant, Kaitlin Storme, George Story, Marlene Story, Dr. Stout, Marian Stout, Dorrence Stovall, Carol Stover, Elmer Stover, Vicky Stowers, Margaret Stragier, Mickey Strange, Thomas Strangman, David Straub, Michael Streed, Brian Street, Linda Strength, Eric Stricker, Fred Strickert, Michael Strickland, Morris Striplin, Ashley Stripling, Brian Strobel, Craig Strohm, Rachel Strong, Benjamin Strong, Jessica Strong, Rachel Strong, Julie Strong, Howard Stroud, Sara Stroud, Armond Stroud, A.E. Stroud, Kathy Stroup, Cindy Strouthos, Stan Struble, Orlo Strunk, Irene Strybosch, Karen Stubblefield, Elizabeth Stuefen,

LeNore Stumpf, James Stumpo, William Sturdevant, Tina Stutts, Raymond Styles, Gary Suffern, Amo Sulaiman, Stephen Sulik, Stephen Sulkey, John Sullivan, Scott Sullivan, Jean Sullivan, Edwin Sullivan, Sherri Sullivan, Harvey Sullivan, Donna Sullivan, Deborah Sullivan, Carolyn Sullivan, Patrick Sullivan, Scott Sumerall, Edwin Summer, Jena Summer, Edwin Summer, Jena Summer, Rebecca Sundberg, Richard Sunderland, Amy Sunkamaitis, Lois Sunley, Claude Surface, Vicka Surovtsov, Kevin Sussman, Gavin Sutherland, Willis Sutter, Tracy Sutterer, Alfred Suttles, Donald Sutton, Cynthia Sutton, Niels-Alf Svensen, Melissa Swaim, Richard Swan, Robert Swanepoel, Jahnn Swanker-Gibson, Helga Swanson, Tyler Swartz, Chad Swayden, Julie Swayze, Adrienne Swearingen, Eloise Sweatman, Marnie Swedberg, Toni Sweeney, Margaret Sweet, Joanne Sweet, Debra Sweet, Joanne Sweet, Margaret Sweet, Dona Swenk, Brooke Swenson, Eric Swenson, Peggye Swenson, Maria Swiatek, Joseph Swicegood, Kenneth Swick, Philip Swift, Michael Swiger, Christopher Swile, Clareatha Swilley, Julian Swinbourne, Lurma Swinney, Stephanie Swinton, Nicole Swisher, Kelly Swisher, Nicole Swisher, Asrar Syed, Sofia Syed, David Syfert, Jana Sylvera, Lawrence Sylvest, Thomas Szarka, Stanley Szczecina, Mark Szekely, Edward Szymczak, Annette Taft, Sarah Tagert, Joseph Taglioli, Gregory Taillon, Kurt Takamine, Dale Talbert, Steve Talbot, Marti Talbott, Marcyle Taliaferro, Rosetta Talley, Sheila Talley, Suzanne Tamberrino, Luke Tamu, Jason Tanamor, Net-Hetep Ta'Nesert, Jennifer Tanis, Jack Tanner, Michael Tanner, Miriam Tanner, Patricia Tanner, Vincent Tanner, Richard Tanos, Alan Tansley, Veronica Tapia, Cami Tapley, Michael Tapp, Debra Tarantino, Cecilia Taranto, Angelique Tarbox, Wendi Tarlton, Joyce Tarpley, Lorraine Tartasky, Ronald Tarter, Carmelo Tartivita, Ed Tasca, Jules Tasca, Rod Tasker, Robert Tassmer, Joanne Tate, Anthony Tatossian, Roberta Tatreau, Kenneth Tatum, Sam Tatum, Danna Tayer, Simon Taylor, Somer Taylor, Susan Taylor, Terry Taylor, B. Taylor, Richard Taylor, Rhonda Taylor, Bruce Taylor, David Taylor, Joyce Taylor, Kelly Taylor, Paul Taylor, Terry Taylor, William Taylor, Anjanee' Taylor, Joe Taylor, Lance Taylor, Phillip Taylor, David Taylor, Marguerite Taylor, Angela Taylor, Carol Taylor, Chadwick Taylor, Claudia Taylor, Daniela Taylor, Paul Taylor, David Taylor, Geoff Taylor, Heather Taylor, James Taylor, John Taylor, Kimberly Taylor, Laurie Taylor, LaVerne Taylor, Lori Taylor, Marguerite Taylor, Darrin Taylor, Verl Taysom, Gypsey

Teague, Mark Tee, Frederick Tegeler, Sandra Temperley, Leonida Teohari, Debra TerHark, Toby Terrar, Doreen Terrarosa, Donna Terres, John Terris, Bobbye Terry, Spencer Terry, Bobbye Terry, Clint Terry, Sherry Terry, Tina Terry-Bails, Rovena Tesfaye, Cody Tesnow, Carmen Tesser, Ryan Tessier, Michael Tessmer, Christina Tetreault, Jenny Thacker, Brian Thames, Theresa Tharp, Alex Thatcher, Steven Thaxton, Remy Theberge, Joseph Thek, Sonja Theodore, Joe Theriot, Michael Thessen, Arlene Thibault, Roger Thibault, Shanice Thibedeau, George Thirteen, Gary Thomann, Samantha Thomas, Wanda Thomas, Carol Thomas, Linda Thomas, Coleen Thomas, Clark Thomas, Pamala Thomas, Darryl Thomas, Daisy Thomas, Anthony Thomas, William Thomas, Rudy Thomas, Cheryl Thomas, Andrea Thomas, Kitina Thomas, Lisa Thomas, Michael Thomas, Nicole Thomas, Nyal Thomas, Pamala Thomas, Phil Thomas, Christopher Thomasel, Lawrence Thomason, Shirley Thomison, Richard Thompson, Teresa Thompson, Richard Thompson, Ruth Thompson, Sovella Thompson, Stacey Thompson, Susan Thompson, Terri Thompson, Virgin Thompson, Michael Thompson, Casey Thompson, Edgar Thompson, Shirley Thompson, Paul Thompson, Terri Thompson, David Thompson, Casey Thompson, Clarence Thompson, Niccolous Thompson, David Thompson, Debra Thompson, Eddie Thompson, Hallie Thompson, Jennifer Thompson, Julius Thompson, Kathleen Thompson, Michael Thompson, Michelle Thompson, Betty Thompson, Jeff Thompson, Carl Thor, Christopher Thordarson, Claude Thormalen, Dustin Thorn, Michael Thornburg, RoseMary Thorne, Jesse Thornsen, Robert Thornton, Jill Thornton, Thomas Thorstenson, Sam Threefoot, R. Thull, Robert Thuman, August Thurmer, Gwandine Thurmond, Earlie Tibbs, Jerry Tice, Brenna Tidwell, John Tieso, Kim Tiggler-Coggins, Bridget Tighe, Karol Tiler, Darryl Tiller, Jennifer Tillery, Lawrence Tilley, Belle Tilley, Lawrence Tilley, Belle Tilley, Linda Tilston, Jerry Tilton, Terry Tilton, Debora Timas, James Timbers, Mary Tinney, Rachel Tinon, Clifton Tinsley, JuLee Tinsley, Amey Tippett, Donald Tipton, Laura Titcomb, Oscar Tobar, Kimberly Tobias, Jason Todaro, Timothy Todd, Candace Toft, Joseph Tofuri, Laura Tolchinsky, Sean Tolley, Karen Tolley, Jesse Tollison, William Tolliver, James Tomaszek, Barry Tomkins, Daniel Tomkinson-Fletcher, Alfred Tompkins, Beatrice Toms, Linda Toney, Mary Tony, Michelle Toogood, William Toombs, Margie Toone, James Torgerson, Abigail Tormanen, Brian Tornatore, Nell Torone, Alicia

Torres, Luana Torres, Elijah Toten, Emil Toth, Kathryn Totten, Violet Towe, Evelyn Towler, Margaret Towne, Bette Towns, Stephen Towns, Brenda Townsend, Rick Townsend, Thomas Towslee, Michael Tozer, Thomas Tozer, Julie Tracht-Tinnermeier, John Train, Samantha Trammell, Noelle Tramontana, Arais Trapp, David Trapp, Jon Traustason, Clayton Travis, Jeffrey Trawford, Angie Treadaway, Christopher Treagus, Alyssa Treff, Ellen Tremiti, Libero Tremonti, Rose Trenbeath, Christy Trent, Arthur Treptow, Doug Trettin, Daniel Trevino, Roger Trexler, Karen Tribble, Coarey Trim, Samuel Trippi, Susan Troendle, Carol Troestler, Michael Troglin, Steven Troncale, Clifford Trottier, Karin Troutman, Thomas Truax, Jason Trudeau, Michelle True, Don Truitt, Jonathan Trumbull, Richard Trusick, David Trustman, Eyrun Tryggvadottir, Ken Tsang, Brea Tschopp, John Tsilimparis, Pavel Tsupruk, Carolyn Tubbs, Don Tucker,

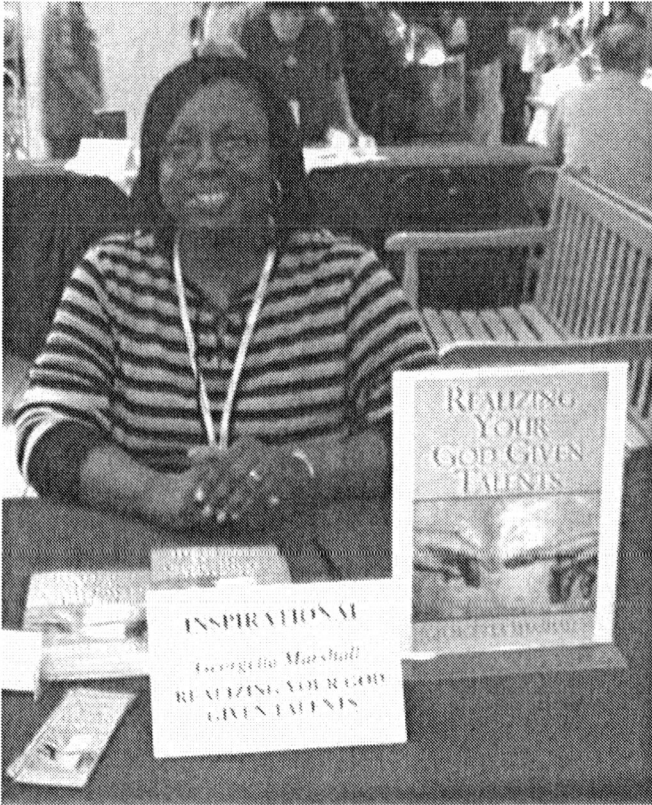

Heather Tucker, Ida Tucker, Julian Tucker, Tracy Tucker, Anniano Tumaliuan, Miriam Tumeo, Omar Tunau, Yelena Tunkel, Darrell Tunsel, Kristina Tunstall, David Turell, Cynthia Turk, Laraine Turner, Taura Turner, Diane Turner, Robert Turner, Tracy Turner, Michael Turner, Melvin Turner, Martin Turner, Kenneth Turner, Karen Turner, Johnny Turner, John Turner, Erin Turner, Deborah Turner, Karen Tuttle, Raymond Tuttle, Gerald Twardowski, Anisha Twitchell, Mary Twitty, Pier Tyler, Amanda Tyler, Cheryl Tyler, Christopher Tyner, Claudia Tynes, Nathan Tyree, Terrence Tyree, David Tyrrell, Wycliffe Tyson, Kelvie Tyus, Nicolaos Tzannes, Victoria Udo, Paul Uduma, Xina Uhl, Paul Uhls, Tim Uhr, Donna Ullom, Steven Ulmen, Kaitlyn Ulmer, Debra Ulrich, Joe Ulrich, Marshall Umpleby, Mary Umpleby, Suzanne Underwood, Maurice Unger, Scott Ungerecht, Daniel Upchurch, Ruth Urich, Arlene Uslander, Mychal Utecht, Karla Utrup, Thomas Utts, June Vaccaro, Chris Vaillancourt, Moisey Vainer, Donna Valdez, Thorunn Valdimarsdottir, Carlos Valdivia, Bethany Vale, Gabriele Valente, Ralph Valentino, Georgia Valenzuela, Roy Valiant, Drew Valla, Mark Valle, Riccardo Valley, Elizabeth Vallone, Randell VanAlst, Dorothea VanArnam, Jim vanBuren, Dani VanBuskirk, Samantha Vance, Valerie Vance, Samantha Vance, Adrienne Van Coeverden-de Groot, Helen VanDaly, Marie-Rose VandeEynde, Marjorie Vandenbree, Richard VanDerBeets, Jackie vanderHorst-Buckley, Melanie Vanderkolk, Karen Vanderlaan, James VanderLinden, Roy VanDerLinden, Helen Vandervort, Robert VanDeventer, Janyce VanEs, Bryon VanFleet, Paul VanHeuklom, Clinton VanHook, Ray VanHorn, Todd Vanisacker, Jennifer VanMassenhoven, Shanon Vannatter, Steven VanNeste, Cynthia Vannoy-Rhoades, Louis VanOrden, Stacy VanOrman, William VanOsdol, Ethel VanPelt, Tara Vanportfleet, Erik van Praag, Marinus vanPrattenburg, Rusty VanReeves, Melody VanSandt, Jane vanTol, David Vantress, David VanWhy, Karen VanWinkle, Josephine Varga, Jeremy Varner, Reva Varner, Jeremy Varner, Gary Varner, Darryl Varner, Reva Varner, Jack Varney, Harry Vasconcellos, Jonathan Vasko, William Vasquez, Edwin Vasquez, Philip Vassallo, Kenneth Vater, Wendy Vaughn, Edward Vaughn, Brandi Vaughn, Richard Vaughn, Brandi Vaughn, Richard Vaughn, Glenda Vautrin, Clinton Veach, Brownie Veazie, Anethea Veenman-Hodges, Gwenith Vehlow, Holly Veigel, Effie Velardo, Alisson Veldhuis, Luis Velez, Deborah

Venable, Lisette Venditto, Carl Veno, Crystal Venters, Edward Ventunelli, Mary Verdick, Vernon Vereen, Richard Vergara, Peter Vergara-Ramirez, Stephen Verigood, Robert Verno, Guy Verreault, Eugene VerSteegh, Janice Vescio, Guinevere Vestich, Peter Vetrano, Helen Vettori, Vickie Viars, Paul Victor, Maureen Vidunas, Harry Viens, Joe Vigliotti, Valerie Vigliotti, Illeana Villafana, Geraldine Villalba, Philip Villamor, Monica Villarrubia, Omar Villasmil, Ann-Marie Vincent, Kimbell Vincent, Kimberly Vincent, Marianne Vincent, Michael Vincent, Mark Vincze, Robert Vine, Edna Vines, Boris Vinokur, Terry Vinson, Louis Virgilio, Tamara Virgilio, Jason Visconti, Peter Viteritti, Jennifer Vivekanand, Luisa Viviani, Natalie Vlasek, Tony Vogiantzis, Clay Void, Fritz Vongucci, Teresa VonReiman, Agathe vonTrapp, Gail Vonwald, Sabiha Vorajee, Helene Vorce-Tish, Edward Voss, Edgar Vovsi, L. Vreeland, Julia Vryheid, Aleksandar Vujadinovic, Ugonna Wachuku, Mary Wacker, John Waddington-Feather, Aubrey Wade, Lawson Wade, Karil Wade, Earl Wade, Marie Wadsworth, Lauren Wadsworth, Liza Wagaman, Shirley Wagand, Christopher Wager, Karen Waggoner, Larry Wagner, Robert Wagner, Stephen Wagner, Richard Wagner, Leta Wahl, James Waite, William Waite, Michael Waitz, Debra Wakefield, Earnestine Walden, Joy Waldenville, Clarence Waldon, Janet Waldrep, Bruce Waldron, Tommy Waldrop, Rhonda Walker, Miriam Walker, Woodrow Walker, James Walker, Allie Walker, Susan Walker, Shirley Walker, Daniel Walker, Gregory Walker, Laura Walker, Carlton Walker, Dawn Walker, Devon Walker, Dorcas Walker, Dorothy Walker, Jason Walker, Jimmy Walker, C. Walker, Karen Wall, Michael Wall, Ben Wallace, Shelley Wallace, Robert Wallace, John Wallace, Rachell Wallace, Mary Helen Wallace, Gillian Wallace, Mary Wallace, Leon Wallace, Kathryn Wallace, John Wallace, Faye Wallace, Antonietta Wallace, Shirley Wallace, Karen Waller, Sarah Walli, Jerald Wallick, Joan Wallis, William Wallner, John Walsh, Glenda Walsh, Jack Walsh, Kathleen Walsh, Thomas Walsh, Tina Walsh, Richard Walsh, Susan Walshe, Barry Walshe, Katy Walsvik, Carol Walt, Robert Walters, Nona Walters, Kenneth Walters, Donna Walters, Julia Walth, Beth Waltman, Eric Walton, John Walton, Wilfred Walton, Wendy Wamsley, Leif Wanager, Cheng Wang, Yuxiang Wang, Thomas Ward, Roxanne Ward, Brenda Ward, Brandon Ward, Zoe Ward, Sherry Ward, Lee Ward, Ervin Ward, Dayna Ward, Christina Ward,

Evelyn Warden, James Wardlaw, Nicholas Warf, Jeffrey Wargo, Rose Warken, Frank Warlick, Montgomery Warman, Elizabeth Warner, Neil Warner, Norman Warner, Rosa Warner, Sandy Warner, Brigadier-General Stephen Warren, Debra Warren, Grady Warren, Ellen Warren, Andrew Warren, Ellen Warren, Leonard Warrick, Mary Warstler, Connie Wasburn, Martha Wasek, Billy Washam, Debra Washburn, Caroline Washington, Faith Washington, Cecil Washington, Christopher Wasson, Chris Wasson, Carole Waterhouse,

Salome Waters, Thomas Waters, Salome Waters, David Watkins, Barbara Watkins, Larry Watkins, Shelagh Watkins, Gwendolyn Watkins, Gloria Watkins, Garrett Watkins, Casey Watkins, Duane Watkins, Richter Watkins, Myriah Watson, Robert Watson, John Watson, Benjamin Watson, Pamela Watson, Sidney Watson, Jerine Watson, Jacqueline Watson, Andrew Watson, Jerine Watson, Kammile Watt, Ian Watteau, Diane Wattles, Daniel Watton, Eric Wattree, John Watts, Debra Watts, George Watts, Pegene Watts-

Cartwright, Clair Waucaush, Kenneth Waxlax, Jessica Wearne, Marvin Weathers, Frank Weaver, Joyce Weaver, Dexter Weaver, Lance Weaver, Casey Weaver, Robert Weaver, Amy Weaver, Marilyn Weaver, Jacqueline Webb, Floyd Webb, Marylou Webb, Margaret Webb, Barbara Webb, Allen Webb, Brandon Webb, Trudy Webber, Brenda Weber, Richard Weber, Robert Weber, Michael Weber, Manjubala Weber, Carolyn Weber, Brenda Weber, Gene Weber, John Webster, Candace Weddle, Melissa Weed, Susan Weekley, Maureen Weeks, Norman Weibel, Ruth Weidig, Janice Weight, James Weigle, Dorothy Weil, Elizabeth Weiland, Mark Wein, Samuel Wein, Florence Weinberg, Debby Weinberger, Craig Weincek, Zachary Weiner, David Weiner, Susan Weinholtz, Janina Weinland, Mark Weinmaster, Raymond Weir, Linsey Weiser, Thomas Weishaar, Anita Weisheit, Murray Weisman, Lionel Weiss, Jennifer Weiss, Lionel Weiss, D. Weissenberger, Helena Welch, Kathleen Welchert, Cheryl Weldon, Jill Weller, Ralph Welliver, Joseph Wellman, Jacqueline Wellman, John Wells, Thomas Wells, Matilda Wells, Franciscus Welman, Nancy Weng, Maria Wennink, Kimberly Wentworth, Kathleen Wermuth, Steven Werner, Derik Wesley, John Wesley, Veronica West, Karen West, Michael West, Richard West, Terry West, Andre West, Travis West, Stephen West, Paul West, Clarence West, Robert West, Charles Westcott, Della Westerfield, David Westfall, Vicki Westfall, William Westhead, Barbara Westley, Ann Westmoreland, Jack Westmoreland, Spencer Weston, Thomas Weston, Sharon Westra, LaTonya Westrick, Robert Wetmore, John Whalen, John Whatcom, Diana Whatley, Marylou Wheatley, Terry Wheeler, Richard Wheeler, Joshua Wheeler, Billy Wheeler, Joshua Wheeler, Doris Wheelus, Stephanie Whelchel, Rodd Whelpley, Wendy Whipple, Jason Whisler, Toni Whitaker, Katarina Whitaker, Francis Whitby, Megan White, Stephanie White, Veronica White, Aaron White, Kenneth White, Diane White, Gail White, Sherri White, Jo White, Marrianne White, Tammany White, Debbie White, Barbara White, Caryn White, Derek White, Donald White, Eugene White, Jackie White, Derek White, Jeannette White, Betty White, John White, Fairy White, James Whited, Susan Whitefeather, Marjorie Whitehead, Raymond Whitehead, Jeffrey Whitehead, Stephen Whitehouse, Ernestine Whitfield, Michelle Whiting, Nancy Whitley, Kimberly Whitlock, Lillian Whitlow, Dawn Whitmire, Evelyn Whitney, Larry Whitney, Sabas Whittaker, Brian

Whitt-Augustine, Robert Whitten, Leone Whittier, Mary Whittle, Kevin Whitworth, Grace Whray, Robyn Whyte, Melissa Whyte, Frank Whyte, Larry Wicker, Martha Wickham, Audrey Wicks, Steven Wickstrom, Robert Widder, Ramon Wideman, Karl Wiebe, Jenny Wiebe, Constance Wiedeman, Fred Wiehe, Richard Wiener, Carol Wierzbicki, Julie Wiese, Robie Wiesner, Bill Wietrick, Dana Wiggens, Chris Wiggins, Doris Wigington, Lawrence Wigley, Garlyn Wilburn, Mary Wilburn, Mary Wilcox, MaryAnn Wilcox, Judith Wild, Mark Wild, Vance Wilder, George Wilder, Lauren Wildrick, Judith Wiles, Anne Wiley, Jeanne Wiley, Cynthia Wilkerson, Judy Wilkerson, Shelton Wilkes, Amanda Wilkin, Joy Wilkins, Sheila Wilkins, Lisa Wilkins, Frank Wilkins, Donald Wilkins, Dallas Wilkinson, Jon Will, April Willbanks, James Willcox, Sue Willett, Carole Willett-Barton, Emma Willey, Roger Willey, Joy Willhight, Dorothy Williams, JuQuan Williams, Wayne Williams, T. Williams, Stephen Williams, Shelly Williams, Sharon Williams, Robert Williams, Eugene Williams, Rita Williams, Philip Williams, Patch Williams, Ruth Williams, Sarah Williams, Pamela Williams, Steve Williams, Joyce Williams, Elizabeth Williams, Virginia Williams, Angel Williams, Douglas Williams, Desiree Williams, Stacey Williams, Jason Williams, Patch Williams, Darlene Williams, Marie Williams, Lawanda Williams, Eugene Williams, Michael Williams, Bertie Williams, Cynthia Williams, Gary Williams, Fifie Williams, Edward Williams, Gerald Williams, Darlene Williams, Daniel Williams, Donna Williams, Charles Williams, Chanda Williams, Billie Williams, Andre Williams, Nea Williams, Lawanda Williams, Chris Williams, Gregory Williams, Mary Williams, Marvin Williams, Lois Williams, Leslie Williams, Lenora Williams, Melissa Williams, Keith Williams, Juan Williams, Josie Williams, Jerry Williams, Jason Williams, Janice Williams, James Williams, Herbert Williams, Sharon Williams-Datcher, Monica Williams-Hazel, Peggy Williamson, Richard Williamson, Linda Williamson, Chad Williamson, Bonnie Williamson, Barbara Williamson, Charlotte Williamson, Bobby Williamson, Dorrie Williams-Wheeler, Cynthia Williford, Patti Willingham, Aaron Willis, Jody Willis, William Willis, Margaret Willis, Steven Willis, Desiree Willman, Sally Willmot, James Wills, Earl Wills, David Wills, Deborah Wilson, Staci Wilson, Stoney Wilson, Wendy Wilson, William Wilson, Gary Wilson, Steve Wilson, Rosalee Wilson, Ritchie Wilson, Robert Wilson, Demetrius Wilson,

Stanley Wilson, Kimberly Wilson, Jon Wilson, Katrina Wilson, Cinda Wilson, David Wilson, Dorothy Wilson, Richard Wilson, Jason Wilson, Kathryn Wilson, Kimberly Wilson, Letisha Wilson, Lianne Wilson, Malcolm Wilson, Maria Wilson, Neil Wilson, Norman Wilson, James Wilson, Erica-Tifany Wilson-Thomas, Michael Winch, Jean Winchester, Doris Windham, Christian-Jerome Windsor, Earl Winebarger, Melody Wines, Marilyn Winfield, James Wingeier, Bruce Wingo, Rebecca Winnard, Tammy Winslett, Loretta Winslett, Tammy Winslett, Victoria Winslow, Caprice Winstead, Vernon Winstead, Yolanda Winston, Lisa Winter, Karen Winter, Alma Winters, Bonnie Winters, Vanessa Winters, Robert Winters, Barbara Winters, Cheryl Winterwest, Katha Winther, Stephen Winzenburg, Hemamali Wirasinha, Judy Wirth, Jason Wisdom, Wayne Wise, Steven Wise, W. Wiseman, Fenwick Witheridge, Jean Witherow, Amy Witkowski, Isaac Witter, Evan Wittig, Willie Wofford, Philip Wohl, Craig Wojack, Antionette Wold, Lori Wolf, Phillip Wolf, Faith Wolf, Cynthia Wolf, Mike Wolf, Denise Wolfe, Cheryl Wolfe-Burley, William Wolfgram, Ruhl Wolford, Donald Wolslagel, Brent Wolters, Nicole Woltz, Carrol Wolverton, Jami Womack, William Womack, Fred Womack, Virginia Wonder, William Wong, Hok-Wai Wong, Sherry Wong, Michael Wood, Gordon Wood, Alan Wood, Joshua Wood, Roy Wood, Robert Wood, Valerie Wood, Lisa Wood, Leanda Wood, Kathy Wood, Gordon Wood, Daniel Wood, Richard Wood, Peter Wood, John Woodall, Kenneth Woodard, Rosanne Woodcraft, Robert Woodcraft, Kyle Woodend, James Woodford, Ralph Woodgate, Charlotte Woodham, Doris Woodland, Betty Woodlee, Robert Woodley, Marie Woodman, Betty Woodrum, James Woods, William Woods, Dena Woods, Wendy Woods, Stephanie Woods, Rita Woods, Richard Woods, James Woods, Glenna Woods, Glenn Woods, Dennis Woods, Billy Woods, Deborah Woods, Cindy Woods, Jill Woods, Charles Woodul, Paul Woodward, Wanda Woodward, Adam Woodworth, Dean Woodworth, George Woolfson, Bill Woolsey, Brenda Woolsey, Nancy Woolums, Cynthia Wootan, Gregory Wooten, Daryl Worcester, Jacki Work, Toney Workman, Roger Worley, Jerry Worrell, Ninel Wortman, Mark Wrede, Delikli Wreh-Wilson, Judith Wren, Clark Wren, Robert Wrench, Charles Wright, Melissa Wright, Ronald Wright, Sheanette Wright, Susan Wright, Benjamin Wright, James Wright, Ronald Wright, James Wright, Mary Wright, Robert Wright, Amberly Wright, Mary

Wright, Alfred Wright, Lisa Wright, Cavin Wright, David Wright, Eugene Wright, Evander Wright, Gene Wright, Ian Wrisley, Mary Wrucke, Isis Wu, Xinglu Wu, Virgil Wulff, Enrique Wulff, Sarah Wunder, Jan Wunderlich, Naomi Wunderman, Robert Wyatt, Becky Wyatt, Thomas Wyckoff, Katherine Wylie, Arthur Wyllie, Doreen Wyman, Karen Wyman, Cherise Wyneken, Bridgette Wynn, Anita Wynn, Jaime Wynn, Heather Wyse, Chrissy Yacoub, Kathyrn Yahr, Mary Yamashiro-Held, Howard Yambura, Robert Yamtich, Frederick Yamusangie, Evelyn Yancey, Lisa Yancey, Kristen Yanish, Jerome Yarznbowicz, Max Yates, Donald Yates, Audrey Yeager, August Yeager, Tina Yeager, Chuck Yeager, William Yeagy, Alexander Yeboah, Janis Yelton, Pamela Yelverton, Herman Yenwo, Nova Yeoman, Diane Yingling, Gail Ylitalo, Victoria Yocom, Jeffrey Yocum, James Yoder, Joan Yonker, Larry York, Benny Yost, Tarra Young, Stephan Young, Tarra Young, Allan Young, Eileen Young, Rosemary Young, Kevin Young, Stephan Young, Herbert Young, Charles Young, Norma Young, Nicola Young, Michael Young, Meredith Young, Frederick Young, Eileen Young, Cleous Young, Christopher Young, Shannon Young, James Youngman, David Yovich, Chul Yu, Gerald Yukevich, Stephen Yulish, Rachael Yunis, Michael Yurk, Joseph Yurkin, Alvin Yusin, Kevin Zabbo, April Zaccaria, Andreas Zachariou, Marqus Zackery, Margaret Zadow, Darlene Zagata, Gregory Zagel, Kimberlie Zakarian, Michael Zangardi, Debra Zapata, Hande Zapsu, Judith Zar, Jacqualynn Zarley, Vic Zarley, Jacqualynn Zarley, Lori Zecca, Randal Zelhart, Ben Zeller, Donna Zeller, Pinbo Zhou, Meng Zhu, Andrea Zicherman, Robert Ziegler, Aaron Ziegler, Robert Ziegler, Richard Zielinski, Nell Zier, Adam Zier, Willadene Zierdt, Jacqueline Zilliox, Joan Zillman, Amy Zimmerman, Wanda Zimmerman, Justin Zimmerman, Daniel Zimmerman, Amie Zinnel, George Zintel, Samuel Zitter, Patricia Zoeller, Gregory Zotos, Atilla Zsarnovsky, Thomas Zukauskas, Charles Zulker, Riang Zuor, Dawne Zupic, Cassandra Zurawski, Nkosiyabo Zvandasara Zhou, Trenee Zweigle, Natalie Zyla, Susan Zytnik-Kunzler, L. Ahumada, James Allen, Terry Allen, Lauro Amezcua-Patino, Stephen Arluck, Michael Arthur, Abhishek Asthana, Fatima Atchley, John B. Ifejika, Barbara N. Ifejika, Colin Barras, Rebecca Baxter, Edwin Becker, Sukhvinder Bedi, Jill Bellas, Daniel Bellomo, Barton Bernales, Joseph Bileti, Linda Blasdell, Susan Blotz, Theresa Bowen, Joan Brickley, Homer Broadstone, Yelena Grigory Bronevetsky, Eric Brown, Michael Brown, Lillian

Brummet, Nancy Brundage , Lorraine Buchanan, Susan Buck, Dennis Burns, John Butler, Dora Cain, Charles Callahan, Susie Camden, Michael Canada, William Carey, Maurice Carlton, Maurice Carlton, Sandra Geraghty Carol Wood, Diane Cassity, Ms. Jon Cellitti, Thomas Champs, Virginia Cheeney, Michael Childers, David Christensen, Jennifer Cline, Shirley Clontz, Jason Coleman, David Coughlan, Lisha Crow, Catherine Crump, David Dailey, Pam DeNiord, Christine DePetrillo, Maria Dever, Michelle DeWitt, Daniel Diadiw, Marie Diaz, George Doerr, Diane Donner, Connie Dunscomb, Tanya Eaves, John Egwuagu, Colleen Elliott, Jennifer Eslick, Joy Farr, Ruth Feldman, Pamela Ferris, Kerry Fickel, Glenda Fields, Rusty Fischer, Diane Fletcher, George Flower, Alessandra Foekel, Robert Freeman, Almeda Froyd, Sarah Fulton, Karen Gallant, Maria Gay, Hosse Ghadiri, Rami Goldstein, W. Good, Georgia Goodridge, Brian Gossard, Adrian Greenlee, Sharon Greenstein, Suzanne Grooms, Craig Hargis, Christina Harkness, Eric Harris, Judith Hays, Bonnie Headington, Tom Hebert, Charlotte Henderson, Ronald Henderson,

Patricia Hendricks, Michael Heydari, Roberta Heydenberk, Mary Hicks, Jennifer Hight, Linda Hoffman, Lavelle Horne, James Howell, A.K.M. Huq, Joanadel Hurst, Heather Hyde-Herndon, Kim Ingraham, Glenn Jacobs, Kenneth James, Phyllis Jessop, Randy Johnson, Kristin Johnson, Debra Johnston, Kristin Jones, Marvin Jones, Patrick Jones, Samuel Joy, Scott Kaiser, Salah Kanaan, Salah Kanaan, Gaynelle Kaywood, Faith Keahey, Faith Keahey, David Keener, Robin Kelley, Gregory Kelly, Betty Kidwiler, Louise Killinger, Leah Kockanowitz, Muriel Kuhn, John Lantz, Mari Laureano, Deborah LePage, Tara Lewis, Elizabeth Lowder , Aja Mack, Nicklas Maddox, Ellen Maidman-Tanner, Barry Mainardi, Sylvia Martin, Beverly Martin-Lowry, Nancy McClellan, Jill McClimon, Betty McElhatten, Jessica McFarlane, Jo Ann McIntosh, John McLean, Jean McNeil, Margie Mears, DJ Mennenga, Gerald Meyer, Ron Meyer, Rosa Pagan Mikala Kobe, Larry Mild, Norma Mixon, Kary Moffitt, Liz Monta, Mary Montgomery, Sherry Moore, D. Morgenstein, Diana Morrell, Patricia Morton, Terry Motteler, Bill Mount, Gregory Mulholland, Mary Murphy, Annie O'Dell, Olivia Olguin, Olivia K. Lab, Lewis Opler, Faith Orange, Robin Orlanda, Mary Orlando, Donald Osgood, Yolanda Pedroza, Keith Perry-Gore, Michael Petti, Marcelle Pichanick, Helen Pierce, David Potter, Carolyn Powell, Roger Pratcher, Brigit Pratcher, Ana Racz, David Rearden, M. Reaves, Mary Reed, Mark Reeder, Janette Reifer-Esprit, Cheryl Riffle, James Rinaldi, Edwina Roady, Michel Rogers, Marlo Rosario-Wood, Lynn Rose, Deborah Rosenkrans, Janice Roswell, Judy Russell, Allen Salowe, Jennifer Santoro, Adam Schack, Beatrice Schalch, Linda Schillig, Jessica Scott, John Scudder, Ronald Sebastian, Deborah Seibert, Egon Sengbusch, George Sewell, Janice Sharp, Eric Shear, Jeanne Siegel, Candace Simms, Kazimierz Slomczynska, Doug Smith, Barbara Soden, Grace Sowells, Cynthia Specht, Cynthia Stein, Ann Stein, Patricia Steiner, Daniel Stiles, Patricia Stively, Richard Swarthout, Eric Tang, Loretta Theriot, Brenda Thomas, Michele Thomas, Ann Thompson, Denise Thompson, Jennifer Thorssell, Jason Traversie, Josephine Tsaligopoulos, Loren Turnage, Michael Tyler, Alice Underwood, Phyllis Varney, Carol Vasquez, Marlon Vines, David Wallis, Rocquie Warde, Debra Wein, Constance Weinmaster, Patricia Welles, Sandra Weston, Melanie Wiehl, Elizabeth Wiens, Glenn Wilkinson, Bobbie Willcox, Robert Willey, Nea Williams, David Williams, Mary Williamson, Joe Wilmetti, Doris Wilson, William

Winter, William Wolfe, Merrill Wolford, Roland Wong, Eva Zarley, Vissilikie Zoyes, Andrea Zug, Oluyinka Adediji, Andria Alexander, Germaine Allen, Layne Bailey, Sandra Bartlett, Roy Beaird, Aleja Bennett, Don Bennett, James Berger, Nephi Blackburn, Heather Brinson, Jenny Brown, Jimmy Calhoun, Raul Camacho, Jay Chandler, Nellotie Chastain, Joyce Colvin, Porzia Danisi, George Dennis, Richard Edges, Colleen Edlebeck, Pamela Evans, Delvenia Fairbanks, Justin Foltz, Sarah Franks, Michele Gonta, Gene Goodwin, Paul Grenert, William Hall, Renee Hand, Opal Harden, Antonette Harris, Bradley Hartman, James Haydock, Timothy Hayes, Stanley Huff, Mary-Anne Ivie, Joni Johnson, Mike Karr, Joseph Kelly, Robert Kennalley, Donna Kilroy, Linda King, Pamela King, Debra Kleinberger, Cleo Lawson, Matthew Lazin, Alan Leatham, Dale Lehman, Carole Lendosky, Penny Lewis, Donald Lewis, Robert Lindquist, Jonathan Lloyd, Kathleen Lunetta, Tony Lynch, Cindi Madsen, Roger Mahaney, Katherine Marple, James Marriott, Ben Matthews, Sherman Mayle, Victoria Mazzotta, Errol McClelland, Sterlynette McIntyre, Joy McQuiston, Jeffrey Miller, Curtis Moore, Linda Morales, Jorin Mulligan, Edward Myers, Joanie Nations, Pamela Nicholson, Angelic Noble, Karen Nutt, Robert Parlier, Gobinder Parmar, Soloman Patrick, Gwendolyn Peterson, Kathy Pippig, Ronnie Ponder, Mildred Prothe, Margretta Ransom, Dean Ream, Theresa Regenold, Linda Rex, Gracianus Reyes, Kathryn Reyes, Kathleen Riley, CC Risenhoover, Tiffany Roberts, Sherri Romig, Dimitri Rowlette, Sheila Roy, Roxanna Russell, Amanda Ryan, Rick Schmidt, Eric Schmidt, Michael Sidden, George Simonis, Daniel Sisk, Al Skinner, Cora Smart-Crisco, H. Smith, Lisa Street, Dee Sugalski, Tammy Thomas, Edward Tilley, Patricia Tinkey, Deidre Turner, PaulaJo Urso, Clinton Vadney, Aleta Varela, Tamera Velasquez, Charles Villa-Lobos, Frances Vlok, Robert Wade, David Walkup, Robert Ward, Jenessa Warren, Richard Williams, James Williams, Churnet Winborne, Tim Wirth, Jim Woodward, and many, many others.

Printed in the United States
30446LVS00002B/97-108